Brecon Beacons

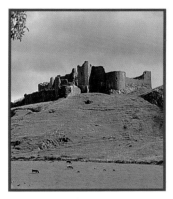

Walks

Originally compiled by
Brian Conduit and Neil Coates
Fully revised by Tom Hutton

D1462826

Acknowledgements

Tom Hutton would like to thank all the staff of the Brecon Beacons National Park Authority and also his partner, Steph, for her company on many of the walks, and Du for her company on all of them – does she ever get tired?

Text:	Brian Conduit, Neil Coates, Tom Hutton
	Revised text for 2010 edition, Tom Hutton
Photography:	Brian Conduit and Tom Hutton
Editorial:	Ark Creative (UK) Ltd
Design:	Ark Creative (UK) Ltd

This product includes mapping data licensed from Ordnance Survey® with the permission of the Controller of Her Majesty's Stationery Office. © Crown Copyright 2010. All rights reserved. Licence number 150002047. Ordnance Survey, the OS symbol and Pathfinder are registered trademarks and Explorer, Landranger and Outdoor Leisure are trademarks of the Ordnance Survey, the national mapping agency of Great Britain.

ISBN: 978-1-85458-557-8

While every care has been taken to ensure the accuracy of the route directions, the publishers cannot accept responsibility for errors or omissions, or for changes in details given. The countryside is not static: hedges and fences can be removed, field boundaries can alter, footpaths can be rerouted and changes in ownership can result in the closure or diversion of some concessionary paths. Also, paths that are easy and pleasant for walking in fine conditions may become slippery, muddy and difficult in wet weather, while stepping stones across rivers and streams may become impassable.

If you find an inaccuracy in either the text or maps, please write to Crimson Publishing at the address below.

First published 1993 by Jarrold Publishing
Revised and reprinted 1997, 2000, 2003, 2005, 2007, 2010

Printed in Singapore. 8/10

This edition published in Great Britain 2010 by Crimson Publishing,
a division of:
Crimson Business Ltd,
Westminster House, Kew Road, Richmond, Surrey, TW9 2ND

www.totalwalking.co.uk

A catalogue record for this book is available from the British library.

Front cover: Hay Bluff and the Gospel Pass
Previous page: Dramatic ruins of Carreg Cennen Castle

Contents

Approximate walk times

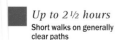 Up to 2 ½ hours
Short walks on generally clear paths

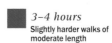 3–4 hours
Slightly harder walks of moderate length

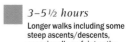 3–5 ½ hours
Longer walks including some steep ascents/descents, occasionally on faint paths

The walk times are provided as a guide only and are calculated using an average walking speed of 2½mph (4km/h), adding one minute for each 10m (33ft) of ascent, and then rounding the result to the nearest half hour.

Walks are considered to be dog friendly unless specified.

Contents

Keymap

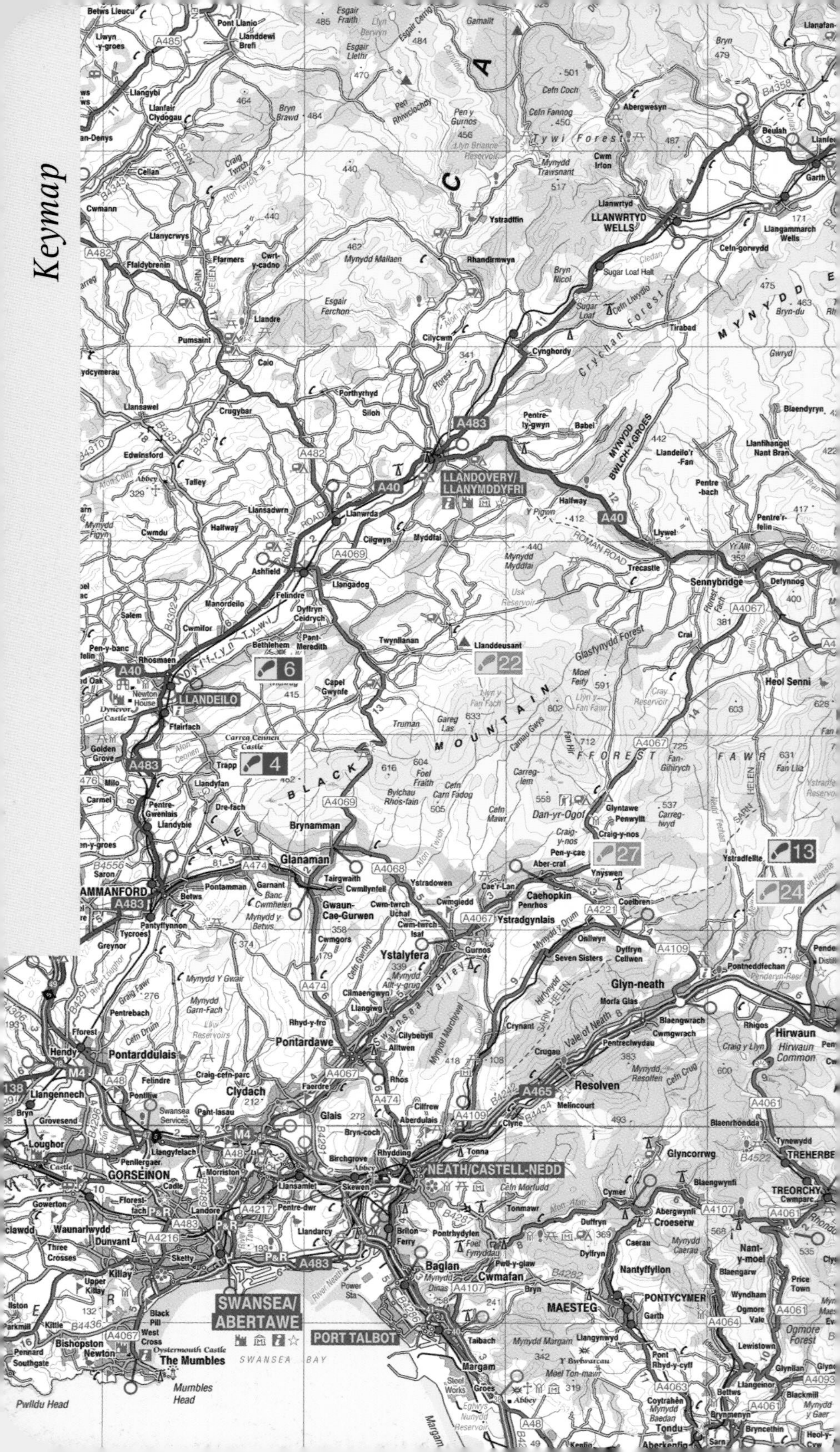

LLANWRTYD WELLS
LLANDOVERY/ LLANYMDDYFRI
LLANDEILO
AMMANFORD
NEATH/CASTELL-NEDD
SWANSEA/ ABERTAWE
PORT TALBOT
GORSEINON
MAESTEG
PONTYCYMER
TREORCHY
TREHERBERT
Tywi Forest
Crychan Forest
Glasfynydd Forest
Ogmore Forest
THE BLACK MOUNTAIN
FFOREST FAWR
MYNYDD BWLCH-Y-GROES
Swansea Valley
Vale of Neath
SWANSEA BAY
Mumbles Head
Pwlldu Head
The Mumbles
Brynamman
Glanaman
Ystalyfera
Pontardawe
Pontarddulais
Clydach
Ystradgynlais
Glyn-neath
Resolven
Hirwaun
Sennybridge
Trecastle
Llangadog
Llanwrda
Pumsaint
Llandeusant
Dan-yr-Ogof
Craig-y-nos
Sugar Loaf
Usk Reservoir
Llyn Brianne Reservoir
6
4
22
27
13
24
A40
A483
A482
A4069
A474
A4067
A465
A4109
M4
A48

Keymap

At-a-glance

Walk	Page	Start	Nat. Grid Reference	Distance	Time	Height Gain
Allt yr Esgair	26	Allt yr Esgair	SO 129226	3½ miles (5.6km)	2 hrs	950ft (290m)
The Blorenge	43	Keeper's Pond	SO 254107	6 miles (9.8km)	3 hrs	1,250ft (380m)
Brecon Beacons Horseshoe	88	Cwm Gwdi	SO 023247	8½ miles (13.7km)	5 hrs	2,890ft (880m)
Carn Goch	24	Carn Goch	SN 681242	3½ miles (4.8km)	2 hrs	820ft (250m)
Carreg Cennen	20	Carreg Cennen Castle	SN 666193	4 miles (6.4km)	2 hrs	590ft (180m)
Craig y Cilau & Llangattock	34	Craig y Cilau	SO 185168	5½ miles (8.8km)	3 hrs	1,115ft (340m)
Craig-y-nos, Cribath and the Henrhyd Falls	84	Craig-y-nos Country Park	SN 839155	8½ miles (13.7km)	4½ hrs	1,935ft (590m)
Cwm Oergwm	52	Llanfrynach	SO 074257	7 miles (11.3km)	3½ hrs	1,020ft (310m)
Cwmyoy	14	Cwmyoy Hall	SO 300226	2½ miles (4.2km)	1½ hrs	655ft (200m)
Fan y Big	77	Torpantau	SO 056175	10 miles (16.1km)	5½ hrs	2,000ft (610m)
Fan Fawr	46	Storey Arms Centre	SN 982203	4½ miles (7.3km)	3 hrs	1,325ft (405m)
Grwyne Fawr	70	Pont Cadwgan	SO 266251	7½ miles (12.1km)	4 hrs	1,720ft (525m)
Hay Bluff & Twmpa	58	Hay Bluff	SO 239373	6 miles (9.8km)	3 hrs	1,390ft (425m)
Llangors Lake	12	Llangors Lake	SO 128272	3½ miles (5.6km)	1½ hrs	130ft (40m)
Llangynidr & the River Usk	17	Llangynidr	SO 155195	3¾ miles (6km)	2 hrs	330ft (100m)
Llyn y Fan Fach and the Carmarthen Fans	66	Llanddeusant	SN 799238	6 miles (9.7km)	4 hrs	2,130ft (650m)
Monmouthshire & Brecon canal	28	Abergavenny	SO 299140	5½ miles (8.9km)	2½ hrs	330ft (100m)
Mynydd Illtud & Cefn Llechid	55	Mynydd Illtud	SN 977262	7½ miles (12.1km)	4 hrs	1,085ft (330m)
Mynydd Llangorse	30	Cockit Hill	SO 160283	5½ miles (8.9km)	3 hrs	1,115ft (340m)
Sugar Loaf	49	Llangenny	SO 239181	6 miles (9.7km)	3½ hrs	1,900ft (580m)
Table Mountain	32	Crickhowell	SO 218183	5 miles (8km)	3 hrs	1,250ft (380m)
Talgarth & Mynydd Troed	63	Talgarth	SO 152336	8 miles (13km)	4 hrs	1,050ft (320m)
Tor y Foel	37	Llangynidr	SO 146200	5½ miles (8.9km)	3 hrs	1,575ft (480m)
The Vale of Ewyas	60	Llanthony Priory	SO 289278	6 miles (9.7km)	3 hrs	1,210ft (370m)
Waterfalls Walk	73	Cwm Porth	SN 928124	9 miles (14.5km)	5 hrs	2,100ft (640m)
Waun Fach	80	Pengenffordd	SO 173296	7 miles (11.3km)	4½ hrs	2,200ft (670m)
Ysgyryd Fawr	22	Ysgyryd Fawr	SO 328164	2½ miles (4km)	2 hrs	960ft (315m)
Ystradfellte & Sarn Helen	40	Ystradfellte	SN 929134	6½ miles (10.4km)	3½ hrs	2,100ft (640m)

Comments

A steady climb through woodland leads to a superb viewpoint looking out over the Usk valley and Brecon Beacons.

A varied walk that starts high and crosses open hilltops before dropping to a nature reserve. The return leg climbs back onto the hilltops.

A long walk that embraces the three main peaks of the Brecon Beacons, including the highest point in southern Britain – sure to be immensely satisfying.

A short walk over impressive hill forts and rugged hillsides in the north west corner of the National Park.

The dramatically sited ruins of Carreg Cennen Castle, perched on its precipitous rock, are in sight for much of this walk.

A varied walk that includes woodland, an attractive stretch of canal, village and a dramatic limestone escarpment.

An energetic, varied and scenic walk that starts in an interesting country park and takes in a summit, a wooded gorge and a dramatic waterfall.

An energetic ramble deep into a lovely wooded valley that offers wonderful views over the high mountains above.

A short but quite steep walk that visits a magical village, complete with crooked church, and then climbs to a spectacular landmark with fine views.

A dramatic walk along the main escarpment of the Brecon Beacons is followed by a section along an ancient trackway and an attractive woodland finale.

A short but strenuous walk that climbs a gentle giant of a mountain with wonderful views over the central Brecon Beacons.

Conifer forest, open moorland and woodland provide plenty of variety, and an added bonus is a lovely secluded medieval church.

From the two most northerly peaks of the Black Mountains the panoramic views are superb. Expect some stiff climbing.

An easy walk mostly across flat, low lying meadows by Llangors Lake. There are some fine views across the lake.

An attractive walk that follows the mighty River Usk on the outward leg and the Brecon and Monmouthshire Canal on the return. Some very rough and slippery paths.

A strenuous but thoroughly invigorating walk that makes a brief foray into the wilderness of the Black Mountain, climbing two of its highest peaks and visiting a wonderful mountain lake.

A canal towpath and the track of a disused railway are utilised for this walk. There are fine views across the Usk valley to the distinctive Sugar Loaf.

Mostly open country with a wooded valley about halfway round, and for much of the way splendid views of the main range of the Brecon Beacons.

Grand views all the time on this enjoyable walk around Mynydd Llangorse, especially across Llangorse Lake to the line of the Brecon Beacons.

A wonderfully scenic walk that climbs from fertile valley floor to windswept mountaintop and back again.

A steady climb from Crickhowell to the top of Table Mountain rewards you with superb views over the Usk valley and surrounding mountains.

An interesting and varied ramble across pastures and onto open mountainsides, visiting an ancient long cairn on the return leg.

A short but quite steep walk over a distinctive mountain that offers wonderful views of the Brecon Beacons.

The steep-sided vale of Ewyas provides a superb setting for the beautiful, secluded ruins of Llanthony Priory, from which point this walk begins.

Wooded ravines and a series of spectacular waterfalls make for a fascinating walk. Expect some difficult paths and hard going in places.

Steady rather than strenuous climbing brings you to the highest point in the Black Mountains. The views from here are superb.

The climb to the summit of Ysgyryd Fawr is relatively easy but the views from it are outstanding. You return via the same gently sloping path.

There are expansive views across the austere landscape of Fforest Fawr and a fine stretch of Roman road.

At-a-glance

Introduction to the Brecon Beacons

A glance at a map reveals two potential areas of confusion that need to be cleared up right from the start: what exactly is meant by 'the Brecon Beacons', and what is the relation between the Black Mountains and the Black Mountain? This possible confusion arises from the fact that within the boundaries of the Brecon Beacons National Park there are four separate mountain ranges. The most easterly is the Black Mountains, the Brecon Beacons themselves constitute only the central range despite giving their name to the whole area, to the west of them lies Fforest Fawr, and the most westerly range of all is the Black Mountain. For the remainder of this introduction 'Brecon Beacons' will be used for the national park as a whole and 'central Beacons' when referring specifically to the main central range.

The National Park has fairly clearly defined boundaries. In the east the most easterly ridges of the Black Mountains overlook the undulating country leading to the Wye Valley and the English border and at times slip over the border. The northern boundary is formed by the hills and moorlands of mid Wales and by the western reaches of the Usk Valley, before the River Usk bears south-eastwards to flow between the Black Mountains and the central Beacons. In the west the broad, lush vale of Towy makes an obvious boundary. But probably the most obvious boundary of all is to the south, although it is more of a historic, economic and environmental boundary: that between rural and industrial South Wales, largely marked by the line of the 'Heads of the Valleys' road between Abergavenny and Swansea.

Despite a basic similarity and uniformity of geology, each of the four ranges that constitute the Brecon Beacons has its own distinctive characteristics. The Black Mountains, the bulk of which lie to the west of the Wye and north of the Usk with a few detached 'outliers' around Abergavenny, comprise a series of long ridges separating narrow, quiet and still remote valleys. In the central Beacons a steep escarpment rises above the Usk Valley to a collection of smooth, rounded summits, the highest in the national park and including Pen-y-Fan 2,907 feet (886m), the highest point not only in South Wales but in the whole of southern Britain. Fforest Fawr, the 'Great Forest of Brecknock', was once a royal hunting ground, a bare, austere, lonely moorland area that lies between the upper reaches of the Taff to the east and the Tawe to the west. In the far west is the wildest and most remote area of the national park, the Black Mountain, brooded over by the bold and unmistakable profile of the Carmarthen Fans, Bannau Sir Gaer and Fan Brycheiniog.

The underlying unity of the Brecon Beacons as a whole comes from the area's basically simple geological structure. Most of it is underlain by Old Red Sandstone which gives it certain physical and scenic characteristics that distinguish it from the more rugged mountain areas of North Wales. This is an area of smooth, sweeping grassy uplands, wide and open vistas and, apart from the abrupt north-facing escarpment, gradual rather than steep or major gradients. The northern escarpment, caused by massive earth movements which thrust the mountains up and then tilted them to the south, is the most striking feature, stretching right across the region from the English border to the vale of Towy but seen at its most dramatic in the central Beacons and Black Mountain.

Only on the southern rim does the sandstone give way to overlapping bands of carboniferous rocks, limestone and millstone grit. Here can be found all the common features of carboniferous limestone scenery: scars, shake holes, gorges, caves, waterfalls and disappearing rivers. Particularly fascinating is the area south of Ystradfellte. Here limestone meets millstone grit, resulting in a series of spectacular falls on the rivers Mellte, Hepste, Neath and Pyrddin, the most concentrated area of waterfalls in Wales.

Youngest of the carboniferous rocks are the coal measures further south which gave rise to the mining industry and led to the tremendous industrial and population growth in the narrow, parallel valleys of the Rhymney, Taff, Dare and Rhondda which south extend like a series of fingers from the mountain core. At their southern end these coal-bearing valleys open out into the Vale of Glamorgan, an undulating limestone plateau ending in a dramatic line of cliffs on the Glamorgan coast.

The Brecon Beacons have their fair share of historic monuments. Prehistoric remains include stone circles, hill forts such as Crug Hywel above Crickhowell and Pen-y-crug above Brecon, and standing stones. Of the latter there are two particularly fine examples, Maen Llia and Maen Madoc, both of which have atmospheric locations, rising amid the lonely and austere moorlands of Fforest Fawr.

Both Roman and Norman conquerors avoided the mountain barrier to South Wales and took easier lowland routes, either to the north via the Usk Valley or to the south via the coast and the Vale of Glamorgan. The Romans have left little in the area apart from some well-preserved sections of road, notably Sarn Helen that runs across Fforest Fawr to the north of Ystradfellte and the 'Gap Road' through the central Beacons, although there is some doubt as to the Roman origins of the latter.

On the other hand, the Normans have left a chain of castles along their invasion routes to mark their line of conquest: Abergavenny, Crickhowell, Tretower, Bronllys and Brecon all fall within the park boundaries. One castle must be singled out as being particularly outstanding: Carreg Cennen, which is perched theatrically on a 300-feet (91m) high limestone crag in the foothills of the Black Mountain and is easily the most dramatically positioned castle in the National Park if not all of Wales.

Introduction

The Normans also established monasteries around the fringes of the area. The most important of these were the Augustinian priory at Llanthony, beautifully situated in the secluded Vale of Ewyas deep in the Black Mountains, and the Benedictine priory at Brecon, elevated to cathedral status in 1923 and bestowing an added distinction on the principal town in the national park. Evidence of an older Celtic Christianity can be found in the fascinating little town of Llantwit Major near the Glamorgan coast, an important centre of learning during the Dark Ages.

Until the 19th century the region as a whole was a thinly populated farming area. By and large the Brecon Beacons area has remained that way, with just a few small villages and a number of pleasant market towns near the periphery of the National Park: Abergavenny, Hay-on-Wye, Crickhowell, Llandovery and Brecon. But the Industrial Revolution produced a virtual population explosion in the mining valleys to the south, as settlements sprang up along the steep valley sides and merged into each other to form a continuous urban development. The demand for high quality Welsh coal also led to the rapid expansion of Cardiff, which at the turn of the century was the world's greatest coal-exporting port, and the vast bulk of the population of Wales became concentrated in this south east corner of the country. In recent years the wheel has turned full circle. The mines have closed down, the waste tips have been landscaped and planted with trees, the valleys are becoming green again and the coal industry has started to recede into the area's heritage.

Although the Brecon Beacons largely escaped the ravages of the Industrial Revolution, the 20th century has had two major physical impacts on the area: the planting of conifer forests and the construction of reservoirs to serve the large towns and industrial areas to the south. Once regarded as alien intrusions in the landscape, they both now contribute to the region's tourist attractions. Nowadays tourism has become a vital part of the local economy.

The Brecon Beacons National Park has much to offer walkers. Apart from the obvious scenic attractions and walking challenges associated with any mountain area, there is a long tradition of *de facto* access to much of the open hillside and moorland. A further advantage is that much of the land, especially in the central Beacons, and including the highest peaks, is common land, owned either by the National Park or the National Trust.

A word of caution is needed, however. Because of their generally smooth and rounded appearance and the absence of craggy outlines, the Brecon Beacons may not look as daunting or formidable as the mountains of Snowdonia, the Lake District or the Scottish Highlands. But do not be misled. *These are true mountains which possess all the potential hazards of other mountain areas and need to be treated with due caution and respect. They have a high altitude and high rainfall, are subject to sudden mists — these are especially dangerous along the edge of the steep northern escarpment — and large areas of Fforest Fawr and the Black Mountain in the west comprise bare, trackless, featureless moorland.* Indeed, the area of the Carmarthen Fans in the Black Mountain is one of the few genuine areas of wilderness remaining in southern Britain and the National Park authorities are keen to preserve its unique quality of remoteness. Because of this, the walks in this book only scratch the surface of this area but experienced walkers might like to explore it for themselves, armed with the appropriate Ordnance Survey Explorer map.

For first time visitors the Brecon Beacons Mountain Centre near Libanus, to the south west of Brecon, is the ideal starting point. You can sit outside on the terrace admiring one of the most striking views in the whole of Wales, a panorama of the highest peaks in the Beacons, the core of the mountain massif. If that does not whet your appetite for exploring this beautiful, wild, fascinating area, nothing will.

This book includes a list of waypoints alongside the description of the walk, so that you can enjoy the full benefits of gps should you wish to. For more information on using your gps, read the *Pathfinder® Guide GPS for Walkers,* by gps teacher and navigation trainer, Clive Thomas (ISBN 978-0-7117-4445-5). For essential information on map reading and basic navigation, read the *Pathfinder® Guide Map Reading Skills* by outdoor writer, Terry Marsh (ISBN 978-0-7117-4978-8). Both titles are available in bookshops or can be ordered online at www.totalwalking.co.uk

 ## Glossary of Welsh Words

This list gives some of the more common elements in Welsh place names, which will allow readers to understand otherwise meaningless words and appreciate the relationship between place names and landscape features. Place names often have variant spellings, and the more common of these are given here.

aber	estuary, confluence	foel, moel	rounded hill
afon	river	glyn	glen
bach, fach	small	hen	old
bont, pont	bridge	llan, eglwys	church
bryn	mound, hill	llyn	lake
bwlch	pass	maen	stone
caer	fort	mawr, fawr	big
capel	chapel	moel, foel	rounded hill
carn, carnedd	cairn	morfa	sea marsh
castell	castle	mynydd	mountain
ceunant	gorge, ravine	nant	brook
coed	wood	newydd	new
craig	crag	pair	cauldron
crib	narrow ridge	pen	head, top
cwm	valley	pont, bont	bridge
drws	doors, gap (pass)	pwll	pool
dyffryn	valley	rhaedr	waterfall
eglwys, llan	church	sarn	causeway
fach, bach	small	traeth	beach, shore
fawr, mawr	big	twll	hole
ffordd	road	ynys	island

Llangors Lake

		GPS waypoints
Start	Llangors Lake	
Distance	3½ miles (5.6km)	SO 128 272
Height gain	130 feet (40m)	Ⓐ SO 125 272
		Ⓑ SO 122 263
Approximate time	1½ hours	Ⓒ SO 132 261
Parking	Free car park at Llangors Lake	Ⓓ SO 126 256
		Ⓔ SO 123 256
Route terrain	Mainly paths across level fields but a short section on a quiet road. Can get boggy and will flood at wetter times of year	
Dog friendly	Care needed on the road	
Ordnance Survey maps	Landranger 161 (The Black Mountains), Explorer OL13 (Brecon Beacons National Park – Eastern area)	

Llangors Lake, or Llyn Syfaddan, is the largest natural lake in South Wales and is noted for its rich flora and fauna, especially bird life. For much of this flat, easy, relaxing walk around its shores the lake is hidden but from time to time lovely views open up across the water to Mynydd Llangorse. After wet weather the low-lying and badly drained meadows bordering the lake are likely to be waterlogged.

From the car park walk straight across the field beside it, looking out for a waymarked footbridge over the Afon Llynfi. The whole of this walk is well waymarked and easy to follow. Cross

Looking across Llangors Lake

the bridge Ⓐ, turn half-left and head across a meadow to a gate at the far end. Continue across a series of meadows, going through a succession of gates and curving gradually to the left all the while. Llangors Lake is to the left and there are fine views of Mynydd

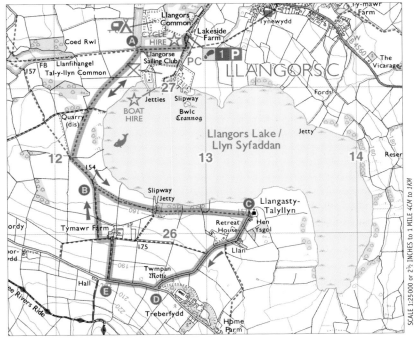

SCALE 1:25000 or 2½ INCHES to 1 MILE 4CM to 1KM

Llangorse and Allt yr Esgair.

On reaching a waymarked post where paths meet **B**, keep straight ahead to walk along the edge of the field, with the lake to your left, to a gate in the corner of a wood. This leads onto a track that veers leftwards to a hide. The walk continues right then left to continue in the same direction with the wood on the left. This soon leads you to a boardwalk, which you follow around the edge of the woodland, and this eventually leads out onto another meadow, where you'll see Llangasty-Talyllyn church ahead. There are also lovely views across the lake.

Go through a gate just to the left of the church **C** and turn right along a track which bears right to continue as a tarmac lane through the hamlet. The church, school and manor house at Llangasty-Talyllyn were all built in the middle of the 19th century for Robert Raikes, the founder of the Sunday School movement, to form a religious

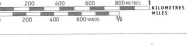

community. Follow the lane for ½ mile, heading gently uphill to a T-junction **D**. Turn right, in the Pennorth direction, and continue for another ¼ mile to a farm drive on the right, signed to Ty-Mawr Camping **E**. Turn right and walk down a tarmac track towards a farm. Just in front of the farm buildings turn left over a stile, walk along the right-hand edge of a field, by a hedge on the right, and turn right over the next stile.

Head gently downhill along the left-hand edge of a field, by a hedge on the left, climb a stile in the field corner, cross an enclosed path and climb another stile immediately ahead. Bear left to continue down the left-hand edge of a meadow to a waymarked post **B** and a gate just beyond. At the post pick up the outward route and retrace your steps to the start. ●

Cwmyoy

		GPS waypoints	
Start	Cwmyoy Hall		SO 300 226
Distance	2½ miles (4.2km)	**Ⓐ**	SO 300 231
Height gain	655 feet (200m)	**Ⓑ**	SO 299 233
Approximate time	1½ hours	**Ⓒ**	SO 298 235
Parking	Cwmyoy Hall, on minor road along the Vale of Ewyas	**Ⓓ**	SO 297 238
		Ⓔ	SO 301 237
Route terrain	A mixture of easy paths across fields and steep rocky tracks		
Ordnance Survey maps	Landranger 161 (The Black Mountains), Explorer OL13 (Brecon Beacons National Park – Eastern area)		

Not many small villages draw quite as much attention as Cwmyoy. Its medieval church is so crooked it's difficult to find a truly upright wall, and the village itself is perched precariously on a steep hillside dominated by a craggy knoll. This walk crosses gently sloping meadows to reach the village, and from the church climbs steeply above the houses, for some staggering views of the surrounding valleys. If the steep pull looks too much, the walk can be shortened by going only as far as the church and then returning by the same route.

Parking is extremely limited in the village of Cwmyoy itself, so the best starting point for this walk is outside Cwmyoy Hall on the other side of the Afon Honddu on the minor road that runs through the Vale of Ewyas. If these spaces are all taken, there is further

Y Craig and St Martin's Church

parking about 1½ miles down the valley.

With your back to the hall, turn right onto the road and walk past a cottage to a stile on the right. Cross this and walk down through the field to a gate ahead. Go through and bear left to follow a faint path to a footbridge over the Afon Honddu, and then continue ahead through the small copse to emerge at the foot of a long field. Walk up the left-hand edge of the field with fine views all around, and continue to a stile at the top that leads out onto a lane **Ⓐ**.

Turn left here and walk past a farm on the left to a sharp right-hand

bend. Continue around this, ignoring a turning on the left, and pass a telephone box on your left before continuing uphill past an old millstone in the wall on the left. Now go around a sharp left-hand bend and you'll see St Martin's Church directly ahead. Continue towards this, passing through a small gate and following an inscribed flagstone path to the main entrance **B**.

The building itself is really quite surreal with barely a true right angle anywhere in its construction. The tower leans at a quite incredible angle and parts of the main wall seem to almost bulge outwards – caused by movements in the underlying rock rather than shoddy workmanship. From the inside it's equally impressive and even the headstones on the surrounding graves lean at various different angles.

It's possible to shorten the walk and avoid a steep and rough climb by retracing your steps back to Cwmyoy Hall from here.

Now follow the path that leads uphill from the church, and go through the gate at the top onto another lane. Turn left for a few paces and then turn right at a waymark to Graig. Climb steeply up the sunken track to a gate at the top and go through this to a junction of paths, by a Hatherall Hill interpretation board **C**. Turn left to follow the broad path along beneath a spectacularly positioned wooden cabin to a gate. Go through this and keep straight ahead on a narrow path that follows a bank and a line of trees, and later a wall. Continue for 200 yds to a junction with a track on the right, above the buildings of Darren Isaf **D**, and turn sharp right onto this to climb steeply up towards the craggy knoll above. Aim to the right of a lone tree and then follow the wall on the right to a stile in the field corner. Cross this into the open access land beyond, and if you've the energy you can scramble up the steep narrow path on the right to the top, where there are wonderful views of the Vale of Ewyas and surrounding mountains. From the stile turn half left to follow a narrow path down through the bracken with a wall to the left. Go past a deep notch in

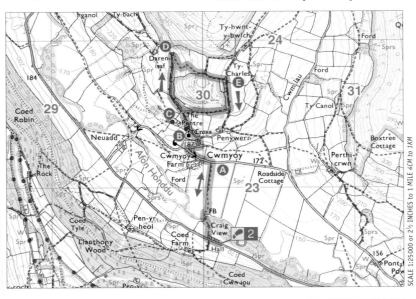

SCALE 1:25000 or 2½ INCHES to 1 MILE 4CM to 1KM

the crags to the right and continue as the track then widens and drops by a wall to a T-junction **E**, where you should turn right to pass beneath a house. Continue with a fence on the right and when this ends, ignore a stile straight ahead and instead turn right to follow the clear path back to the junction of paths by the interpretation board.

Turn left down the sunken track and retrace your earlier steps back past the church and down through the village to the footpath at **A**. Turn right here and continue back to Cwmyoy Hall. ●

St Martin's Church

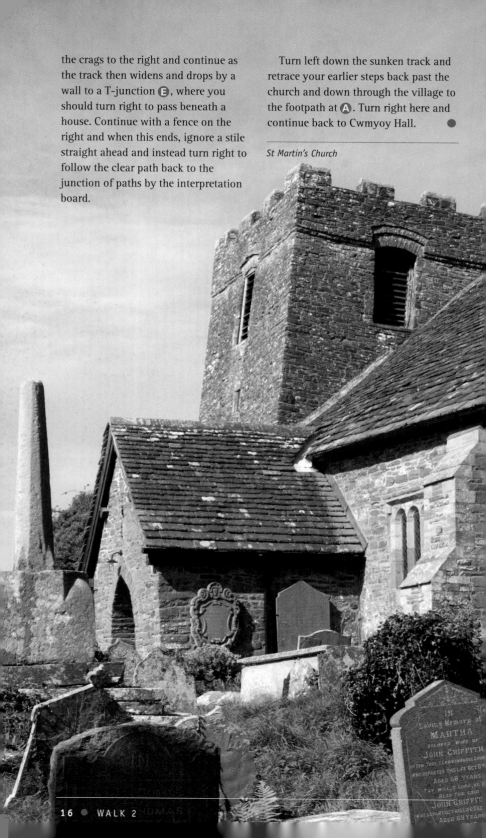

Llangynidr and the River Usk

Start	Llangynidr, main car park	**GPS waypoints**	
Distance	3¾ miles (6km)	🖉	SO 155 195
Height gain	330 feet (100m)	Ⓐ	SO 165 198
Approximate time	2 hours	Ⓑ	SO 158 202
Parking	Llangynidr Community Car Park (free)	Ⓒ	SO 152 202
		Ⓓ	SO 145 200
		Ⓔ	SO 146 198
Route terrain	A mixture of rough rocky paths and a well-surfaced canal towpath	Ⓕ	SO 160 197
Dog friendly	A couple of awkward stone stiles		
Ordnance Survey maps	Landranger 161 (The Black Mountains), Explorer OL13 (Brecon Beacons National Park – Eastern area)		

The River Usk begins high on the grassy uplands of the Mynydd Du, in the far west of the National Park. By the time it starts to meander southwards, it has become a magnificent waterway; wide and wild, with cataracts and rapids at almost every turn. As it approaches the village of Llangynidr, it starts to run parallel to the Brecon and Monmouthshire Canal, making it possible to link rough riverbank footpaths with the canal towpath to make a rewarding short circular walk.

🖉 Walk out of the small gate at the end of the car park and turn right onto the main road. Then turn straight away left, down Cyffredyn Lane and follow this down, over a bridge over the Brecon and Monmouthshire canal, which provides your return route.

Continue along the lane until you round a sharp right-hand bend, where you'll see a waymarked, walled footpath leading left. Follow this down to the River Usk Ⓐ and turn left to walk along the bank, on a sandy and sometimes rocky path. Cross a stile and continue in the same direction across a meadow, with great views down over the river.

Continue in the same direction now, crossing a succession of stiles and taking great care on a few rocky sections that can be very slippery when wet. After ½ mile the path turns slightly away from the riverside to pass an impressive waterfall Ⓑ. Stay with it as it drops back down again and keep ahead for another ½ mile and you'll come to a tarmac drive, with a gate ahead marked Pen Isha Coed. Walk up to the gate and then turn right infront of it to locate a narrow path that continues with bushes to the right, and a fence to the left. Keep ahead until you reach the road next to Llangynidr Bridge Ⓒ. This magnificent structure,

River Usk near Llangynidr

which spans the River Usk just north of the village, was originally built between 1587 and 1630, and would have originally carried packhorses, hence its narrow profile and the need for quite severe traffic restrictions.

Cross the road and follow the waymarked footpath straight ahead. It runs behind gardens for a short distance and then drops down to the banks of the river again. Now continue upstream, first in woods and later with better views. Ignore a path that leads up left,

marked with a red-topped post and continue for a few more paces, where a set of steps leads away from the river for a final time **D**.

Turn right at the top, and follow the narrow drive up to a road that runs alongside the canal, by a lock. There are five locks at Llangynidr, which were actually constructed to a slightly unusual size, but as the canal had no links with any other canal system, this did not really cause a problem. Turn right here to follow the road into Llangynidr for refreshments in the **Coach and Horses**, which you'll see to the left **E**.

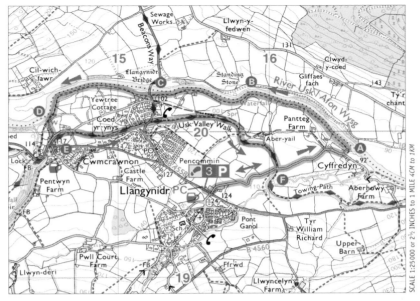

There's a fine viaduct over the Afon Crawnon, just a few paces farther along the canal from the main road.

If you do not want to visit the village, bear left, with the lock to your right, and follow the canal towpath easily eastwards. This is a good place to spot kingfishers, which can usually be heard before they are seen. You'll soon pass beneath a bridge, where the waterway runs under the B4560, a few yards above Llangynidr Bridge. You'll now need to walk beneath one more bridge before finally leaving the canal by a stile on the left, just before you reach another **F**. This rejoins Cyffredyn Lane, where you need to turn right to retrace your steps back up into the village and the car park. ●

SCALE 1:25 000 or 2½ INCHES to 1 MILE 4CM to 1KM

Lock on the Brecon and Monmouthshire Canal

Carreg Cennen

		GPS waypoints
Start	Carreg Cennen Castle	SN 666 193
Distance	4 miles (6.4km)	Ⓐ SN 666 188
Height gain	590 feet (180m)	Ⓑ SN 671 177
Approximate time	2 hours	Ⓒ SN 673 180
Parking	Free car park at Carreg Cennen	Ⓓ SN 675 192
Route terrain	Mainly clear paths across sheep pasture and through deciduous woodland	
Dog friendly	No dogs in castle grounds and many awkward stiles	
Ordnance Survey maps	Landranger 159 (Swansea & Gower), Explorer OL12 (Brecon Beacons National Park – Western area)	

The major attraction of this popular and well-waymarked walk in the western foothills of the Black Mountain is the ever-changing views of Carreg Cennen Castle, perched on its precipitous rock, from many different angles. The finale is superb – a steady ascent through woodland to the castle entrance.

One of the most dramatically sited castles in Britain, Carreg Cennen occupies a 300 feet (91m) - high exposed vertical limestone outcrop above the Cennen valley. It is everyone's idea of what a ruined castle should be like; it is even complete with an underground passage, hewn from the rock, which leads down into a cave. Originally a Welsh fortress, stronghold of the Lords Rhys, it was taken by the English and rebuilt and strengthened in the late 13th and early 14th centuries. Most of its extensive remains belong to that period.

At the far end of the car park go through a gate into the farmyard of Castle Farm. Do not continue ahead between the farm buildings towards the castle, but turn right just before the house to walk across a gravel area to a gate. Head downhill across a field, making for a stile and footpath sign in the bottom left-hand corner – like most of the signs on this walk it has a castle

symbol on it. Climb the stile and turn left along a narrow lane.

Ignore the first stile on the right and follow the lane downhill, curving left to a second stile just before a cottage, at a public footpath sign to Llwyn-bedw Ⓐ. Turn right over the stile, head downhill across a field, bearing slightly right to climb a stile in the field corner, and continue along a steep downhill path to climb another stile at the bottom. Go across the next field, cross a footbridge over the River Cennen and bear slightly left to head uphill to a stile. Climb it and continue steeply uphill, keeping parallel with a wire fence and line of trees on the left, towards a farm. Turn right at the top, before the buildings and continue beyond them before going through a gap in the hedge to join a drive. Turn right on to this and follow it easily away from the farm, through an area of scattered trees. After fording a stream, the track bends to the right and then curves left to reach a footpath sign a few yards ahead.

Turn left here over a stile and walk along a track, by a hedge bank on the right, bearing slightly left to cross a footbridge over a narrow stream and continuing to a stile. Climb it and bear slightly right along an enclosed track; this later emerges briefly into a more open area before continuing as a tree-lined route by the infant River Loughor on the right, a most attractive part of the walk. Climb a stile and if you want to see the source of the Loughor which issues from a cave here, another stile immediately to the right gives access.

Continue along the track, which curves slightly left and winds gently uphill, by a wire fence on the right. It then turns left to continue initially by a hedge bank on the right, and later veers left away from it to a stile. Climb the stile, bear right to pass between two hollows and head across to climb a stile onto a lane **B**.

Turn left, climb a stile beside a cattle-grid and continue along the lane as far as a right-hand bend **C**. Here keep ahead along a track, by a wire fence and hedge bank on the right. To the right are the Pillow Mounds – artificial rabbit warrens made by local people in the 19th century to ensure a regular supply of fresh meat. As the track curves right to the house, keep left to cross a stile and follow the waymarked path along with a fence to the left. This eventually swings right and becomes fenced on both sides as it heads towards the brow of a

hill. Continue over the hill and down again to a stile that leads onto a sunken track. Follow this down to join a broad track at a hairpin bend and turn left to take the lower track, and then, as the track turns sharply left, bear right to cross a stile and drop down a stony, tree-and hedge-lined path, climbing another stile and keeping by a stream on the right. Turn right to cross a footbridge over the stream, turn left along the other bank, climb a stile and keep ahead to cross another footbridge over the River Cennen **D**.

Turn right and almost immediately turn sharp left, at a footpath sign to Carreg Cennen, onto a path that heads steadily uphill through the lovely, slop-ing Coed y Castell (Castle Wood) towards the castle. Continue past the castle entrance at the top and follow the path as it descends, turning right through a kissing-gate, on through another one and down through Castle Farm to return to the start. ●

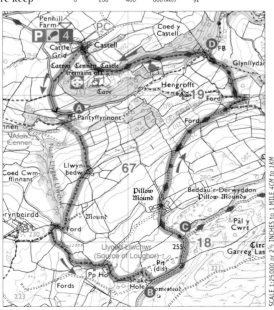

SCALE 1:25000 or 2½ INCHES to 1 MILE 4CM to 1KM

Ysgyryd Fawr

Start	Ysgyryd Fawr	**GPS waypoints**
Distance	2½ miles (4km)	SO 328 164
Height gain	960 feet (315m)	Ⓐ SO 327 166
		Ⓑ SO 327 169
Approximate time	2 hours	Ⓒ SO 331 182
Parking	National Park free car park on B4521 between Abergavenny and Skenfrith	
Route terrain	Well marked paths through woodland followed by a deer path along a narrow ridge. Some steep ground	
Ordnance Survey maps	Landranger 161 (The Black Mountains), Explorer OL13 (Brecon Beacons National Park – Eastern area)	

The distinctive bulk of Ysgyryd Fawr, alternatively called the Skirrid or Holy Mountain, lies to the north east of Abergavenny and is the most easterly detached outlier of the Black Mountains. Its 'holy' connections derive from its shape: various legends claim that the cleft in its ridge was created either by Noah's Ark or at the time of the Crucifixion, but the more prosaic explanation is that it was the result of a massive landslip. The walk to its summit, a steep climb initially through woodland and later along an open, grassy, narrow ridge, gives splendid views in all directions. Although it is possible to descend from the summit to a path that encircles the hill, the northern slopes are so steep that it is better to return by the same route used on the ascent, with the opportunity to enjoy the fine views again from a different angle.

Approaching the summit of Ysgyryd Fawr

Start by walking around the barrier at the side of the car park, and walk along the track, which soon bends around to the right and climbs gently between hedges to reach a double gate with a stile on its left. Climb over the stile and walk past a bench and up the forest track for another 20 yds to a turning on the right Ⓐ, marked by a short post with an arrow on the top. Follow this path upwards, soon

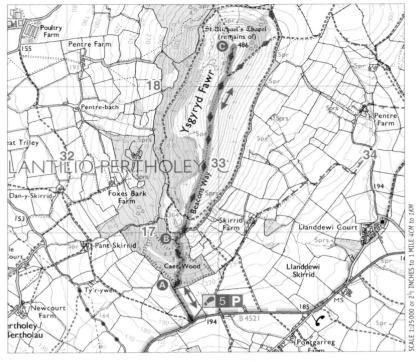

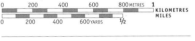

0	200	400	600	800 METRES	1
					KILOMETRES
					MILES
0	200	400	600 YARDS	½	

climbing a few wooden steps, and then continue for another 20 yds to a junction with another broad forest track. Keep straight ahead to cross this and continue upwards on a broad footpath that is again marked by a small post on the right.

This section of path is a lot longer than the previous one, continuing deep into the woods. Stay with it and eventually you'll emerge onto another forest track, which you cross again to continue the climb. Follow the path upwards again and you'll soon come to a large gate, with a walker's gate to the right of it **B**.

Go through the gate and turn right to walk along a level path, with a wall to your right. Continue for 100 yds and turn left onto a path that can be seen winding up the hillside.

The path continues quite steeply uphill, eventually emerging onto a small, open grassy area. Turn sharp right, shortly turn left to follow a well-worn path up to the ridge, and continue along the ridge to the triangulation pillar at the summit **C**. The walk along this narrow, grassy ridge is most enjoyable, a gradual and easy climb with magnificent views on both sides. The finest views of all are from the summit (1,595 feet/486m): a great arc takes in Abergavenny, the Usk Valley, Blorenge, the Sugar Loaf, the Black Mountains, and the more gentle countryside to the east looking towards the English border and the Wye and Monnow valleys. In the Middle Ages a chapel was built here for the pilgrims who were attracted by the hill's religious connections but it is virtually impossible to see any traces of it now.

From the summit retrace your steps to the start. ●

Carn Goch

		GPS waypoints
Start	Carn Goch	SN 681 242
Distance	3½ miles (4.8km)	Ⓐ SN 690 243
Height gain	820 feet (250m)	Ⓑ SN 696 242
Approximate time	2 hours	Ⓒ SN 692 228
Parking	Free parking area on narrow lane that leads south from Bethlehem	Ⓓ SN 688 228 Ⓔ SN 681 234
Route terrain	A mix of paths over farmland and rough mountainside	
Ordnance Survey maps	Landrangers 159 (Swansea & Gower) and 160 (Brecon Beacons), Explorer OL12 (Brecon Beacons National Park – Western area)	

Situated in the far north west corner of the National Park, Carn Goch is one of the largest and most impressive hill forts in Wales. It's actually two hill forts in one: Y Gaer Fach (the small fort) and Y Gaer Fawr (the large fort), which are positioned on adjacent hilltops high above the Twyi Valley. The name Carn Goch translates to the Red Cairn and likely a reference to the huge burial cairn that crowns the larger fort. The land is owned and maintained by the National Park Authority. This walk links an exploration of the two hill forts with the hills to the south, which rise higher but are somehow not quite as impressive. It finishes easily, first dropping through sheep pasture and then following a narrow lane.

From the left-hand end of the parking area, take the clear path that leads behind the interpretation signs and follow it steadily uphill, passing an impressive standing stone that is in fact a memorial to Plaid Cymru MP Gwynfor Evans, and despite its authentic appearance was actually erected in July 2006. Continue to the top where you cross a bank of stones – the smaller fort's western ramparts. Keep ahead; still following a vague path and you'll drop past another bank of stones, the eastern ramparts, onto the broad saddle that divides the two hilltops.

Stay with the path to cross this saddle, then climb up onto the earthworks that once protected the western end of Y Gaer Fawr. Turn sharp left when you reach the top and follow a steep and stony ramp up through the ramparts onto easier ground. Now keep straight ahead towards the huge cairn Ⓐ. The views from this section are quite breathtaking and it's easy to see how well-protected the fort would have been in such an imposing position.

Keep the giant cairn to your left and drop into a hollow with a grassy ridge to your right. Head towards the far end of this ridge where a gap in the stone ramparts leads out onto a rough but gentle slope. Bear half right to follow a vague track down across the hill, eventually reaching the road opposite the drive to Tan-y-lan Farm . Turn right onto the road and as you approach Garn Wen Farm, keep left to cross a stile that leads onto a narrow path with the house up and to the right.

Follow this through a gate, where it broadens and then keep straight ahead climbing up through further gates to a small square field, where you turn left to a junction with another track, and then turn right onto it, to continue in the same direction. At the next gate, turn right to follow the field edge to a stile and cross this and keep to the left hand, top edge of the field to pass through a gap in the wall on your left to another stile **C**.

Cross this into woodland and keep ahead to gradually drop down to join a broad track at the bottom. Turn right to go through a gate, and then turn left to drop to a stile **D**. Cross this and continue down the tree-lined track, which follows the line of a stream. Keep straight ahead, crossing a succession of stiles and trying to keep to the easiest and driest ground and you'll eventually cross a stile that leads into an open field.

Keep straight ahead to the bottom of this and then continue with the row of trees to your right, bearing half left at the bottom of this field to cross another stile. Now follow a marker post diagonally across the field towards a wall corner and then deflect slightly left again to drop to a gate **E**.

Turn right onto the road and follow it past Cwmdu Cottage and around to the left. Drop to cross a bridge and then continue to a junction, where you turn right. Now follow this lane easily back to the cattle-grid by the car park, where you turn right to finish. ●

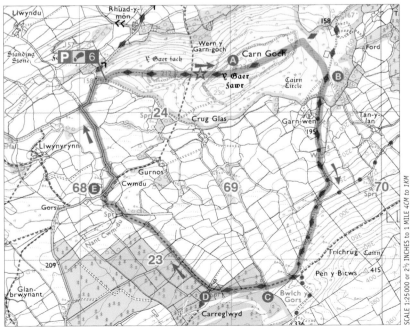

Allt yr Esgair

Start	Allt yr Esgair	**GPS waypoints**
Distance	3½ miles (5.6km)	SO 129 226
Height gain	950 feet (290m)	Ⓐ SO 123 251
Approximate time	2 hours	Ⓑ SO 131 231
Parking	Free car park and picnic area off A40 ½ mile south of Llansantffraed	
Route terrain	Wooded paths, steep and occasionally muddy in places, and a short section that crosses an open hilltop	
Ordnance Survey maps	Landranger 161 (The Black Mountains), Explorer OL13 (Brecon Beacons National Park – Eastern area)	

Allt yr Esgair is a narrow, wooded ridge that lies between the Usk Valley and Llangorse Lake. From its highest slopes there are extensive views and attractive woodland clothes its lower slopes. There is plenty of climbing but none is too steep or strenuous.

Begin by going through a gate beside the car park, at a public bridleway sign to Allt yr Esgair, onto an enclosed track, and almost immediately turn left through a metal gate. Head diagonally uphill across two fields, go through a

The Brecon Beacons from Allt yr Esgair

gate and continue uphill in the same direction to enter an attractive wooded area. All the way there are fine views through the trees to the left across the Usk Valley to the Brecon Beacons. Go through a gate and continue through the woodland, to climb steadily to reach a track.

Turn left along this lovely, grassy, fairly flat track which keeps along the left-hand edge of woodland; below on the left Llansantffraed church and the village of Talybont-on-Usk can be seen. Continue through another gate and keep ahead, staying on the main track, to eventually join another track at a waymark post. Keep left onto this, waymarked Penorth, to continue in the same direction, and go through a succession of gates, passing the ruined Paragon Tower, an early 19th-century hunting lodge, on the right. Keep ahead along a narrow path that winds through gorse, trees, bracken and rough grass; keeping roughly in the same direction the whole time. When it emerges into an open meadow walk straight ahead across it, bearing right at the far end into trees above a covered reservoir. In front is a superb view of Llangorse Lake backed by Mynydd Llangorse.

Once in the trees, turn sharp right **Ⓐ** onto a path marked 'Pedestrians only' that leads steeply up through brambles and gorse. The path, sunken and enclosed in places, heads quite steeply uphill, eventually merging with the path for horses and cyclists, and following a dry stone wall up onto the open hilltop, by some large rocks. Here is the finest view of all, over the Usk Valley to the Brecon Beacons

Keep ahead, and descend to a gate, then continue to the right of a plantation to a fork. Bear right towards a wall corner and then continue with the wall to your left and a fence to your right. Keep ahead through another gate and drop down through a meadow to another gate. Go through this onto a tree-lined track and take the first turning on the right **Ⓑ**. Follow this down until it bends to the right and heads down to a farm.

Just before reaching the farm, turn

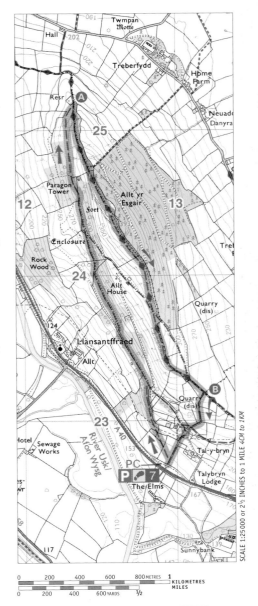

SCALE 1:25000 or 2½ INCHES to 1 MILE 4CM to 1KM

```
0      200    400    600    800 METRES   1
                                         KILOMETRES
0      200    400    600 YARDS    ½        MILES
```

sharp left, waymarked A40, and go through a gate to a T-junction of paths, where you turn right. A few yards ahead turn left (not sharply left through a metal gate) down an enclosed, stony, sunken, tree-lined path. Go through a gate and continue down to go through another gate to return to the start. ●

The Monmouthshire and Brecon Canal

		GPS waypoints
Start	Abergavenny Castle	🖉 SO 299 140
Distance	5½ miles (8.9km)	Ⓐ SO 291 139
Height gain	330 feet (100m)	Ⓑ SO 287 138
Approximate time	2½ hours	Ⓒ SO 286 132
Parking	Nearby Byfield Road car park, fee on Tuesdays	Ⓓ SO 285 130
		Ⓔ SO 268 137
Route terrain	Good paths across riverside meadows, canal towpaths and well-surfaced disused railway line. Crosses a busy road	
Dog friendly	Care needed on the road	
Ordnance Survey maps	Landranger 161 (The Black Mountains), Explorer OL13 (Brecon Beacons National Park – Eastern area)	

As most of this walk is either across riverside meadows, along a canal towpath or along the track of a disused railway, it is bound to be easy and relaxing. The sections along the banks of the River Usk and the towpath of the Monmouthshire and Brecon Canal are especially attractive and there are some fine views over the Usk Valley to the Sugar Loaf and Ysgyryd Fawr.

Encircled by the outlying hills of the Black Mountains Abergavenny guards one of the main routes into the heart of South Wales, a position appreciated by the Norman conquerors, who built the castle. In the Middle Ages Abergavenny Castle was one of the main border strongholds, but nowadays little remains and the 'keep' is a 19th-century imitation. Abergavenny lies on the eastern edge of the National Park and makes an excellent walking centre.

🖉 The walk begins at the entrance to the castle grounds. Facing the entrance, turn right and head down the lane beside the castle walls. After about 100 yds the lane ends and ahead are two paths; take the right-hand, lower, one which descends by a wall on the right, and turn right at the bottom onto a paved path. Pass through a gate and continue across a meadow to reach the bank of the River Usk. Ahead is a grand view of Blorenge.

Turn right onto another paved path that follows the river along to Usk Bridge Ⓐ, turn left over the bridge and immediately turn right onto a lane, which is a footpath that leads to the cemetery. The lane passes to the right of the cemetery and then swings

left **B**, downhill, to pass through a tunnel that leads beneath the Heads of the Valleys Road. Continue past a garden centre and uphill slightly to meet the road on the outskirts of Llanfoist village, close to the Llanfoist Crossing car park **C**.

Cross the road and continue up the lane ahead, which is signposted 'Blorenge and Usk Valley Walk', passing to the right of Llanfoist church and heading steadily uphill between trees. At a fork bear right to an aqueduct but just before reaching it turn right up steps to join the canal towpath **D**. Turn right to follow the towpath for $1\frac{1}{2}$ miles by the tree-fringed, tranquil waters of the canal, high above the Usk Valley with fine views to the right over Abergavenny and the Sugar Loaf, and below the steep, thickly wooded lower slopes of Blorenge on the left. The canal was built between 1797 and 1812 to provide a link between Brecon and the Bristol Channel and carried coal, iron, lime and agricultural produce. After the inevitable decline and fall into disuse, it was restored and reopened in 1970 as a recreational waterway.

At the first bridge turn left over the canal and turn right to walk along the other bank, passing under a second bridge and continuing past a marina by Govilon Boat Club. At a third bridge **E** climb steps to leave the canal and turn right along the track of a disused railway, part of a line built in the 1860s to link the coal mines around Merthyr Tydfil, Tredegar and Ebbw Vale to the Monmouthshire and Brecon Canal. Follow the track for just under $1\frac{1}{2}$ miles; it is lined most of the way with attractive willows and silver birches and there are more fine views of Blorenge and the Usk Valley. On reaching Llanfoist Crossing, pass through a wooden barrier and turn left **C** beneath the Heads of the Valleys Road to retrace part of the outward route to the Usk Bridge on the edge of Abergavenny.

Cross the bridge and for the final section you can either continue along the outward route by taking the paved path beside the river, or alternatively head diagonally across the meadows, along a clear path that ducks into trees, close to some houses. Follow this to a kissing-gate in the far corner and continue through the Byfield Road car park to the road, where you turn right to return to the castle. ●

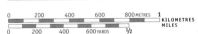

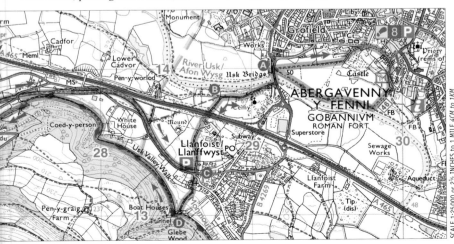

Mynydd Llangorse

		GPS waypoints
Start	Cockit Hill	
Distance	5½ miles (8.9km)	✎ SO 160 283
Height gain	1,115 feet (340m)	Ⓐ SO 168 266
		Ⓑ SO 165 261
Approximate time	3 hours	Ⓒ SO 159 250
Parking	Small parking area on bend at	Ⓓ SO 152 265
	highest point of minor road	
	1¾ miles (2.8km) east of Llangors village	
Route terrain	Clear paths and tracks around and across a high mountain. Some muddy stretches	
Ordnance Survey maps	Landranger 161 (The Black Mountains), Explorer OL13 (Brecon Beacons National Park – Eastern area)	

This circuit of Mynydd Llangorse provides superb and ever-changing views for remarkably little effort. The only strenuous section is the steep climb between Ⓐ and Ⓑ out of the valley of Cwm Sorgwm on to the moorland plateau. The walk along the western slopes is particularly enjoyable.

✎ First head southwards down the lane and after a few yards bear right onto a track which keeps parallel to the lane but later bears gradually right away from it. Follow the track along the side of Cwm Sorgwm and below the eastern slopes of Mynydd Llangorse for about 1¼ miles. About 100 yds before reaching a metal gate, bear right Ⓐ onto a grassy path which heads up the hillside, clips a fence corner and then continues more steeply uphill.

Follow the path all the way up to a sharp right-hand bend and go around this before climbing a little more on to the plateau above. Now continue along a grassy path through bracken and heather to a prominent cairn Ⓑ. The only strenuous part of the walk is now over and from the cairn there are superb views over the Black Mountains and the Usk Valley.

Continue past the cairn over the open, breezy moorland on top of Mynydd Llangorse. Stay on the main path all the while, keeping right at one fork, and then left at second, to reach a crossroads of paths and tracks just in front of a small group of stunted trees, a rarity on this windswept plateau. Here turn left onto a broad grassy track and follow it past a boundary stone on the right after a few paces. Continue across open moorland, gradually curving left and heading gently downhill to a crossroads marked by a cairn Ⓒ. Turn right and follow the clear track, which runs parallel to a fence on the left and where it ends continue ahead. The path curves to the right to contour along the western slopes of Mynydd Llangorse. Descend to go through a gate, continue, passing to the right of a cottage and on across a meadow, before descending again through conifer woodland. Bear right, go through a gate and continue

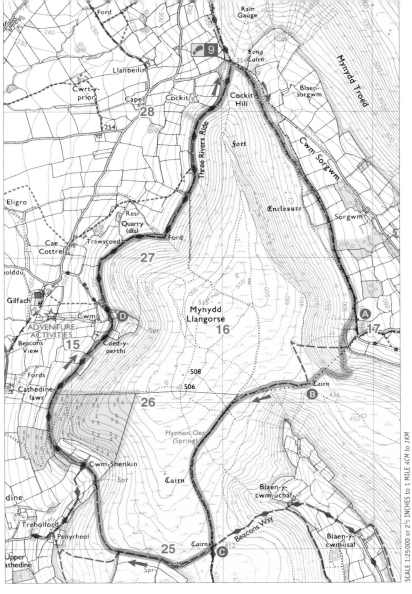

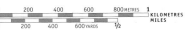

down through the wood. Cross a track and keep ahead along an attractive tree-lined path, by the bottom edge of woodland and with a wire fence on the left.

Go through a gate to leave the wood and continue, keeping by a fence on the left for almost the remainder of the walk. The western slopes of Mynydd Llangorse are more wooded than those on the eastern side and this part of the walk makes a striking contrast with the early section.

Ford a stream ❶ and continue, taking the right-hand, upper path at the fork just in front. Continue along the same line, with a fence to your left and open hillside to the right, and cross another stream, now with the distinctive bulk of Mynydd Troed ahead. Eventually the path veers slightly right away from the fence and then leads back to the start.●

Table Mountain

		GPS waypoints	
Start	Crickhowell		SO 218 183
Distance	5 miles (8km)	**A**	SO 221 183
Height gain	1,250 feet (380m)	**B**	SO 223 192
Approximate time	3 hours	**C**	SO 227 205
Parking	Pay and Display in Crickhowell	**D**	SO 225 207
Route terrain	Easy paths over sheep pasture mixed with rougher mountain paths. Some steep climbs	**E**	SO 218 208
		F	SO 215 189
Ordnance Survey maps	Landranger 161 (The Black Mountains), Explorer OL13 (Brecon Beacons National Park – Eastern area)		

It is easy to see how Crug Hywel, with its distinctive flat top, lying just north of Crickhowell, gets its nickname of Table Mountain. From Crickhowell the 1,481-ft (451m) summit – crowned by an Iron Age fort and with a superb viewpoint – is reached via lanes, farm tracks and field and moorland paths. Both ascent and descent are gradual and relatively easy.

Crickhowell, with its many Georgian houses, gets its name from the mountain Crug Hywel. Crickhowell's most famous son is the surveyor Sir George Everest, after whom Mount Everest is named.

Begin in the main car park, off Greenhill Road. Walk back out onto Greenhill Road and turn left to walk uphill to a mini roundabout, where you turn right. Take the next left, Great Oak Road **A**, which is signed to Grwyne Fechan, and follow this road uphill for just over ¹/₂ mile, heading for Table Mountain in front. Where the road bends slightly right turn left through a metal gate **B**, at a public footpath sign, and take a tarmac track towards a farm.

Go through a metal gate, continue through the farmyard and in front of the farmhouse turn right through another metal gate. Keep straight ahead, with a hedge to your left, to a stile that leads onto an enclosed hedge-lined

track. Turn left onto this and walk uphill to a stile. Climb it, continue along the right-hand edge of a field, climb another stile and head steadily uphill along the right-hand edge of the next field, by a wire fence and line of trees on the right, to climb a set of steps and another stile. Turn left onto a tarmac drive and leave it almost immediately to the right to climb a stile and continue along the right-hand edge of the next field, by a hedge on the right.

Climb a stile in the top corner and turn right to follow both the yellow waymark and a 'To the Mountain' sign along a pleasant, tree-lined path, passing to the left of a farmhouse. The next stile admits you to the open moorland of Table Mountain. Keep straight ahead to follow a clear, grassy path gently uphill between bracken over the lower slopes of the mountain, with a wall down to the right curving slightly left to a fork **C**. Here bear left along the upper path to continue contouring along the side of the mountain, and at the highest point on the shoulder take the path to the left for a brief detour to the summit. Pass through the rocks that mark the ramparts of the Iron Age fort to reach the summit cairn **D**, where there is a tremendous all-round view.

Continue to the highest point of the table, and follow a clear but steep path down beneath a rocky outcrop to level ground below. Keep ahead to meet the main path at a crossroads, and turn left, to drop slightly to a wall. Now follow the wall rightwards, following a path that meanders across the moorland, crossing several small streams and heading downhill. Pass a waymark post by a tumbledown building and continue, soon dropping steeply to a sheepfold in a corner. Enter this and turn left, as signposted, to a gate **E**.

Now continue down a walled track for a few paces, where you come to a short awkward section of about 20 yds along the bed of a stream – there are plenty of rocks to step on to keep your feet dry. Eventually the path spills into a narrow field, where you should keep ahead, with the stream now to your left, to woodland at the bottom. On the edge of the trees turn left to ford the stream and turn right through a metal gate to follow a sunken path downhill along the left-hand edge of the narrow, steep-sided, wooded valley of Cwm Cumbeth to a gate. Go through and continue along the edge of this delightful wooded valley, passing through a gate before coming to a fork with a new metal gate on the left, and a wooden stile to the right. Cross the wooden stile, which is signed Beacons Way, and follow the path straight down with the fence to your right, through a couple of fields and into a compound to the right of a barn.

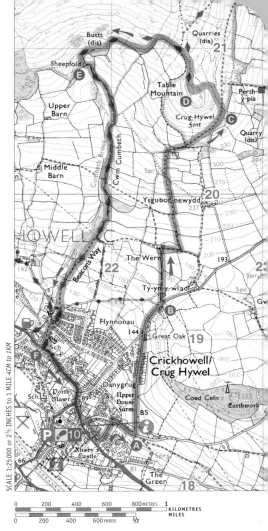

SCALE 1:25000 or 2½ INCHES to 1 MILE 4CM to 1KM

Cross the stile to the left of the stable buildings, and turn left onto a lane, and then immediately right, though a gate, onto a housing road. Walk straight across this to follow a tarmac footpath downhill between houses and cross another road, to follow another tarmac footpath to a junction with a third road. Turn right onto this and swing left to walk past a school. Where the road ends, keep ahead on a narrow pathway that leads down to the main road **F**. Turn left and walk past the **Bear Hotel** before bearing left up Standard Street and then right, back into the car park.●

Craig y Cilau and Llangattock

		GPS waypoints
Start	Craig y Cilau	
Distance	5½ miles (8.8km). Shorter version 4½ miles (7.2km)	☑ SO 185 168 Ⓐ SO 187 174 Ⓑ SO 206 172
Height gain	1,115 feet (340m). Shorter version 1,015 feet (310m)	Ⓒ SO 207 177 Ⓓ SO 210 177
Approximate time	3 hours (2½ hours for shorter versions)	Ⓔ SO 207 171 Ⓕ SO 205 159 Ⓖ SO 200 159
Parking	On verge below Craig y Cilau	
Route terrain	Clear paths and tracks around and across a high mountain. Some muddy stretches	
Ordnance Survey maps	Landranger 161 (The Black Mountains), Explorer OL13 (Brecon Beacons National Park – Eastern area)	

Craig y Cilau forms part of the northern edge of Mynydd Llangatwg, a steep, dramatic limestone escarpment overlooking the Usk Valley. Not only is it a fine viewpoint but it is of considerable botanical, geological and historic interest. The walk starts just below the escarpment and the first part of it is along field paths and quiet lanes, mostly through or along the edge of woodland, and includes a short but very attractive section along the towpath of the Monmouthshire and Brecon Canal and a visit to the village of Llangattock. Later there is a steep climb onto the escarpment, followed by a splendid walk across the face of it before the descent to return to the starting point. The shorter version of the walk omits the village of Llangattock.

📷 Face uphill from the cattle-grid and look down to your right to find a waymarked stile. Climb this and keep close to the line of trees on your right, go through a metal gate in the bottom right-hand corner and follow a stony path into woodland. Keep straight ahead to drop to the bottom of the wood, and after emerging into a field bear left to keep parallel to its left-hand edge, which is bordered by woodland, descending steeply to the valley floor.

At the bottom, just before reaching a ford, turn right Ⓐ along a track which climbs gently above the wooded valley on the left. Where the track peters out keep ahead along the left-hand edge of a succession of fields, by the woodland of Coed y Cilau on the left, climbing a series of stiles. Eventually go through a metal gate, continue along an enclosed track, and after passing through another metal gate the track curves first to the right and then to the left to Cilau Farm.

At the boundary of the farm complex turn right at a fingerpost and climb the waymarked stile at the corner. Walk the field edge behind the barns and farmhouse to a stile onto a tarred lane. Turn left and then take the stile on the right at the corner, keeping along the left edge of the subsequent field. Climb another stile, bear half right across the next field, making for a stile and public footpath sign on its right-hand edge, and climb the stile onto a lane. Turn left, cross the canal bridge **B** and turn right down to the canal.

For the shorter version of the walk, omitting Llangattock, turn left here and walk along the towpath to the next bridge about 100 yds ahead. Pass under it and turn left up to a lane, turning left to rejoin the full walk at **E**.

Turn right under the bridge and then continue along the right bank of the canal for nearly ½ mile, as far as the next bridge. This is a delightful stretch of the Monmouthshire and Brecon Canal: it is tree-lined, tranquil and with some lovely views through gaps in trees on the right of Llangattock church, the Usk Valley, Crickhowell and on the horizon the distinctive, flat top of Table Mountain.

At the bridge **C** turn right through a gateway, and turn right downhill along a lane, following it around a right-hand bend into Llangattock, an attractive village of narrow streets, old cottages and a solid-looking medieval church. The lane passes a new housing development all the way up to a sharp right-hand bend and go around this

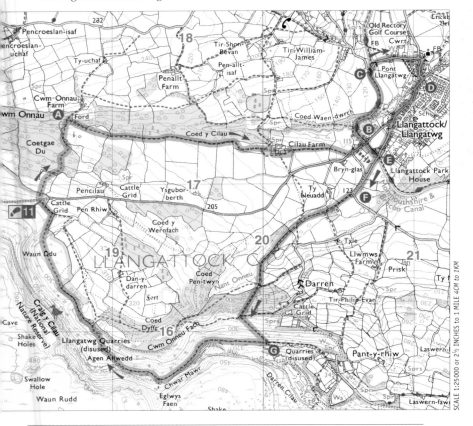

Craig y Cilau

before climbing a little more on to the plateau above. Now go through the village to a T-junction . Turn right along the road signposted to Beaufort and keep straight ahead at a fork, by a chapel on the right. Cross a canal bridge and continue along the lane for another ¼ mile. In front looms the forbidding-looking escarpment of Craig y Cilau.

Where the lane bends left turn right over a stile, at a public footpath sign, almost immediately following the direction of another public footpath sign to the left. Walk along a grassy path, by a hedge on the left; this was once part of a tramway that carried stone from the quarries on Mynydd Llangatwg to Llangattock Wharf on the Monmouthshire and Brecon Canal. The path later becomes enclosed and continues through woodland. Go through a metal gate, keep ahead to go through another and continue along this attractive, partially tree-lined path. Soon after passing to the right of a cottage the path bears left to cross a stream and continues along the right-hand edge of a field to a stile at the foot of a steep incline. This incline was the means by which wagons loaded with limestone were lowered down the escarpment into the valley from where they were carried via the tramway to the canal.

Climb the stile and then climb the incline, which is in two parts. This is by far the most strenuous and tiring part of the walk. On reaching a flatter open area at the top of the first incline keep ahead for a few yards and then turn left to climb a second incline, slightly less steep and stony than the first one, turning sharp right at the top onto a track . Now comes the most scenic and one of the easiest parts of the walk along this broad, flat, well-surfaced track, also a former quarry tramway, as it contours across the face of the escarpment, with magnificent views to the right over the Usk Valley, Crickhowell, Table Mountain and the Black Mountains, and a spectacular view in front of the line of the curving escarpment. A notice says that you are entering Craig y Cilau National Nature Reserve, noted for its cave systems, rare flora and limestone woodland.

The old trackbed passes below the entrance to Eglwys Faen cave and then curves beneath an old quarry face. At the far end of this look carefully for a waymark post indicating a path forking off to the right. Take this, which descends gradually across the steep slope. In 200 yds you will reach a waymarked split in the path. Keep right dropping through woodland of gnarled hawthorns to reach a wood. Keep this on your right; the path undulates through tumbled boulders and beneath contorted old ash trees to gain an open area of common.

Head diagonally across this, passing just to the right of two fenced areas and aiming for an obvious path up the hillside ahead. Pass by another Nature Reserve sign and trace the fence through to a rough lane. Turn left onto this to return to the cattle-grid and the starting point of the walk. ●

Tor y Foel

		GPS waypoints	
Start	Llangynidr		SO 146 200
Distance	5½ miles (8.9km)	Ⓐ	SO 144 197
Height gain	1,575 feet (480m)	Ⓑ	SO 134 193
Approximate time	3 hours	Ⓒ	SO 114 194
Parking	Small free parking area at Lower Lock	Ⓓ	SO 113 204
		Ⓔ	SO 127 200
Route terrain	Mainly easy to follow, waymarked paths and tracks over farmland and open hilltops		
Ordnance Survey maps	Landranger 161 (The Black Mountains), Explorer OL13 (Brecon Beacons National Park – Eastern area)		

The lonely outlier of Tor y Foel is wedged between the central Brecon Beacons and the Black Mountains, and although it offers fine views over both massifs, it actually belongs to neither. It's one of those mountains that can be seen from just about anywhere; and its distinctive lofty, yet rounded outline is easily recognised, no matter where it's viewed. The hill is at its most impressive from the Usk Valley, where the steep north and west flanks really do look quite daunting. Yet it's not difficult to climb, especially from the east, where good, well-waymarked paths lead through a succession of sheep pastures all the way to the summit. This walk makes the most of these paths to tackle the peak from east to west. It returns on scenic paths that drop easily into the Usk Valley, finishing on a delightful stretch of the Monmouthshire & Brecon Canal.

The walk starts at Llangynidr's Lower Lock, which is one of five locks in the Llangynidr area. There's parking here for a few cars. Follow the towpath away from the lock with the canal to your left and walk beneath the bridge carrying the B4558. Now round a long right-hand bend and when you reach the first of the next locks

Tor y Foel from Table Mountain

Ⓐ, bear left, over the little bridge, to follow a clear footpath up through woodland to a stile, which is waymarked with a Beacons Way disk. Continue through the woodland to another stile which leads out onto open pasture, and keep straight ahead across the field to another stile, still following the Beacons Way. Bear right to follow the hedge to another stile and cross this and turn left to follow the field edge up to a drive.

Go straight across this and continue in the same direction, towards the top corner, where you need to cross another stile. Now continue in the same direction, all the time following Beacons Way signs, until you reach a lane ahead of a farmhouse. Turn right onto this and follow it up and around to the left, where you need to turn right onto a tree-lined track **Ⓑ**.

Now follow this straight up, keeping to the right-hand edge of the field the whole time, with great views ahead to Tor y Foel. Continue like this until a stile ahead leads into a narrow finger of

SCALE 1:25000 or 2½ INCHES to 1 MILE 4CM to 1KM

open hillside, with a plantation to your right. Now continue straight ahead, passing the end of the plantation and climbing steeply up onto the summit

Waun Rhycl and the Talybont Reservoir from Tor y Foel

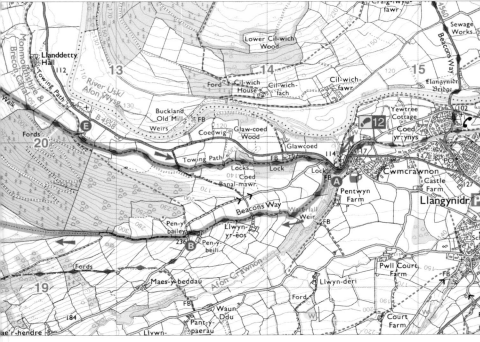

C. The very top is marked by the smallest of cairns but the views are absolutely magnificent with the Talybont Forest and Reservoir stretched out at your feet and the imposing bulk of the main Brecon Beacons dominating the vista directly ahead. There are also fine views down to the south, to the Crawnon Valley – a rarely visited glen that slices decisively into the limestone wastes of Mynydd Llangynidr.

To descend, turn right, away from the main path onto a narrower, fainter path that descends towards the north west. Follow this easily down to the narrow road below and turn right onto this to follow it downhill for 500 yds to an obvious, broad muddy track on the right. Take this, and climb uphill slightly, before curving left and dropping to a gate **D**. Now follow the path across the hillside towards the middle of a band of trees ahead. Go through a gate and continue across another field, dropping all the time until

you have the hedge to your left. Now continue through another gate and along the bottom edge of another field to yet another gate. Carry on in the same direction, dropping all the time, and cross a stream before going though another gate at the bottom corner of a wood. Keep heading in the same direction, passing through further gates until you eventually reach a hedged track that leads easily down to a bridge over the Monmouthshire & Brecon Canal **E**. Cross the bridge and turn right onto the towpath to walk easily along with the canal to your right.

You'll soon reach the first of three locks in quick succession, and after another few minutes, you'll reach a boatyard and another lock, where you crossed the canal earlier. Keep straight ahead to curve back round beneath the B4558 and continue back to the start. ●

Ystradfellte and Sarn Helen

Start	Ystradfellte	
Distance	6½ miles (10.4km)	
Height gain	2,100 feet (640m)	
Approximate time	3½ hours	
Parking	Free car park in Ystradfellte	
Route terrain	Mainly good paths and tracks with a short section on a very quiet lane. *One section of moor would require careful navigation in poor visibility*	
Ordnance Survey maps	Landranger 160 (Brecon Beacons), Explorer OL12 (Brecon Beacons National Park – Western area)	

GPS waypoints

- SN 929 134
- Ⓐ SN 924 138
- Ⓑ SN 926 154
- Ⓒ SN 925 166
- Ⓓ SN 911 148
- Ⓔ SN 907 138
- Ⓕ SN 912 141

This is a surprisingly tough walk through an austere, atmospheric limestone landscape with wonderful views over the empty expanses of the Fforest Fawr mountain range. The highlights include a lovely section of Sarn Helen – an old Roman road that runs almost the full length of Wales – and the impressive standing stone of Maen Madoc, resplendent with a Roman inscription.

The isolated hamlet of Ystradfellte comprises little more than a church, a pub, a post office and a few houses, but it makes an excellent walking centre.

🖉 Go through a gap at the top of the car park and turn left onto a tarmac track that leads uphill through a metal gate. Where the tarmac track turns right to Tyle Farm continue uphill along an enclosed track, passing through two metal gates to emerge onto open moorland Ⓐ.

Ignoring a public footpath sign to the left, keep ahead, by a wall on the right, along a grassy path which heads straight across an austere, open landscape of grass, heather and isolated trees, littered with limestone boulders. Go through a metal gate and continue between the crags of Carnau Gwynion to another metal gate. Go through that

to walk along a wide, walled, grassy track from which there are superb views ahead over mountains, moorland and forest. Go through a gate and follow the track to a road Ⓑ. Keep ahead along the road for ¾ mile, entering conifer plantations and passing Blaen Llia car park.

Just after the car park entrance there is a grand view ahead up the valley and to the right across the bare slopes of Fan Dringarth. About ¼ mile past the car park turn sharp left Ⓒ onto a broad track (waymarked Sarn Helen), go through a metal gate and follow the track through conifers. This track follows a well-preserved stretch of Sarn Helen, a Roman road that linked South and North Wales. Here it runs across the open moorlands of Fforest Fawr between the forts of Nidum (Neath) and Y Gaer, near Brecon. After going through another metal gate, leave the trees and continue across open moorland, with fine sweeping views across the valley of the River Neath, passing the isolated standing stone of Maen Madoc. It is probably of Celtic origin but the Romans later carved a Latin inscription on it. The track winds downhill, bending right through a metal gate to reach a bridge that spans the Afon Nedd Fechan 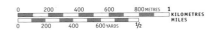.

Cross the bridge and continue along Sarn Helen, at first climbing steeply on a very rough surface. Continue all the way up to a gate at the corner of a plantation. Go through and bear half

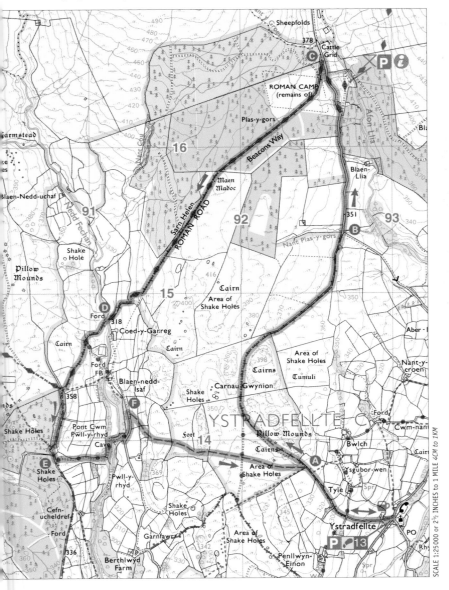

The isolated standing stone of Maen Madoc

left onto a good track that's signed Sarn Helen, and follow this with the wood to your right past a turning that comes in from the right to another gate by a large shake hole. Go through this and after a few more paces, turn left onto a clear track that heads downhill **E**.

Follow this steeply downhill and around to the left and then right to cross an old bridge over the Afon Nedd Fechan. Climb steeply away from the bridge and at the top, turn left onto a lane. Follow this for a few paces to a gate and a footpath sign to Ystradfellte **F**. Go through and turn sharp right to head diagonally uphill across a field to go through a gate in the top corner and continue in the same direction across the next field and through the trees to another gate. Continue once more across open grassy moorland, passing a waymark post and passing through two more gates; the second close to the brow of a hill. Pass to the right of the remains of an Iron Age fort and go through another gate. Now keep straight ahead across the moorland – there is no obvious path – heading downhill and making for a circular fence in front enclosing a shake hole – a depression in the limestone – one of many in this area.

Cross a track, pass to the left of the circular fence and bear slightly left – again there is no obvious path – aiming to the top of the hill, from where you should be able to make out the wall corner **A**. Here bear right through a metal gate and retrace your steps downhill to Ystradfellte. ●

The Blorenge

Start	Keeper's Pond (Pen-ffordd-goch Pond)
Distance	6 miles (9.8km)
Height gain	1,250 feet (380m)
Approximate time	3 hours
Parking	Keeper's Pond free car park, just off the B4246, halfway between Llanfoist and Blaenavon
Route terrain	Mainly clear paths and tracks over rough mountain-side. *One steep descent and one short, steep climb*
Ordnance Survey maps	Landranger 161 (The Black Mountains), Explorer OL13 (Brecon Beacons National Park – Eastern area)

GPS waypoints

- SO 254 107
- Ⓐ SO 264 119
- Ⓑ SO 269 127
- Ⓒ SO 282 116
- Ⓓ SO 278 112
- Ⓔ SO 277 122
- Ⓕ SO 263 107

The formidable bulk of the Blorenge towers high above Abergavenny and the Usk Valley and is unique in being the only peak of any significance in the National Park that actually sits south of the A465 Heads of the Valleys road. It's famous not just for the magnificent views but also for some fascinating industrial history, standing as it does, above the small town of Blaenavon, famous for both iron and coal production. The surrounding area also features in the classic Rape of the Fair Country *novel by Alexander Cordell. An inn bearing his name is just down the hill from the start and finish.*

Keepers pond was once used to feed steam engines at the Garnddyrys Forge, about ¾ mile on the hillside below. It got its name from the gamekeeper's cottage that was once situated nearby.

From the car park, walk down to the pond and turn left, keep it to your right. Now follow the clear path around the southern tip, where you'll find a well-surfaced, wheelchair-friendly path that carries on along the western shore, keeping the pond to the right the whole time. Continue to the very far end and cross a footbridge before bearing slightly right to continue on a clear grassy path that runs easily along with the main ridge up to the right.

This gradually veers around to the right to reveal great views over the Usk Valley and the town of Abergavenny. Stay with it, passing through a shallow, stony cutting at one stage, until you reach a junction marked with a small post Ⓐ. Turn left here, signed to Llanfoist and Govilon, and follow it steeply down for a few paces until the gradient eases slightly and it bears around to the right again to continue around the hillside, dropping slightly as it goes. It ends at a junction with a broader, clearer track above a wood Ⓑ. Turn right onto this, which is actually the line of an old tram road known as Hill's Tram Road after the local Iron

Master, Thomas Hill, and follow it easily around the hillside, ignoring a footpath that drops down to the left. Pass a tunnel to your right and stay with the track, which continues to contour around the hillside, until you eventually reach a gate that leads into the Punchbowl Nature Reserve.

Keep straight ahead again and soon you'll come to the lovely pond at the heart of the Punchbowl 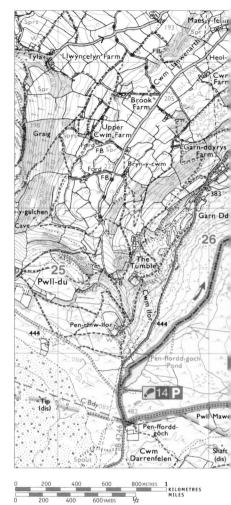. Keep the water to your right and keep straight ahead to climb steeply on a rough track that leads beneath towering beech trees before levelling slightly at a gate. Go through this and continue to another gate alongside a plantation. Keep ahead again and another gate leads out onto a narrow lane.

Turn right onto the lane, and after passing the end of the plantation on the right, turn right again onto a narrow path, waymarked to the Blorenge **D**. Follow this upwards, with the wall to your right, and continue to a small marker post where the wall veers right, away from the path. Keep straight ahead climbing steadily upwards and keeping right when you join another path that comes in from the left. Stay with this all the way to the top, where it passes through some small grassy humps, once piles of quarry spoil, and levels out, with wonderful views to the right.

Continue until you reach a small brick hut **E** and here turn left to climb steeply up a peaty and stony path that soon levels again. Now stay with this main path all the way to the summit, which is marked with a trig point concealed in the rocks. To descend, keep ahead to follow a continuation path towards the two huge masts that you can see in the distance. As you get close to the masts and the car park beneath them, look for a faint path to the right that leads to a seat. Cross the bank

behind the seat and you'll find a plaque that marks the spot of Foxhunter's Grave.

Foxhunter was a champion show jumper that won Britain's only gold medal in the 1952 Olympic Games, in Helsinki, ridden by Welshman, Sir Harry Llewellyn. Together they won nearly 80 international trophies until Foxhunter died in 1959. He was buried at this spot, high on the Blorenge and Sir Harry's ashes were scattered there with him some 40 years later.

Turn left onto the path here and

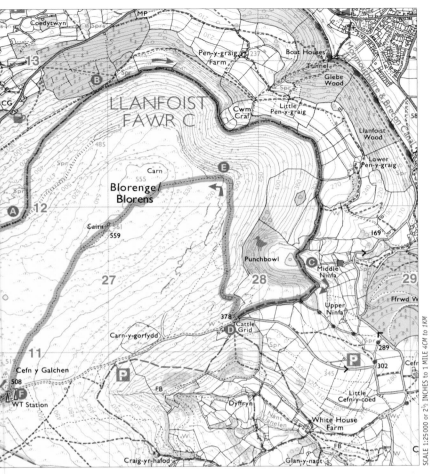

SCALE 1:25 000 or 2½ INCHES to 1 MILE *4CM to 1KM*

follow it easily to the car park . Carry on out onto the road and turn right to follow this all the way down to a junction with the B4246. Turn right onto this and then right again to return to Keeper's Pond. ●

Keeper's Pond

Fan Fawr

		GPS waypoints	
Start	Storey Arms Centre		SN 982 203
Distance	4½ miles (7.3km)	Ⓐ	SN 987 195
Height gain	1,325 feet (405m)	Ⓑ	SN 984 184
Approximate time	3 hours	Ⓒ	SN 988 180
Parking	Free parking opposite the Storey Arms on the A470 between Brecon and Merthyr Tydfil	Ⓓ	SN 969 193
Route terrain	Mainly faint and rough paths across moorland and high mountains. Some boggy sections		
Ordnance Survey maps	Landranger 160 (Brecon Beacons), Explorer OL12 (Brecon Beacons National Park – Western area)		

The contrast between the mountains of Fforest Fawr and the central Brecon Beacons could not be more marked. While hundreds of walkers ascend the summits of Corn Du and Pen y Fan every day, far fewer turn their sights west, to the steep grassy slopes of Fan Fawr. This walk, a short but quite strenuous ramble, scales this peak ascending its shapely and easy-angled south-east ridge. Like most of the Fforest Fawr massif, the paths are faint and the ground is boggy in places, so it's best not tackled in poor visibility.

The Storey Arms was once a coaching inn, ideally placed at the top of the pass that would have carried most of the traffic through the mountains in those days. Today the building is an adventure centre, surrounded by busy car parks that make ideal starting places for walks to the highest mountains in the National Park.

Summit Cairn, Fan Fawr

From the higher of the two car parks, opposite the Storey Arms, cross the road and walk along the opposite verge until you can fork slightly left to walk through the slip road that actually makes up the lower car park. Continue to the very bottom, where a stile leads into a conifer plantation. Follow the narrow path to another stile that leads back onto the verge and then cross the road to continue for a few paces on the other side. At a tall Taff Trail waymark, drop to the right to continue on a narrow path that runs beneath a bank. Stay with this to a waymarked kissing-gate **A** that leads out onto open moorland next to the Afon Taf Fawr.

Cross a footbridge and follow a boggy path along the river bank to the edge of a wood, where you should turn right to climb steeply up to a clearer track that then follows the line of the wood leftwards. Stay with this, keeping the wood to the left the whole time and

after dropping into a deep river gulley and climbing back out again, you'll come to a waymarked stile in the fence on the left **B**. Cross this and turn almost immediately right onto a broad forest track that runs high above the Beacons Reservoir before dropping to the A4059 **C**. Turn right, onto a verge, and follow the road uphill with the wood to the right for around 100 yds. Cross a cattle-grid and pass the end of the wood, then turn right onto a faint path that improves as it goes. Bear half

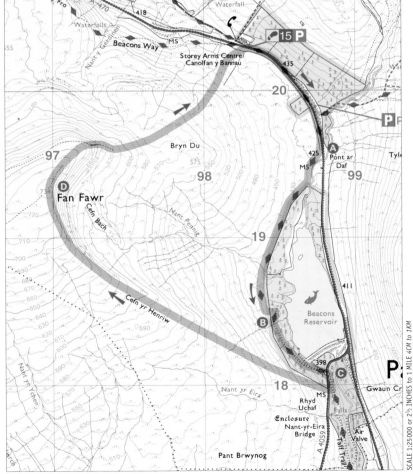

SCALE 1:25000 or 2½ INCHES to 1 MILE 4CM to 1KM

Fan Fawr from Pen y Fan

left to follow the path, all the way up onto the south-east ridge of Fan Fawr; with magnificent views ahead to the steep eastern escarpment. Continue to the very top, and trace your way around the escarpment edge to the true summit, which is marked with a diminutive cairn **D**.

Although less-walked than Corn Du and Pen y Fan, which dominate the skyline on the other side of the valley, Fan Fawr offers equally spectacular views including, of course, a true high-level close-up of the highest peaks

themselves. From the cairn, continue around the escarpment edge, with fantastic views into the valley below, and stay with the path as it starts to drop steeply down the eastern flanks of the mountain.

Eventually it levels and continues easily onto the boggy plateau of Bryn Du, where the path starts to become vague again. Keep ahead, aiming all the time for the left-hand side of the wood you can see opposite, on the flanks of Corn Du. After a few paces the car park comes into sight and you should be able to follow faint paths and sheep tracks all the way back down to the road. ●

Sugar Loaf

		GPS waypoints
Start	Llangenny	SO 239 181
Distance	6 miles (9.7km)	Ⓐ SO 240 179
Height gain	1,900 feet (580m)	Ⓑ SO 244 194
Approximate time	3½ hours	Ⓒ SO 253 189
Parking	Limited parking by the church or ask for permission at the Dragon's Head pub	Ⓓ SO 272 187 Ⓔ SO 260 182 Ⓕ SO 243 178
Route terrain	Mainly clear paths and tracks over farmland and rough mountainside. Some steep sections	
Ordnance Survey maps	Landranger 161 (The Black Mountains), Explorer OL13 (Brecon Beacons National Park – Eastern area)	

The Sugar Loaf is one the most popular mountains in the Brecon Beacons National Park, and its distinctive conical summit can be seen from miles around, especially when approaching from the east. It's a wonderful viewpoint, all the better for being set back a little from the main Black Mountains massif, which it views from across the pretty valley of the Grwyne Fawr. This walk climbs to the summit from a small village on the floor of this scenic valley.

Walk back towards the main bridge, by the **Dragon's Head** pub, cross it, then turn left to climb over a stone stile in the wall on your left Ⓐ. Follow the path easily along the banks of the river into Pendarren Park, and keep ahead, following the well-signed footpath, until you reach a second footbridge, where you go through a gate and turn immediately right to follow a clear path up to join another clear grassy track that you turn left onto to follow around the hillside to a farm. Cross a stile into the yard, and keep slightly right to another stile, that leads onto a lane Ⓑ.

Turn right and walk along the road for ¼ mile to a narrow lane on the left. Take this and walk up past a house on the right, and then, as you reach another farm, bear left onto a way-

marked bridleway. Follow this around the hillside to a junction between two gates, and bear right to walk steeply uphill to another gate, which gives access to open hillside. Keep ahead, with the fence, then wall, on your right and aim for some rough ground at the foot of Sugar Loaf's obvious west ridge ahead Ⓒ. Keep ahead to follow a clear path up onto this ridge and stay with it to the crest where another path forks in from the right. Now follow the crest all the way up to the summit of the Sugar Loaf, with fine views over the mountain all the way.

Cross the summit ridge to the trig point Ⓓ, where you get splendid views over the Usk Valley to the Blorenge, as well as the Black Mountains to the west, and Ysgyryd Fawr to the east. You'll also see Abergavenny tucked beneath the foot of the mountain, and the distinctive gash of the Clydach Gorge heading uphill from the village of Gilwern, on the other side of the Usk. Now bear right to follow a clear path steeply down the face of the mountain. There are a few different paths dropping down, but if you keep to the right as much as possible, with a distinct valley between you and the ridge you've just climbed, you cannot go far wrong. As the ground levels, fork right, to drop through bracken to a stream in the valley bottom, by the corner of a coniferous wood **E**.

Cross the stream and turn immediately left to walk down to a gate. Now keep ahead on a clear path that crosses sheep pastures. Eventually, bearing left onto a sheltered track, that drops to a junction with another track. Turn right onto this and follow it down past a lovely house to the road head. Turn right to climb steeply up to the waterworks and then bear left, over a stile, to follow a footpath straight across a field. Cross another stile and keep to the bottom of the next field to a stile on the left. Cross

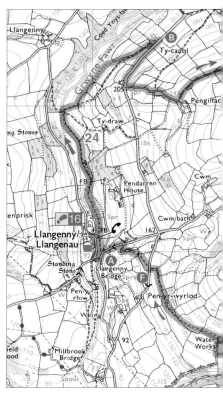

this and turn right to follow the field edge through a wooded area and past a ruined building. Now keep ahead and you'll follow a sunken track all the way out to another road **F**.

Sugar loaf from Mynydd Llangatwg

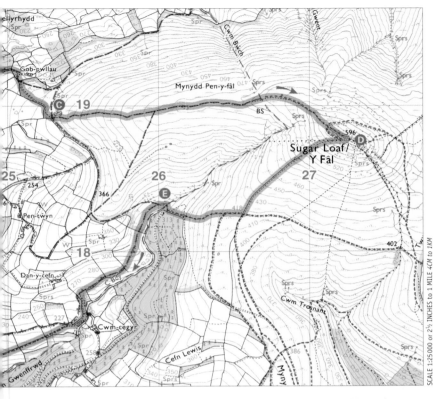

Cross this, and climb over the stile opposite. Now bear half-right to cross the next field and cross another stile to drop down beside a house. Bear right at the bottom, and follow the drive out to the road, where you should turn left to drop to the bridge where you started. ●

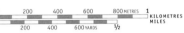

Cwm Oergwm

		GPS waypoints
Start	Llanfrynach	
Distance	7 miles (11.3km)	SO 074 257
Height gain	1,020 feet (310m)	Ⓐ SO 075 257
Approximate time	3½ hours	Ⓑ SO 064 239
Parking	Street-side parking in Llanfrynach	Ⓒ SO 058 228
Route terrain	Quiet lanes, wooded paths, rough	Ⓓ SO 047 214
	paths over moorland. An awkward	Ⓔ SO 047 216
	stream crossing that's best not	Ⓕ SO 049 220
	tackled after extensive rain	Ⓖ SO 057 233
		Ⓗ SO 057 240
Ordnance Survey maps	Landranger 160 (Brecon Beacons),	Ⓙ SO 065 249
	Explorer OL12 (Brecon Beacons	
	National Park – Western area)	

The high mountains of the central Brecon Beacons are defined as much by the wonderful, steep-sided cwms that radiate from them, as by the summits themselves, and this walk delves deep into the eastern-most of these beautiful valleys: Cwm Oergwm, offering fine views of the towering peaks of Fan y Big and Cribyn, as well as visiting a delightful chain of small cascades on the Nant Menasgin.

With the toilets to your right and the church to your left, walk along the road for a few paces and turn right by the telephone box Ⓐ. Follow this across the bridge and then turn first right, up a narrow lane (Tregaer Road). Follow this hedged lane easily up into the valley, with the occasional tantalising glimpse of the high mountains ahead, and continue for just over 1 mile past the farm at Caerau and past another house, where tarmac gives way to a dirt track at a gate Ⓑ.

Continue for ¼ mile to a fork and go straight ahead, through a waymarked gate, into forest. Keep ahead for another ½ mile to ford a stream and go through a gate that leads out onto National Trust ground Ⓒ. Bear slightly right to follow a green track by a tumbledown wall and

stay with this to another gate. Keep straight ahead again and you'll

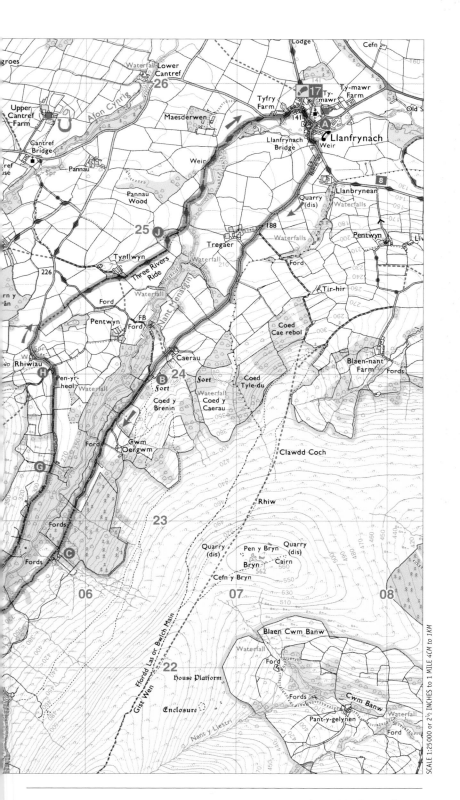

SCALE 1:25000 or 2½ INCHES to 1 MILE 4CM to 1KM

eventually come to another gate that leads out onto open moorland, with the peaks of Fan y Big and Cribyn towering above you at the head of the valley.

Continue on a rough path, with a tumbledown wall to your right, and when the path veers right to drop to the Nant Menasgin, bear right onto an obvious path to follow it, with a huge boulder to your left. Drop down to the stream and cross at the obvious ford **D**, where you'll see a lovely succession of waterfalls tumbling down the hillside above. If the stream is in spate, it may be easier to cross above the waterfalls, but if the levels are too high, it may be better to return the way you came.

A rough path leads away from the stream on the other bank. Follow this up for around 100 yds and keep your eyes peeled for a much fainter path forking off to the right **E**. Take this, and follow it around the hillside, neither climbing nor dropping.

This leads to a gate **F**, waymarked with a bridleway arrow, which you should go through to continue in the same direction. Keep ahead to another gate and then fork slightly left to follow waymarks uphill alongside a tumbledown wall. Ignore a fork to the left and continue to a metal farm gate. Do not go through this but instead head to the left of it and continue to a small bridlegate **G**.

Follow this up, where it becomes a sunken track and stay with this until, after a dark, tree-lined section, you see a gate ahead, blocking the obvious

Cascades on the Nant Menasgin, Cwm Oergym

route. The bridleway has been diverted here so bear slightly right into the field, and then turn left to continue parallel to the original track, beneath some houses, to a waymarked gate just beyond **H**.

Turn right onto the lane, and then, after 300 yds, turn right, through a waymarked gate, onto a footpath. Take this diagonally left across the field to a stile in the corner, and then keep the hedge to your right to drop to a lane. Cross this and go through the gate ahead to continue straight down the left-hand edge of the field to another gate. Go through this and keep ahead to another, and then bear slightly left to drop to a series of waymark posts above a stream **J**.

Bear right as directed and continue to another post that sends you left, through a gate and over a brook. Now follow the obvious path ahead, with the Nant Menasgin to your right, and eventually break out into sheep pastures, where you continue with the stream and trees to your right in the same direction to a gate that leads onto a narrow lane. Turn right onto this and then turn right again to return to Llanfrynach. ●

Mynydd Illtud and Cefn Llechid

		GPS waypoints
Start	Mynydd Illtud. Brecon Beacons Mountain Centre 1½ miles (2.4km) west of Libanus	🖉 SN 977 262 Ⓐ SN 970 253
Distance	7½ miles (12.1km)	Ⓑ SN 959 259 Ⓒ SN 956 264
Height gain	1,085 feet (330m)	Ⓓ SN 944 257
Approximate time	4 hours	Ⓔ SN 949 280
Parking	Brecon Beacons Mountain Centre at Mynydd Illtud (Pay and Display)	Ⓕ SN 954 278
Route terrain	Mainly clear paths and tracks over farmland and rough mountainside. Short sections on quiet lanes	
Ordnance Survey maps	Landranger 160 (Brecon Beacons), Explorer OL12 (Brecon Beacons National Park – Western & Central area)	

From the open, spacious common land of Mynydd Illtud at the start and finish of the walk there are splendid views of the main ridge of the Brecon Beacons, and there are more open and extensive views from the slopes of Cefn Llechid, especially over the Usk Valley. As a contrast there is the pleasant wooded valley of Cwm Camlais and easy and enjoyable walking along a wide drove road. This walk provides varied scenery and grand views for relatively little effort as there are no steep climbs or difficult terrain to be negotiated.

The Brecon Beacons Mountain Centre, opened in 1966, is situated 1,100 feet (335m) up on Mynydd Illtud, a large area of open common which gives grand panoramic views over the mountains.

🖉 Begin by turning left out of the entrance along a road and at a T-junction leave the road by keeping straight ahead and continuing along a gravel track which keeps along the edge of the rather marshy common, near a wire fence and line of trees on the left. After ¾ mile, just after the top of the hill and before a stile on the left, 250 yds short of some farm buildings, turn

right Ⓐ onto a very obvious broad, grassy track. This heads across the common in a north-westerly direction, between the two marshy areas of Traeth Mawr and Traeth Bach, to reach a road just to the right of a large pool Ⓑ.

Cross the road, continue along the broad, grassy, enclosed track opposite – it is likely that this was an old drove road – and after nearly ½ mile take the first turning on the left, marked by a post Ⓒ. Go through a wooden gate, head downhill along a hedge-lined, enclosed path that leads down to a lane. Turn left along this narrow, winding lane for ¾ mile, following it around several sharp bends to reach the A4215.

A few yards before the road turn right ⓓ through a gate onto a sunken path between hedge banks and follow it gently uphill through a series of gates and stiles, eventually emerging onto the open, windswept Cefn Llechid Common. Keep straight ahead at a crossroads of grassy tracks on a waymarked bridle-way and continue through bracken, enjoying the extensive all-round views. On the skyline to the left the triangulation pillar marks the highest point on the common 1,314 feet (400m); it is worth a brief detour for the magnificent views. After passing several pools the route starts to descend, by a hedge bank and wire fence on the right, with superb views ahead over the Usk Valley.

Leave the track to the right to go through a wooden gate, a few yards to the left of a fence corner, and continue quite steeply downhill along a sunken path, by a wire fence on the right, passing through a succession of gates and stiles to reach a narrow lane ⓔ. Turn right along it for ½ mile, heading downhill, and where the lane bends left in front of Cwm-Camlais-uchaf Farm ⓕ keep ahead through the farmyard, bearing right through a metal gate at

Trees above Cwm Camlais

the far end to continue along a winding track. The track soon joins the lovely, tree-lined stream of Cwm Camlais which rushes over rocks and small falls. Turn left over a footbridge at a

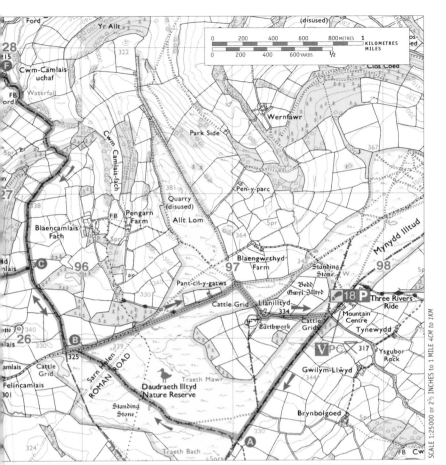

SCALE 1:25 000 or 2½ INCHES to 1 MILE 4CM to 1KM

confluence of streams, bear right and head across to join an enclosed path. Bear left to follow this path uphill through woodland above the valley of Cwm Camlais-fach. Go through a metal gate, and then another, and turn right to continue along an enclosed path between hedged banks.

A few yards after the hedge banks peter out, with a gate directly ahead, look out for where the sunken path reappears on the left and follow it uphill to a gate on the edge of a plantation. Go through the gate to walk along the right inside edge of the plantation, by a wire fence on the right, and just before reaching the corner of it turn right through another gate to continue along

an uphill sunken path. Later the path levels out and continues as a wide, green, tree-lined enclosed track – the old drove road again – follow it through a series of gates and stiles, later picking up part of the outward route and continuing to the road **B**. This is easy and most enjoyable walking, with the magnificent panorama of the Brecon Beacons spread out ahead of you all the while.

Leave the outward route at the road by turning left along it across Illtud Common and after ¾ mile turn right along a lane signposted to the mountain centre. Follow it back to the start, passing to the left of the ruined church of Llanilltyd. ●

Hay Bluff and Twmpa

		GPS waypoints
Start	Hay Bluff	
Distance	6 miles (9.8km)	✎ SO 239 373
Height gain	1,390 feet (425m)	Ⓐ SO 244 366
		Ⓑ SO 235 351
Approximate time	3 hours	Ⓒ SO 220 346
Parking	Free car park beside stone circle on the Gospel Pass road between Hay-on-Wye and Abergavenny	Ⓓ SO 231 356
Route terrain	Clear paths over high mountains and open moorland, with a return leg along a quiet lane	
Ordnance Survey maps	Landranger 161 (The Black Mountains), Explorer OL13 (Brecon Beacons National Park – Eastern area)	

The adjacent open expanses of Hay Bluff and Twmpa – the alternative name for the latter is Lord Hereford's Knob – are the most northerly peaks of the Black Mountains and from them there are extensive views of the long ridges of the mountains and over the Wye Valley to the hills of mid Wales. The walk involves two ascents: the first to the summit of Hay Bluff (2,220ft/677m) is steep, the second to the summit of Twmpa (2263ft/689m) is easier and more gradual. It is best to choose a fine, clear day for this walk, to enjoy the grand views to the full and because otherwise route-finding in such open terrain could be difficult.

✎ From the car park and stone circle cross the road and head uphill across grass to the summit of Hay Bluff which lies directly ahead. At about half

The glorious view from the summit of Twmpa

height, you'll meet a good path rising up from your left; turn right onto Offa's Dyke Path and follow it to the top. Turn left onto a good gravel path and follow this to the triangulation pillar Ⓐ from which the views over the Black Mountains, Brecon Beacons, Wye Valley and hills of mid-Wales are magnificent. Now retrace your steps back along the path to the top of the initial climb and instead of descending again, keep straight ahead to continue along the edge of the escarpment of Ffynnon y Parc, heading towards the prominent steep face of Twmpa. The track eventually descends to the road and parking area at Gospel Pass Ⓑ. Cross the road and keep straight ahead to follow a continuation path easily up onto the hillside on the other side of the pass, this now leads onto Twmpa. Near the top the path passes between two piles of stones – remnants of cairns – and continues to a third one which marks the summit, another superb viewpoint. From here continue along the edge of the escarpment, bearing slightly left and gently descending. Later the broad, grassy path levels out; follow it almost to the rim of the chasm ahead.

Turn right here **C** onto a clear path which heads steeply downhill. You'll reach a deep groove, after which the original bridleway bends around to the left, but you need to keep straight ahead, descending steeply, until the ground levels at a junction with a clear cross path, approximately 200 yds from the fence below, and directly below two small clumps of trees. Turn right onto this, which climbs slightly to start with, and continue beneath the obvious nose of Twmpa. Later you join a wider path, bearing right and still keeping below

the curving slopes of Twmpa. From here there are particularly dramatic views of Twmpa on the right and the long ridge of Hay Bluff ahead.

On joining a narrow lane turn right along it to walk through a pleasant area of trees, ford two streams at a left-hand bend **D** and follow the lane for just over 1 mile to get back to the starting point. This is a delightful, unspoilt, old-fashioned country lane which appears to be used more by walkers and riders than vehicles; it heads gently uphill across open country below Hay Bluff. ●

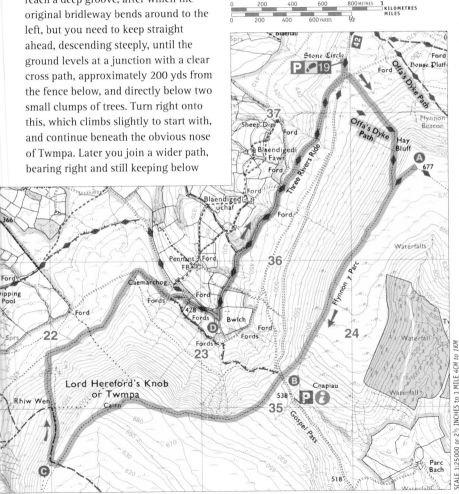

The Vale of Ewyas

		GPS waypoints
Start	Llanthony Priory	
Distance	6 miles (9.7km)	SO 289 278
Height gain	1,210 feet (370m)	Ⓐ SO 285 279
		Ⓑ SO 270 299
Approximate time	3 hours	Ⓒ SO 268 296
Parking	Car park at Llanthony Priory (free)	Ⓓ SO 273 266
Route terrain	Clear paths over high mountains and less clear paths over farmland. A long section on a very quiet road	
Ordnance Survey maps	Landranger 161 (The Black Mountains), Explorer OL13 (Brecon Beacons National Park – Eastern area)	

The Vale of Ewyas, a narrow, remote, steep-sided valley on the eastern edge of the Black Mountains, provides a romantic, secluded setting for the ruins of Llanthony Priory. Initially the walk follows a pleasant track northwards along the bottom of the valley before turning westwards to cross the River Honddu and climb onto open moorland. A delightful ramble follows, along the western slopes of the valley to Bal-Bach, a fine viewpoint over both the vale of Ewyas and the neighbouring Grwyne Fawr Valley. On the final descent the priory ruins are in sight most of the time. This highly scenic and quite energetic walk is best done on a fine day as in misty conditions route-finding on the open moorland stretch could be difficult.

The austere-looking ruins of Llanthony Priory perfectly match their setting in the peaceful, lonely vale of Ewyas enclosed by the bare slopes of the Black Mountains. The Augustinian priory was founded in the early 12th century and much of the late 12th and early 13th-century church survives, notably the west front, the north arcade of the nave, the central tower and parts of the east end. Little remains of the domestic buildings, although the small parish church nearby incorporates the monks' infirmary. Uniquely, the south west tower of the priory church is now part of the **Abbey Hotel**, surely one of the most unusual hotel sites in the country.

Leave the car park by walking between the priory ruins on the right and the church on the left. Go through a gate straight ahead, and follow the waymark across the field in the direction of Capel-y-ffin, making for a gate to the left of a barn – formerly the priory gatehouse – onto a road and bear right along it, passing the **Half Moon Inn**. Where the road bears left to Capel-y-ffyn, keep straight ahead Ⓐ. After passing through a gate, with a drive up to the right, the lane becomes a tree-lined path for a while, before reverting to a tarmac track at the next gate. Along this stretch

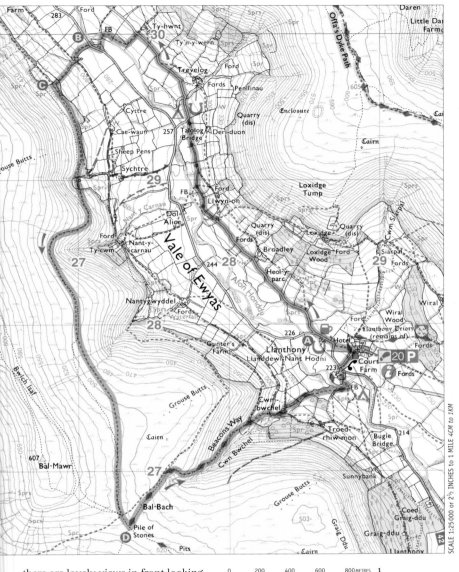

SCALE 1:25000 or 2½ INCHES to 1 MILE 4CM to 1KM

there are lovely views in front looking towards the head of the valley.

At a public footpath sign to Hay Road turn left through a metal gate and head downhill along the left-hand edge of the field, by a wire fence bordering a stream on the left, later bearing right away from the field edge and going through a gap in a line of trees. Continue down to the bottom and bear right to a stile by some sheep pens.

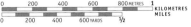

Cross this and continue for a few paces to a footbridge over the River Honddu. Cross this and climb a stile above it to continue to a gate and then the road.

Turn right and after a few yards, where the road bears slightly right, turn left **B** up some steps, climb a stile and head uphill along the left-hand edge of

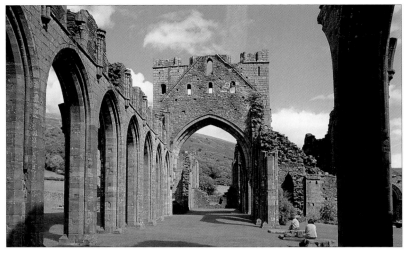

Llanthony Priory

a field, by a wooded gully and stream on the left. Near the top of the field, bear left over a stile, with a house to your left, and then turn immediately right to walk steeply up the right-hand edge of the field with a bramble-filled gulley to your left. At the top, climb a stile and turn left ● to keep alongside a wire fence on the left, soon picking up a clear path which can be seen a few yards to the right. This path winds along the bottom edge of open moorland, keeping roughly parallel with the wire fence on the left. There are superb views over the valley and at times the ruins of Llanthony Priory can be glimpsed.

Where the path forks above a farm building, take the right-hand, upper path which heads away from the wire fence to join a wider, clearer path. Bear left along it, go through a metal gate and keep ahead to pass through another one. The path now starts to climb and becomes more rocky as first it bends right above the edge of a steep valley, and then it bears left across the head of the valley to continue across the lovely, open, heathery moorland on the western slopes of the Vale of Ewyas.

Make for the cairn that can be seen on the skyline ahead; this is Bal-Bach where there is a junction of tracks and paths and a view to the right over the forested Grwyne Fawr Valley ●. Here turn left downhill along a broad, well-used path. At a fork take the right-hand path, shortly turning right and heading downhill along the left-hand side of the narrow, steep-sided valley of Cwm Bwchel. *Be careful as the path is steep and rocky.* As it descends there are glorious views of the priory ruins in front. At a footpath sign keep ahead in the Llanthony direction, climb a stile and continue downhill to climb another. Keep ahead, go through a gate, with the farm to your right, and continue past a stile, where the path bears left away from the fence to a waymark post in a gap in the trees ahead. Continue down to another stile and climb it then turn right to climb another. Take the footbridge over the stream and keep ahead to another stile. Now turn left to drop down to a gate in the corner. Go through this and follow the path down to cross an iron footbridge over the river. Turn right along a track through a farmyard to a road. Cross the road and follow the lane opposite to return to the priory. ●

Talgarth and Mynydd Troed

		GPS waypoints
Start	Talgarth	� SO 152 336
Distance	8 miles (13km)	Ⓐ SO 146 334
Height gain	1,050 feet (320m)	Ⓑ SO 144 325
Approximate time	4 hours	Ⓒ SO 152 304
Parking	Free car park on the A479	Ⓓ SO 160 295
Route terrain	Mainly clear paths and tracks over farmland and rough mountainside. Short sections on quiet lanes	Ⓔ SO 150 315
		Ⓕ SO 142 321
Ordnance Survey maps	Landranger 161 (The Black Mountains), Explorer OL13 (Brecon Beacons National Park – Eastern area)	

Mynydd Troed sits in a kind of no man's land between the main massif of the Black Mountains, and the lower-lying ground that surrounds Llangorse Lake. It's a shapely peak, especially when seen from the north, where its sharp northern ridge and slender summit conspire to give it an almost pyramidical appearance. This walk approaches the mountain from this direction, deflecting easily around the peak itself on good paths. It then returns to the small town of Talgarth via the impressive Penyrwrlodd Long Cairn.

🔖 Leave the car park via an exit in the bottom corner that leads onto the main road, at the same end as the main entrance. Cross the road and turn left then right through a gate towards the rugby pitch. Turn immediately left onto a track and follow it past a barn and through a gate. Continue diagonally across the next field to a stile and then continue ahead on a rough, hedged track that then veers left to a gate onto the road.

Turn right and then left Ⓐ, just before crossing a bridge, onto a signed footpath. Follow this around the edge of the field and through a stile then continue ahead, keeping the River Llynfi to your right, to the far end of the field, where you'll join a lane. Turn right and then left onto a drive, marked

Pont Nichol. Walk up the drive and pass beneath the house, which sits on the site of the old railway crossing. Now fork left to a stile that leads into a wood and follow the path through the woodland and up to another stile that leads onto the B4560, close to College Farm Ⓑ.

Turn right to walk along the road and into Trefecca village. Trefecca was the home of Hywel Harris, one of the leaders of the Welsh Methodist Revival and the settlement he founded, now known as Trefecca College, is passed later on the walk. Leave the village and then take the no through road on the left, which leads up to Trefecca Fawr. Follow the lane around to the right and then continue through Felin Cwm Dingle to a sharp left-hand bend, where you should go straight ahead through a gate into a field.

Continue with the wood on your left and go through another gate and up through the next field to a stile. Cross this and turn right, over a stream, and then left to follow a line of trees up and then right, aiming all the time towards the farm buildings. Continue to a gate in front of the farm but do not go through, instead turn left to keep the hedge to your right, and walk up to a stile that leads onto the road **C**. Turn right to walk past Whole House Farm and continue past the farmhouse to a track on the left. Follow this up through three fields and upon entering the third, bear half left to aim for the bottom left corner, where you join a lane. Turn right and walk past the turn to Garn y Castell and around a sharp left-hand bend. Now keep your eyes open for a narrow path that leads into a copse on the left. Follow this path through two gates and out onto the open ground at the foot of Mynydd Troed **D**.

Turn left and follow the obvious track along the foot of the mountain until it dips leftwards towards a gate that leads onto a road. Turn left onto the lane and then turn right at the next junction and continue past Penyrheol and Trewalkin farms. Continue for another 100 yds and bear left, through a gate. Now head across the field towards the left-hand end of the farm ahead. Cross a stile and go straight across a track and then over another stile, to enter another field. Keep to the right to another stile and then head diagonally right, over the brow of the hill and down to the far corner, where you'll see another stile beneath a small plantation of

Looking across at Y Grib from Mynydd Troed

evergreens. Cross this and then a stile on the right to enter the site of the Penyrwrlodd Long Cairn **E**.

This is an amazing example of a long barrow burial cairn, which despite its colossal size was only discovered in 1972. Human remains suggest it was constructed around 3800BC, which makes it one of the oldest cairns in southern Britain. Among the many finds it has yielded is a small length of hollowed out sheep bone with holes drilled in it – possibly a very early musical instrument.

Go back over the stile and turn right down to another stile. Continue with the hedge on your right and pass through a gate to continue to a cluster of buildings. Keep these to your left and locate a path that ducks into bushes on the right. Continue down, with the hedge to your right, to a gate and stile close to a new barn. Turn left onto the lane and follow it down past Trefecca College to the B4560 **F**.

Cross the road and continue down the lane opposite, which turns into a steep, stony track and drops to cross the dismantled railway. Bear left then right to cross a footbridge over the Afon Llynfi. Now head up the steep bank ahead to join a lane by the farm buildings at Tredustan Hall. Turn right onto the lane and follow it easily back towards Talgarth, taking a right and then a left at the two junctions.

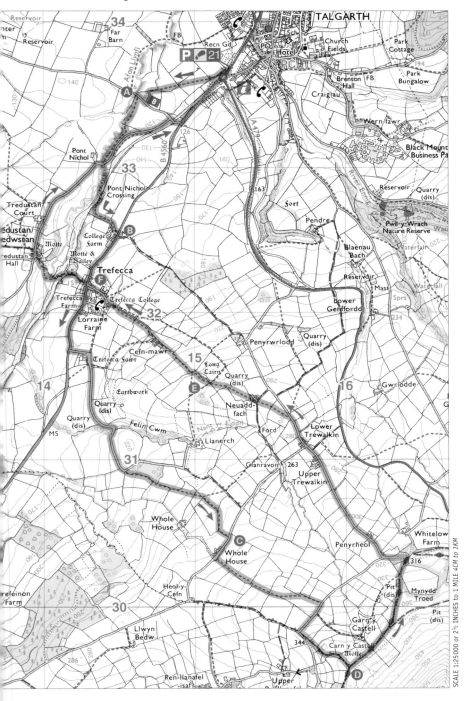

Llyn y Fan Fach and the Carmarthen Fans

		GPS waypoints
Start	Near Llanddeusant	✎ SN 799 238
Distance	6 miles (9.7km)	Ⓐ SN 814 237
Height gain	2,130 feet (650m)	Ⓑ SN 821 223
Approximate time	4 hours	Ⓒ SN 811 218
Parking	Free parking on a dead-end lane that leads east from Llandeusant	Ⓓ SN 797 220
		Ⓔ SN 803 220
Route terrain	A mixture of faint and clear paths over high mountains. Some steep going. Easy return along a broad track	
Ordnance Survey maps	Landranger 160 (Brecon Beacons), Explorer OL12 (Brecon Beacons National Park – Western area)	

The Black Mountain (singular) is the western-most massif of the Brecon Beacons National Park and is often described as its last surviving wilderness, with sweeping, craggy escarpments that tower commandingly above glistening lakes, and a peaty upland plateau that bears few paths. This walk links a good waterworks track with a spectacular ridge-top path to create a short but extremely rewarding tour of the high escarpments at the western edge of the range, often known as the Carmarthen Fans.

✎ From the car park, cross the access track and climb the steep hillside

Bannau Sir Gaer and Llyn y Fan Fach

almost directly above a small signpost. At the top of this short, steep slope, the ground levels and you should locate a faint path that contours eastwards

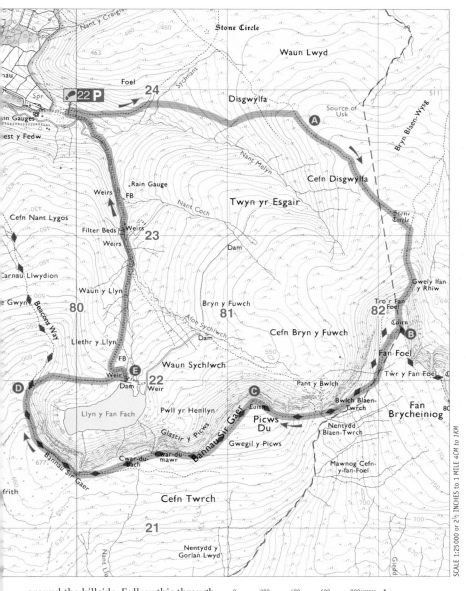

around the hillside. Follow this through the gorse, climbing slightly all the time, and then drop to cross a stream. Keep ahead on the same trajectory and you'll drop to cross a bigger stream, this one the Sychnant brook.

Leaving this behind and keeping the deep gorge of the Nant Melyn beneath you to the right, stay on the path as it contours just south of east around the

hillside. Stay with the path, which does start to become faint until you reach a small stream gully. Here, turn left and climb alongside it all the way to the crest of the broad ridge above and to your left. You'll cross a path near the top but ignore this and you'll find another on the crest itself . Onto it, bear right and track along the ridge top towards the mountains on the horizon.

You're now aiming for the steep and obvious spur of Fan Foel, which lies south east of you just over 1 mile away. Follow the main track which is faint in places over Waun Lwyd and then, as the ridge starts to narrow, keep to the crest where you'll meet a very distinct path coming up from your left. Continue towards the steep spur and follow the path sharply up it to a cairn on the grassy plateau above **B**. This is Fan Foel, and although it's a few feet

smaller than Fan Brycheiniog, just a short distance to the south, it still makes a magnificent viewpoint.

From the cairn, bear right to follow the edge along, and drop easily at first, and then steeply, into the deep col of Bwlch Blaen-Twrch, which marks the boundary between Powys and Carmarthenshire. From here, climb steeply up the hillside ahead to the summit cairn of Bannau Sir Gaer **C** – another wonderful viewpoint. Stay with the path and continue with the escarpment edge to your right, above precipitous cliffs, into a small saddle, directly above Llyn y Fan Fach. Climb slightly again and then continue around the lake until you see a good path

The lofty escarpment of Bannau Sir Gaer

dropping down a grassy spur towards the dam . Take this and drop to the lake itself.

Llyn y Fan Fach is often referred to as the magic lake after a mythical story of a lady of the lake. The lady, both beautiful and wise, with special healing powers, appeared regularly to a shepherd boy named Rhiwallon. He fell for her and persuaded her to marry him. She agreed, but only on the condition that he should never strike her with iron. They duly married and had a son before Rhiwallon did strike her with iron and, true to her word, the lady vanished back into the black waters, taking their livestock with her. Their son, named after his father, went on to become a great healer. This is most likely a twist on a tale that is told in many places and is thought to reflect on the advance of the Iron Age in Britain and of the Bronze Age people's distrust of their strange new neighbours. It's likely that a Bronze Age lady would have had a good understanding of healing using natural medicines but what's particularly interestingly about this version of the story is that much later on, there actually was a line of successful physicians operating from nearby Myddfai.

From the dam, pick up the well-surfaced track that heads back downhill. This will lead you past the waterworks filter beds, which you pass on the right, and back to the car park.

Grwyne Fawr

		GPS waypoints
Start	Pont Cadwgan	
Distance	7½ miles (12.1km)	SO 266 251
Height gain	1,720 feet (525m)	Ⓐ SO 268 237
Approximate time	4 hours	Ⓑ SO 260 237
Parking	Forestry Commission car park at Pont Cadwgan	Ⓒ SO 262 226
		Ⓓ SO 278 224
Route terrain	A real mix of forest roads, well-marked footpaths over sheep pasture and less well-established footpaths over high mountains. *Best tackled in good visibility*	Ⓔ SO 283 226
		Ⓕ SO 281 235
Ordnance Survey maps	Landranger 161 (The Black Mountains), Explorer OL13 (Brecon Beacons National Park – Eastern area)	

The Grwyne Fawr Valley is one of a series of long, narrow, parallel valleys that separates the ridges of the Black Mountains. The walk begins by heading uphill through the conifers of Mynydd Du Forest on the western side of the valley, emerging onto open moorland to reach the grand viewpoint of Crug Mawr (1,805ft /550m). A descent to the delightful, secluded Partrishow church is followed by a high-level return route along the eastern side of the valley. Forest, moorland, wooded valley and extensive views all combine to create a most varied and satisfying walk, and although there is some climbing along the route, none of it is steep or strenuous.

Leave the car park, cross the bridge (Pont Cadwgan) onto the road and take the forest track opposite which bears left and climbs steadily. Follow the track around a right-hand curve, keep ahead to a crossroads of tracks and bear left to continue along a winding track signed to Fford Las Fawr through a pleasant area of mixed woodland. Go through a gate, keep ahead to a farm, turn left at the end of the farm buildings, by a public bridleway sign, and continue between trees for 100 yds to a clear path leading right Ⓐ, steeply uphill. Follow this, keeping straight ahead across two forest tracks, until you reach a gate at the top that leads onto open moorland Ⓑ. Turn left onto a path that runs along the forest edge to the corner of the plantation, from where a triangulation pillar can be seen ahead on the summit of Crug Mawr. Bear half right for a few paces to join a clear path that heads towards it across the heathery moorland, ascending gently. From the summit Ⓒ there is a magnificent panoramic view that includes the Sugar Loaf, Ysgyryd Fawr, the Grwyne Fawr valley, the western ridges of the Black Mountains, the Usk Valley and the main Brecon Beacons beyond.

Retrace your steps to the corner of the forest, bear right and follow a path that winds downhill, keeping roughly parallel to the edge of the trees and later dipping below them. Where the path levels out pick up and continue along a pleasant, grassy track that curves to the right, following the bottom edge of Crug Mawr. Go through a gate, head down an enclosed, stony track to a lane, bear right and follow it downhill around some sharp bends to Partrishow church, ignoring a stile marked Beacons Way and continuing to the ornate gates ⒹÐ where you turn left into the churchyard. This is a delightful, unspoilt, secluded church in a lovely, remote mountain setting, and is particularly noted for its superb 15th-century carved oak screen. It also has a medieval painting of a skeleton on the west wall of the nave

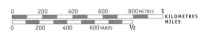

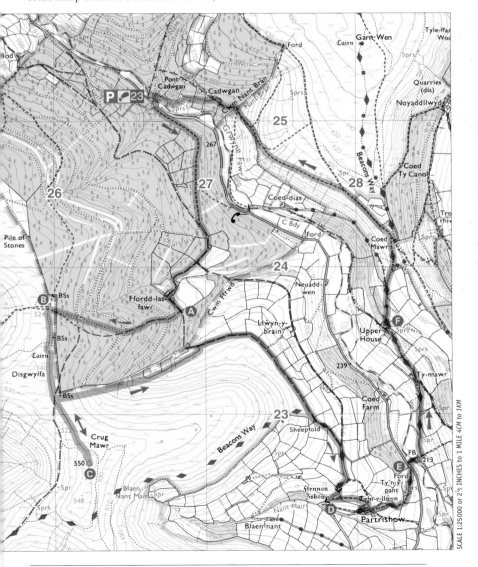

and a parish chest hewn from a solid tree trunk.

Pass to the right of the church, go through a gate at the far end of the churchyard and continue across a sloping field. Bear right on joining a track, follow it around a sharp right-hand bend and continue down to the attractive 15th-century buildings of Tyn-y-llwyn Farm. Turn left, passing beneath the farmhouse, and go through a metal gate on the left, above the drive and next to a small outhouse, to walk across a field to a stile. Climb it, bear right downhill across the next field to climb another stile, bear left and continue downhill, passing between two ruined buildings and on down a most attractive tree-lined path to climb a stile onto a road **E**.

Cross over the road, take the downhill tarmac track opposite, which is sign-posted 'Tabernacle Chapel', turn right to cross the stream and continue, passing to the right of the chapel. Shortly afterwards the track bends to the left and climbs gently along the eastern side of the valley. Go through a metal gate, keep ahead, pass to the right of a farm and continue, going through several more metal gates, up to the next farm, Upper House.

Go through a metal gate into the farmyard, turn right **F**, in the direction of a yellow waymark, between the farmhouse and a barn, then turn left and continue up, going through another metal gate. Walk along an uphill track, passing

through a metal gate onto open moorland, and bear slightly right to keep alongside a wall on the right. Where the wall turns to the right keep ahead along an obvious grassy track towards the ridge in front.

On meeting a broader track just before a group of conifers bear left onto it to continue along the side of the valley – this is a superb high level walk with grand views. About 50 yds after a fence on the right ends there is a fork; take the left-hand, narrower path which eventually descends into the valley of Cwm Nant Brân, meeting a wall on the left and keeping alongside it downhill. Cross a small stream, go through a gate and then continue along a wooded path gently uphill to a farm. Turn left to pass between gateposts and, ignoring a waymark to the right, follow the track ahead which descends between thick conifers to the starting point. ●

Partrishow church

Waterfalls Walk

		GPS waypoints	
Start	Cwm Porth		
Distance	9 miles (14.5km)	✎	SN 928 124
Height gain	2,100 feet (640m)	Ⓐ	SN 924 109
		Ⓑ	SN 928 099
Approximate time	5 hours	Ⓒ	SN 910 079
Parking	Pay and Display car park, on minor road 1 mile (1.6km) south of Ystradfellte	Ⓓ	SN 900 076
		Ⓔ	SN 898 091
		Ⓕ	SN 907 105
Route terrain	Clear but rough paths with some very steep and exposed sections and a slippery walk beneath a waterfall	Ⓖ	SN 912 116
		Ⓗ	SN 918 116
Dog friendly	Great care needed near the steep drops and waterfalls		
Ordnance Survey maps	Landranger 160 (Brecon Beacons), Explorer OL12 (Brecon Beacons National Park – Western area)		

There can be few more exhilarating and satisfying walks than this. On the southern edge of Fforest Fawr, where the sandstone that underlies most of the National Park gives way to limestone, the rivers Mellte, Hepste, Pyrddin and Nedd Fechan plunge over a series of waterfalls, the highest concentration of falls in Wales. All are spectacular but probably the most exciting part of the walk comes when you walk behind the great sheet of water at Sgŵd yr Eira. The walk is lengthy and quite energetic, with plenty of ascents and descents and some fairly difficult sections over rocky terrain and muddy paths, some above very steep drops. Take your time and watch your step, for this is a walk to be enjoyed to the full and worth taking slowly.

✎ Leave the car park and go through the left-hand of two entrances opposite (signed footpath). Walk past a stile, which is signed 'Cavers only' and go through a kissing-gate to drop to the grassy banks of the river. Now bear left to follow the stony and often muddy path along the side of the river, passing through two gates and rising and dropping a few times. Eventually you'll pass a footbridge over the river, at which point you drop to cross a small brook and then climb steeply into a wood, with a fence on your left. At the top, keep ahead towards another fence a few paces away and follow this down to the viewing area above the waterfall of Sgŵd Clun-gwyn Ⓐ.

The next section is steep and rocky and there are some very steep drops. If you do not feel confident about tackling it, head back uphill the way you came to the edge of the conifer plantation, and then bear right and right again to follow red-topped markers through the wood to Sgŵd yr Eira Ⓑ.

From here, turn effectively left, to walk past a green warning notice and then down and up to another. Now continue on the narrow path which contours around the steep hillside above a very steep drop. At one point it dips beneath overhanging cliffs and, shortly after this, it drops very steeply to the right to the viewing area close to the second waterfall, Sgŵd Isaf Clun-gwyn. *This section is steep and slippery so take great care.*

From the waterfall, continue along the bank of the river and head downstream, past a path that goes up to the left, until you reach another waterfall, Sgŵd Pannwr. Turn left here, and follow a faint path steeply uphill, where it joins another coming in from the left. Continue upwards, over a short boardwalk section, and up to a T-junction, where you should turn right to follow red-topped posts. Follow the path easily around the hillside to a junction marked with a tall fingerpost. Turn right, down a steep flight of steps which twist and turn sharply, and follow the steps down to the bottom of the gorge.

Turn left to Sgŵd yr Eira – *take care, the path is difficult in places.* Now comes the most exciting part of the walk; you turn right to pass behind the fall **B**. *Be careful – the rocks are slippery, and if the falls are very full they create a strong back draft which can make things very wet.* On the other side climb quite steeply along a rocky, curving path, turning sharp right at a yellow waymark to continue twisting and turning up steps. At the top turn right at a public footpath sign, following directions to Pontneddfechan and Craig y Ddinas, and continue along the top of the gorge. Soon the path bears left away from the river to continue through a mixture of woodland and more open moorland; keep following the

regular waymarks and footpath signs to Craig y Ddinas (Dinas Rock). At a public footpath sign for Dinas Rock car park, keep straight ahead along the broad ridge of Craig y Ddinas, above two rivers **C**. Soon the path heads downhill to the car park. Cross the road and follow the footpath opposite that leads along the banks of river to a bridge. Turn right to cross this and then turn left to follow the road into Pontneddfechan.

Walk through the village and in front of the **Angel** pub turn right **D**. This is a delightful section, keeping beside the rushing waters of the Afon Nedd Fechan. Climb a stile and shortly afterwards the track narrows to a path; follow it as far as a footbridge just beyond the confluence of the Afon Nedd Fechan and the Afon Pyrddin **E**. Turn right over the bridge to a footpath sign on the other side and turn left for a short detour to view Sgŵd Gwladus, which some would consider the most beautiful of all the falls in its lovely, wooded amphitheatre.

Retrace your steps to the footbridge and keep ahead to another one a few yards ahead. Do not cross it but continue above the left bank of the River Neath, following the footpath sign to Pont Melin-fach. This is another lovely section of the walk, passing several small falls and with fine views up the river. Turn right over a footbridge and continue by the river, passing Sgŵd Ddwli, eventually climbing a stile and bearing left through a car park to a bridge (Pont Melin-fach) **F**. Cross the bridge and take the stile on the left. Immediately, turn right up a narrow path, clamber up over roots and then swing left with the path to trace a course through the woods. In 400 yds it drops almost to river level; here keep right, up a stony path-cum-streambed. In 150 yds you'll pass a redundant,

Sgwd Ddwli on the Afon Nedd Fechan

waymarked stile confirming the public footpath. The clear path undulates high above the Nedd Fechan, crossing two more stiles and numerous side streams to reach the bridge at Pont Rhyd-y-cnau **G**.

Here turn right at the footpath sign to Gwaun Bryn-bwch, along a track winding steadily uphill through woodland. Emerging from the trees, continue uphill and go through a metal gate onto a lane. Turn right along the lane, which bends right to a T-junction. Turn left and after a few yards bear right **H**. At a blue-waymarked post turn left off the track, go through a wooden gate and downhill along an enclosed path, passing through a series of gates to reach the road opposite the car park at the start.

Fan y Big

		GPS waypoints
Start	Torpantau	🚩 SO 056 175
Distance	10 miles (16.1km)	Ⓐ SO 057 205
Height gain	2,000 feet (610m)	Ⓑ SO 036 206
Approximate time	5½ hours	Ⓒ SO 031 205
Parking	Forestry Commission Upper Waterfalls free car park at Torpantau	Ⓓ SO 033 181
		Ⓔ SO 035 173
		Ⓕ SO 049 167
Route terrain	Mainly clear paths over high mountains. Some steep going. Easy return along a broad track and quiet lane	
Ordnance Survey maps	Landranger 160 (Brecon Beacons), Explorer OL12 (Brecon Beacons National Park – Western area)	

After an initial steep climb, the rest of this walk in the heart of the Brecon Beacons is relatively relaxing. The climb is to the ridges of Craig y Fan Ddu and later Graig Fan Las, which the walk follows to reach the main north-facing escarpment of the Beacons. After a dramatic stretch along the curving rim of the escarpment to the summit of Fan y Big, the route descends to the 'Gap Road' and follows this trackway, which is thought to be Roman, above the Neuadd reservoirs. Finally there is a pleasant, scenic stroll along the Taff Trail through the woodlands of Taf Fechan Forest. Although this is a comparatively easy mountain walk, much of it is along the edge of steep escarpments and therefore do not attempt it in winter or in misty weather unless properly experienced and equipped for such conditions.

🚩 Begin by walking back to the car park entrance and crossing a cattle-grid before turning right onto an uphill path, by a wire fence on the right and above a stream and waterfalls on the left. Follow the wire fence as it curves round to the right and after it ends keep straight ahead, more steeply uphill, to reach a cairn at the top of the ridge. To the right there are superb views over the Talybont valley to the long ridges of the Black Mountains on the horizon.

Continue along the well-surfaced path that runs along the ridge top of Craig y fan Ddu with the impressive, sweeping, smooth curve of the ridge of Graig Fan Las ahead. Later bear right to ford a stream and continue, curving gradually right along Graig Fan Las and enjoying the magnificent open, empty views to the right over mountain and forest. When you eventually reach the main escarpment of the Brecon Beacons turn sharp left Ⓐ.

Keep along the clear, well-used path to the summit of Fan y Big, following the edge of the escarpment as it bends left and later curves right around the head of the valley of Cwm Oergwm. This is a typical Beacons landscape of sweeping, bare, smooth curves, steep escarpments, flat summits and wide vistas, with views beyond of the gentler scenery of the Usk Valley and the houses of Brecon. On reaching Fan y Big's rather unremarkable summit **B** turn sharp left, still walking along the edge of the escarpment, to descend into the broad col of Bwlch ar y Fan which lies between Fan y Big and Cribyn. Ahead looms the abrupt and daunting-looking peak of Cribyn, to the left the Upper Neuadd Reservoir can be seen

and to the right there is a view down Cwm Cynwyn to the Usk Valley.

At the col turn left **C** along a broad, flat, stony track, which is thought to be of Roman origin and is usually referred to as the 'Gap Road' because it makes use of the gap in the escarpment. Follow this trackway above the Upper Neuadd Reservoir and after $1\frac{1}{2}$ miles, where the main track turns right **D**, there is a choice of routes. *If the stream below is fordable, bear left and head steeply down a rocky track to ford it, head up the other side and continue along the right-hand edge of conifers to descend gently to a road. Otherwise, follow the main track to the right down to a metal gate, turn left onto a path in front of it, cross the stream, climb a stile and continue along the road ahead.* The track and road meet at a junction **E**, where you should turn left to take the track ahead, which is part of the Taff Trail. It runs to the left of the road, by a wire fence on the right and along the edge of the conifers of Taf Fechan Forest. Ahead are most attractive views towards Talybont reservoir. The track passes through several gates and continues through woodland, eventually bending right to cross a stream and rejoin the road **F**. Turn left and follow the road uphill for just over $\frac{1}{2}$ mile to return to the starting point. ●

On the escarpment of the Brecon Beacons

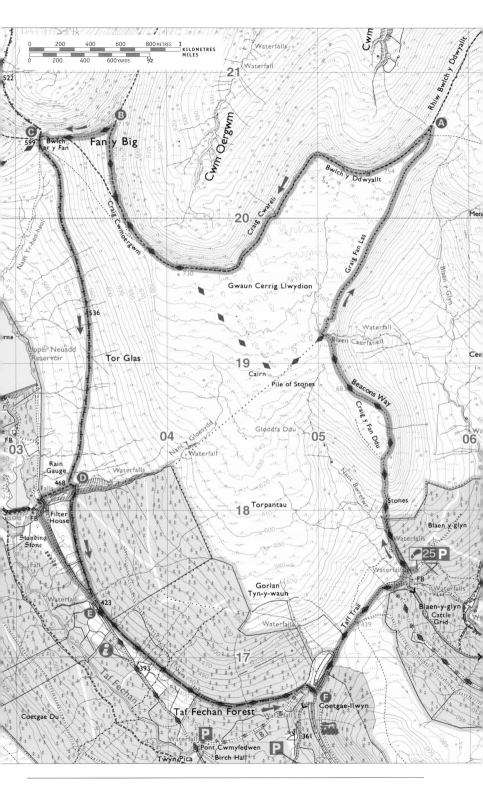

Waun Fach

		GPS waypoints
Start	Pengenffordd	📝 SO 173 296
Distance	7 miles (11.3km)	Ⓐ SO 178 301
Height gain	2,200 feet (670m)	Ⓑ SO 195 310
Approximate time	4½ hours	Ⓒ SO 212 308
Parking	Castle Inn car park (pay in the pub)	Ⓓ SO 215 299
		Ⓔ SO 204 286
Route terrain	Clear and often boggy paths over high mountains and open moorland. *Navigation would be difficult in poor visibility*	Ⓕ SO 186 289
Ordnance Survey maps	Landranger 161 (The Black Mountains), Explorer OL13 (Brecon Beacons National Park – Eastern area)	

After a short, steep climb at the start of the walk to the scanty remains of Castell Dinas, a magnificent viewpoint, the rest of the route to the 2,660 ft (810m) summit of Waun Fach, the highest point in the Black Mountains, is a lengthy and steady rather than strenuous ascent, much of which involves an exhilarating ramble along a switchback ridge. Route-finding could be difficult and potentially hazardous in bad weather, especially misty conditions, therefore save this walk for a fine day when the extensive views can be enjoyed to the full.

📝 Head down the set of wooden steps at the back of the car park and turn right onto a rough track. Follow this for a few paces and then turn left, over a stile, onto a permissive path that leads to Castell Dinas. This drops steeply down to a small stream, which you cross, before making your way up the steep left-hand edge of the field on the other side. Continue, all the time on the same line until you reach the lower ramparts of Castell Dinas, a Norman Castle built on the original site of an Iron Age Hill Fort Ⓐ. There's nothing much left of the castle but it's a great spot with views in all directions, including straight ahead along the full length of Y Grib, which rises like a dragon's back from the deep saddle at your feet.

Drop steeply into the saddle, cross the track that runs across it, and then climb up onto the ridge, ahead. Now simply follow the crest upwards on an easy path that vaults a few small rocky outcrops along the way. A small cairn marks a subsidiary top at 1,607 feet (490m), and beyond this, the path drops into a pronounced saddle named Bwlch Bach a'r Grib – which translates to the 'Small Gap in the Ridge'. Climb steeply away from this and enjoy a lovely level section that leads to a final steep climb over a succession of small rocky steps.

Cairn on Y Grib

Keep ahead the whole time, sticking to the crest as much as possible, until you eventually reach the magnificent cairn that crowns the true top of the ridge **B**.

Keep straight ahead crossing a broad plateau and then climbing steeply on a fainter path that eventually leads onto the main Black Mountains ridge, just a short distance north of the outlying summit of Pen y Manllwyn. Bear right onto a broad peaty path that leads to this summit, marked with a small cairn **C**, and then continue in the same direction to climb steadily, through a

succession of peat hags, to the obvious summit of Waun Fach – marked by a plinth that once carried a trig point **D**. This is the highest point in the Black Mountains but it does not offer much in the way of views or shelter so it's probably best to keep moving.

Bear right to leave the boggy hollow and locate another peaty path that runs easily along a broad ridge with the Grwyne Fechan Valley dropping steeply away to the left. Follow this path easily around the head of the valley to the small summit of Pen Trumau, where it then drops steeply into a huge, deep saddle that's marked by large cairns **E**.

View towards Pen y Manllwyn from Waun Fach

This is a fabulous viewpoint and by far the best place to appreciate the real size and stature of Waun Fach as well as its twin peak, Pen y Gadair Fawr, which has a much more distinctive outline despite being slightly lower.

Turn right to drop down from the cairns and then keep left at a fork after 200 yds. The

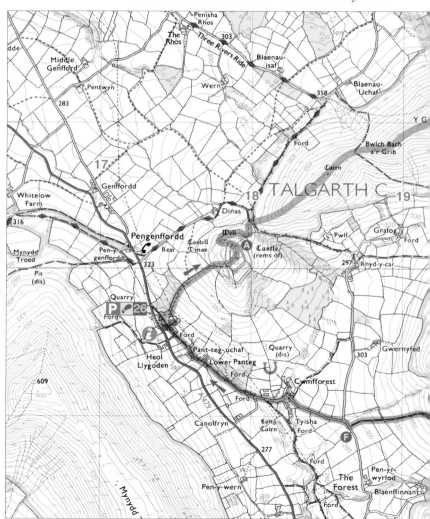

rough path now leads steeply down through sheep pasture, finally leaving the open moorland at a gate and dropping, between dry stone walls to a road **F**. Turn right and then left to drop steeply down to a bridge over the Afon Rhiangoll and then climb up the other side, where you'll see a rocky track leading off to the right, on a sharp left-hand bend. Take this and follow it for $^1/_2$ mile, past the stile that you crossed at the start and back up the steps to the car park.

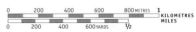

Craig-y-nos, Cribarth and the Henrhyd Falls

		GPS waypoints
Start	Craig-y-nos Country Park	⬛ SN 839 155
Distance	8½ miles (13.7km)	Ⓐ SN 828 141
Height gain	1,935 feet (590m)	Ⓑ SN 829 133
Approximate time	4½ hours	Ⓒ SN 829 125
Parking	Pay and Display car park	Ⓓ SN 834 126
Route terrain	A true mix of paths that cross mountains and woods. Some sections may be awkward in poor visibility. Some short sections of road walking and one longer stretch of quiet lane	Ⓔ SN 854 120 Ⓕ SN 851 124 Ⓖ SN 847 129 Ⓗ SN 848 147 Ⓙ SN 843 157
Ordnance Survey maps	Landranger 160 (Brecon Beacons), Explorer OL12 (Brecon Beacons National Park – Western area)	

Craig-y-nos Country Park, formerly the grounds of a large house, is the starting point for this lengthy and unusually varied walk in Glyn Tawe, the upper reaches of the Swansea Valley on the southern fringes of the Black Mountain. The walk includes open hillside, a summit, woodland, riverside, a narrow ravine and the highest waterfall in South Wales, as well as having the historic interest of Craig-y-nos and the former quarrying activities in the area. In addition to being lengthy, this is quite an energetic walk with several ascents and descents but well worthwhile for the superb views and scenic contrasts.

In 1878 the tempestuous, internationally famous opera singer Adelina Patti fell in love with the romantic setting of Craig-y-nos Castle in the upper Swansea valley and the following year she bought it. Over the next 12 years she enlarged and modernised the early 19th-century castle and laid out over 40 acres of ornamental grounds. Such was her fame and wealth that at the nearby station she had her own railway carriage and a private waiting room for herself and her many distinguished visitors, who included the Prince of Wales, later

Edward VII. After her death in 1919 the castle became a hospital and it is now a restaurant and function centre. In 1976 the grounds – woodland, meadow, lakes and river – were acquired by the Brecon Beacons National Park and restored as a country park.

🖊 Park at Craig-y-nos Country Park. Turn left on to the main road and follow it for about 400 yds passing in front of the 19th-century castle buildings and the coach house. Continue to a gate on the right, opposite a lay-by on the left, and pass through it to follow the grassy track uphill, signed to the open hill. Bear sharp right after a few paces and follow the narrow track up the steep hillside in a series of zigzags, that are marked with white-topped posts. Turn left on reaching the fence at the top, and keep this to your right to continue climbing steeply to a stile over a wall.

Climb the stile and turn right to follow the wall up over the side of the limestone crag, then down past a stile to a gate in the wall on the right. Turn left to follow a faint path easily upwards passing through a natural amphitheatre with a rock-covered hillside directly ahead. Keep right near the top, to locate a clearer path, and then follow this leftwards, in front of the rock-strewn hill, to meet a clearer, grassy, quarry track. Turn right onto this and continue around the hillside for a few paces, meeting a wall on the left. The triangulation pillar on the summit of Cribarth 1,390 feet (423m) can be seen ahead; bear right and head up to it Ⓐ for the magnificent all-round view that takes in the hilly moorlands of Fforest Fawr, almost the whole length of the Swansea valley, the hills that guard the northern end of the former mining valleys and the barren, empty wilderness of the Black Mountain.

From the summit keep straight ahead to wind your way between outcrops and back down to the original track, which should be followed downhill, with a wall on the left. At a wall corner a disused quarry tramroad can be seen contouring along the side of the hill ahead but at this point you turn left and make your way between boulders to a stile and footpath sign about 50 yds ahead. Climb the stile and, following the direction of a yellow waymark to the right, continue along a grassy path that contours around the slopes of Cribarth, keeping parallel to a wall and a wire fence on the right.

The path gradually bears left following the curve of the hill and heads down to a short marker post, and beyond that to a stile. Do not climb over the stile but instead turn left, in the direction of a public footpath sign to Ynyswen, and continue through rocks, bracken and heather along the southern flanks of Cribarth. Keep ahead at a junction of paths, marked by a wooden post, and cross a short boardwalk to a stile in the fence on the left. Cross this and keep ahead along the right-hand edge of the field to another stile. Cross this and turn right to go through a metal gate at the top of the woodland Ⓑ. Fork immediately right and descend through the beautiful, steep-sided Abercrave Wood to reach a metal gate in front of a barn.

Go through, keep ahead, pass through the right-hand one of two metal gates straight ahead and continue along a track by a stream on the right. Keep to the right of farm buildings and then turn right along a tarmac drive. At a junction by the **Abercrave Inn** turn sharp left down a road and take the first turning on the right along a road that first bends sharply to the right and then turns left to cross a bridge over the River Tawe.

On the other side of the bridge turn left at a public footpath sign, go through a kissing-gate to the left of a house and continue along a tarmac path beside the river. Go through a second kissing-gate, pass under a road, go through a third one and keep ahead to a footpath sign. Turn left to keep alongside the river, below sloping woodland, and a few yards farther on follow the direction of a waymarked post to bear slightly right uphill and continue through woodland above the river. Head up to keep by a hedge bank and line of trees on the right, climb a stile, continue along the left-hand edge of a field, above the top edge of the wood and by a wire fence on the left, and climb another stile onto a lane C .

Turn left along the lane for nearly ½ mile, keep left at a fork, descend steeply and follow the lane around a right-hand bend to Llech Bridge. Cross the bridge, continue along the lane for about 50 yds and at a public footpath sign turn right over a stile D. There is now an attractive stretch along an undulating path by the side of the beautiful gorge of the River Llech to the Henrhyd Falls. The path is mostly high up above the river, with steps in places and several stiles and footbridges. Approaching the falls the route continues by bearing left along an uphill path, but for a better view keep ahead, turn right over a footbridge and turn left to continue to the impressive falls which at just under 100 feet (30m) are the highest in South Wales. They are now owned by the National Trust. Retrace your steps to take the steep uphill path, go through two gates at the top and continue through a car park to a road E. Turn left along the road (or to visit the pub, turn right over the bridge) and keep ahead for nearly ½ mile.

At a left-hand bend by a mast F *there is a choice of routes. If you would prefer to avoid a stretch of boggy walking (for instance after wet weather), go round the left-hand bend and continue for just under ½ mile until you reach a road leading off to the right. Go down this, and after about ¼ mile and two slight bends to the right you rejoin the main route at* G *below.*

If you don't mind covering boggy ground, climb the stile at F and keep ahead – there is no obvious path – across an area of rough pasture, bearing slightly left and heading down to cross

a footbridge. Continue in the same direction to a stile, climb it and head gently uphill towards the right-hand edge of the line of trees in front. Here bear right alongside a fence on the left, go through a gap in a wire fence ahead and, keeping by a hedge bank and fence on the left, bear left and head downhill by a stream on the right.

Climb a stile onto a lane G, turn right over a bridge and follow the lane for ½ mile, heading downhill. There are superb views of Cribarth and along the Tawe Valley to the prominent Carmarthen Fans on the skyline. Where the lane turns left to cross Pen-y-cae Bridge keep ahead, at a public bridleway sign, along a tarmac drive. In front of a metal gate fork left onto an enclosed, tree-lined path and continue to a lane. Keep ahead along the lane, which later joins a wider one.

Just after passing an outdoor centre on the right, bear left H along a tarmac, hedge-lined track. Where this ends in front of a farm bear left again through a metal gate, passing to the left of the farm-house, and continue along an enclosed path. Later the path keeps along the right-hand edge of woodland, by a wire fence on the left and below steep rocky slopes on the right. At a fork **J**, go left through a wooden gate and drop to a bridge over the River Tawe. Do not cross but instead turn left, with the river to your right, and walk easily along the banks, through trees, to a bridge on the right. Cross this and bear right then left at the pond, to return to the start.

Brecon Beacons Horseshoe

Start	Cwm Gwdi	
Distance	8½ miles (13.7km)	
Height gain	2,890 feet (880m)	
Approximate time	5 hours	
Parking	Free car park in Cwm Gwdi	
Route terrain	Mainly good paths over high mountains but one short untracked section and some steep climbs and drops. The return leg follows quiet, narrow lanes	
Ordnance Survey maps	Landranger 160 (Brecon Beacons), Explorer OL12 (Brecon Beacons National Park – Western area)	

GPS waypoints

- 🖊 SO 023 247
- Ⓐ SO 032 244
- Ⓑ SO 023 222
- Ⓒ SO 023 213
- Ⓓ SO 011 215
- Ⓔ SO 007 213
- Ⓕ SO 011 252

This walk, which includes the three main peaks of the Brecon Beacons, is arguably the finest mountain walk in South Wales and one of the best in the country. A lengthy, gradual, steadily ascending approach leads to the foot of Cribyn, then the final climb up to its summit (2,608ft/795m) is steep and exhausting. A descent into a col is followed by another steep, though short, pull up to Pen y Fan (2,907ft/886m), the highest point in the Brecon Beacons and the highest point in Britain south of Snowdonia. A much gentler descent and ascent leads onto the distinctive flat summit of Corn Du (2,863ft 873m). The return route drops down to the beautiful little lake of Llyn Cwm Llwch, and this is followed by a relaxing stroll through the lovely valley of Cwm Llwch. This is a walk worth taking plenty of time over; the approach and return are every bit as enjoyable as the three peaks themselves and the views are magnificent. But do not attempt it in poor, especially misty, weather, unless experienced in such conditions and able to use a compass.

🖊 Begin by walking down a muddy path that leads left out of the top car park. Cross a stile on the right and a footbridge over the Nant Gwdi. Turn right to follow the path up through scrubby woodland, with the brook to the right, and keep heading up until you emerge from the trees onto an open hillside. Bear left to contour around the hillside, keeping the steep bracken covered slopes to your right, and the wooded lower slopes to your left. Continue around until you see a gate down to your left Ⓐ, and trend rightwards to follow a clear path up into Cwm Sere, with fantastic views up the valley to Cribyn and Pen y Fan.

Follow this path effortlessly up the

valley for about 1½ miles, until the path gradually drops to meet the Nant Sere above some waterfalls **B**. Cross the stream above the falls, and make your way directly up the steep hillside beyond. Continue climbing to the top, where you'll meet a good path that runs along Bryn Teg. Turn right onto this and climb easily at first, and then steeply, to the summit of Cribyn **C**. The reward is a magnificent view which includes Fan y Big, the Black Mountains, Llangorse Lake, Brecon, the Usk Valley, the hills of mid Wales, Pen y Fan, Corn Du and the peaks and reservoirs to the south.

Turn right and make for the summit of Pen y Fan along a clear, broad, path, heading steeply down into a col and equally steeply uphill again, with a final, rocky scramble to the cairn that marks the summit **D**. From here there is an even more spectacular view because it includes Fforest Fawr and the Black Mountain to the west and the beautiful little lake of Llyn Cwm Llwch below. Now bear left and make your way to the third of the trio of summits, the flat-topped Corn Du – thankfully there is only a modest descent and ascent this time.

From the summit cairn on Corn Du **E** keep in the same direction and after an initial steep descent turn right to continue along the edge of the escarpment above Llyn Cwm Llwch. The memorial passed by is to Tommy Jones, a five-year-old boy whose body was found here in 1900. He was visiting his grandparents who lived in Cwm Llwch, and became separated from his father as they walked from the rail station in Brecon. The obelisk was moved slightly a few years ago to try and stem the erosion that surrounded it. Shortly after the monument follow the path that descends quite steeply towards the left-hand side of the lake. From this path there are spectacular views of the great natural amphitheatre formed by Corn

Pen y fan – the highest point in southern Britain

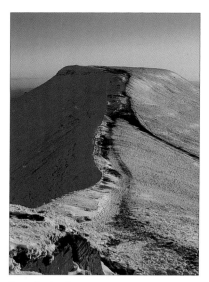

Pen y fan in winter

Climb a stile, then cross a footbridge over a tributary stream and continue beside the stream to a parking area. Pass through it, go through a metal gate and

Du and Pen y Fan that encloses the lake, and of the lovely green valley of Cwm Llwch with Brecon and the gentler landscapes of the Usk Valley beyond.

Upon reaching the outlet of Llyny Cwm Llwch bear slightly left to continue through the valley, keeping to the left of the stream all the way. This is an outstandingly attractive and relaxing section of the walk; the path is clear and easy to follow and there are constant superb views. At first you head fairly gently downhill across open grassland to climb a stile by a National Trust sign for Cwm Llwch. Then continue through the increasingly more gentle and wooded terrain and just in front of a cottage turn left over a waymarked stile. Turn right to climb another one, keep ahead by a wall on the right, and soon after the wall ends curve first to the right and then turn left to continue along a delightful, tree-lined track enclosed by low walls, with the stream close by.

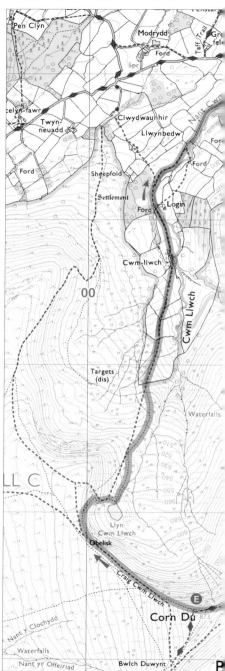

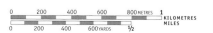

continue along the track ahead, which soon becomes a tarmac track. At a crossroads turn right **F**, cross the stream and follow a narrow lane for 1 mile, keeping ahead at a junction, to the entrance to Cwm Gwdi Training Camp. Turn right through the entrance to return to the start.

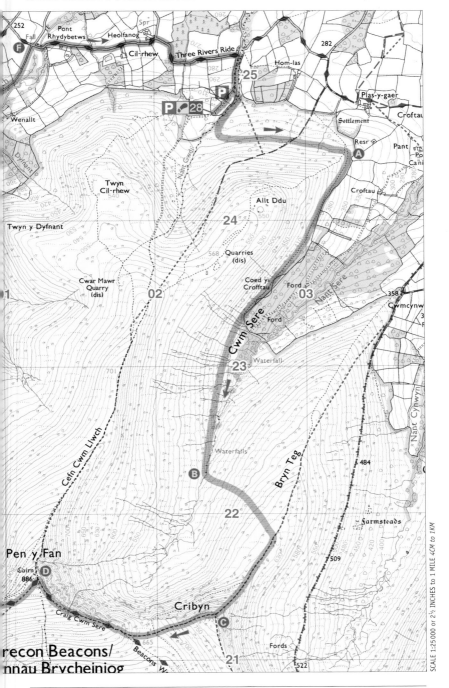

SCALE 1:25000 or 2½ INCHES to 1 MILE 4CM to 1KM

Further Information

 ## Safety on the Hills

The hills, mountains and moorlands of Britain, though of modest height compared with those in many other countries, need to be treated with respect. Friendly and inviting in good weather, they can quickly be transformed into wet, misty, windswept and potentially dangerous areas of wilderness in bad weather. Even on an outwardly fine and settled summer day, conditions can rapidly deteriorate at high altitudes and, in winter, even more so.

Therefore it is advisable to always take both warm and waterproof clothing, sufficient nourishing food, a hot drink, first-aid kit, torch and whistle. Wear suitable footwear, such as strong walking boots or shoes that give a good grip over rocky terrain and on slippery slopes. Try to obtain a local weather forecast and bear it in mind before you start. Do not be afraid to abandon your proposed route and return to your starting point in the event of a sudden and unexpected deterioration in the weather. Do not go alone and allow enough time to finish the walk well before nightfall.

Most of the walks described in this book do not venture into remote wilderness areas and will be safe to do, given due care and respect, at any time of year in all but the most unreasonable weather. Indeed, a crisp, fine winter day often provides perfect walking conditions, with firm ground underfoot and a clarity that is not possible to achieve in the other seasons of the year. A few walks, however, are suitable only for reasonably fit and experienced hill walkers able to use a compass and should definitely not be tackled by anyone else during the winter months or in bad weather, especially high winds and mist. These are indicated in the general description that precedes each of the walks.

 ## Walkers and the Law

The Countryside and Rights of Way Act (CRoW Act 2000) extends the rights of access previously enjoyed by walkers in England and Wales. Implementation of these rights began on 19 September 2004. The Act amends existing legislation and for the first time provides access on foot to certain types of land – defined as mountain, moor, heath, down and registered common land.

Where You Can Go
Rights of Way
Prior to the introduction of the CRoW Act, walkers could only legally access the countryside along public rights of way. These are either 'footpaths' (for walkers only) or 'bridleways' (for walkers, riders on horseback and pedal cyclists). A third category called 'Byways open to all traffic' (BOATs), is used by motorised vehicles as well as those using non-mechanised transport. Mainly they are green lanes, farm and estate roads, although occasionally they will be found crossing mountainous area.

Rights of way are marked on Ordnance Survey maps. Look for the green broken lines on the Explorer maps, or the red dashed lines on Landranger maps.

The term 'right of way' means exactly what it says. It gives a right of passage over what, for the most part, is private land. Under pre-CRoW legislation walkers were required to keep to the line of the right of way and not stray onto land on either side. If you did inadvertently wander off the right of way, either because of faulty map reading or because the route was not clearly indicated on the ground, you were technically trespassing.

Local authorities have a legal obligation to ensure that rights of way are kept clear and free of obstruction, and are signposted where they leave metalled roads. The duty of local authorities to install signposts

Countryside Access Charter

Your rights of way are:

- public footpaths – on foot only. Sometimes waymarked in yellow
- bridle-ways – on foot, horseback and pedal cycle. Sometimes waymarked in blue
- byways (usually old roads), most 'roads used as public paths' and, of course, public roads – all traffic has the right of way

Use maps, signs and waymarks to check rights of way. Ordnance Survey Explorer and Landranger maps show most public rights of way

On rights of way you can:

- take a pram, pushchair or wheelchair if practicable
- take a dog (on a lead or under close control)
- take a short route round an illegal obstruction or remove it sufficiently to get past

You have a right to go for recreation to:

- public parks and open spaces – on foot
- most commons near older towns and cities – on foot and sometimes on horseback
- private land where the owner has a formal agreement with the local authority

In addition you can use the following by local or established custom or consent, but ask for advice if you are unsure:

- many areas of open country, such as moorland, fell and coastal areas, especially those in the care of the National Trust, and some commons
- some woods and forests, especially those owned by the Forestry Commission
- country parks and picnic sites
- most beaches
- canal towpaths
- some private paths and tracks Consent sometimes extends to horse-riding and cycling

For your information:

- county councils and London boroughs maintain and record rights of way, and register commons
- obstructions, dangerous animals, harassment and misleading signs on rights of way are illegal and you should report them to the county council
- paths across fields can be ploughed, but must normally be reinstated within two weeks
- landowners can require you to leave land to which you have no right of access
- motor vehicles are normally permitted only on roads, byways and some 'roads used as public paths'

Further Information

---

extends to the placing of signs along a path or way, but only where the authority considers it necessary to have a signpost or waymark to assist persons unfamiliar with the locality.

The New Access Rights
Access Land

As well as being able to walk on existing rights of way, under the new legislation you now have access to large areas of open land. You can of course continue to use rights of way footpaths to cross this land, but the main difference is that you can now lawfully leave the path and wander at will, but only in areas designated as access land.

Where to Walk

Areas now covered by the new access rights

– Access Land – are shown on Ordnance Survey Explorer maps bearing the access land symbol on the front cover.

'Access Land' is shown on Ordnance Survey maps by a light yellow tint surrounded by a pale orange border. New orange coloured 'i' symbols on the maps will show the location of permanent access information boards installed by the access authorities.

Restrictions

The right to walk on access land may lawfully be restricted by landowners. Landowners can, for any reason, restrict access for up to 28 days in any year. They cannot however close the land:

- on bank holidays;
- for more than four Saturdays and

Sundays in a year;
- on any Saturday from 1 June to 11 August; or
- on any Sunday from 1 June to the end of September.

They have to provide local authorities with five working days' notice before the date of closure unless the land involved is an area of less than five hectares or the closure is for less than four hours. In these cases land-owners only need to provide two hours' notice.

Whatever restrictions are put into place on access land they have no effect on existing rights of way, and you can continue to walk on them.

Dogs

Dogs can be taken on access land, but must be kept on leads of two metres or less between 1 March and 31 July, and at all times where they are near livestock. In addition landowners may impose a ban on all dogs from fields where lambing takes place for up to six weeks in any year. Dogs may be banned from moorland used for grouse shooting and breeding for up to five years.

In the main, walkers following the routes in this book will continue to follow existing rights of way, but a knowledge and understanding of the law as it affects walkers, plus the ability to distinguish access land marked on the maps, will enable anyone who wishes to depart from paths that cross access land either to take a shortcut, to enjoy a view or to explore.

General Obstructions

Obstructions can sometimes cause a problem on a walk and the most common of these is where the path across a field has been ploughed over. It is legal for a farmer to plough up a path provided that it is restored within two weeks. This does not always happen and you are faced with the dilemma of following the line of the path, even if this means treading on crops, or walking round the edge of the field. Although the latter course of action seems the most sensible, it does mean that you would be trespassing.

Other obstructions can vary from overhanging vegetation to wire fences across the path, locked gates or even a cattle feeder on the path.

Use common sense. If you can get round the obstruction without causing damage, do so. Otherwise only remove as much of the obstruction as is necessary to secure passage.

If the right of way is blocked and cannot be followed, there is a long-standing view that in such circumstances there is a right to deviate, but this cannot wholly be relied on. Although it is accepted in law that highways (and that includes rights of way) are for the public service, and if the usual track is impassable, it is for the general good that people should be entitled to pass into another line. However, this should not be taken as indicating a right to deviate whenever a way becomes impassable. If in doubt, retreat.

Report obstructions to the local authority and/or The Ramblers.

 ## Useful Organisations

Council for National Parks
6-7 Barnard Mews,
London SW11 1QU
Tel. 020 7924 4077
www.cnp.org.uk

Brecon Beacons National Park Authority
Plas y Fynnon, Cambrian Way,
Brecon LD3 7HP
Tel. 01874 624437
www.breconbeacons.org
National park information centres:
Abergavenny: 01873 853254
Brecon: 01874 623156
Brecon Beacons Mountain Centre, near Libanus: 01874 623366
Craig-y-nos Country Park: 01639 730395
Llandovery: 01550 720693

Glamorgan Coast Heritage Centre
Dunraven Park, Southerndown CF32 0RP
Tel. 01656 880157
www.valeofglamorgan.gov.uk

Campaign for the Protection
of Rural Wales
T'y Gwyn,
31 High Street,
Welshpool
SY21 7YD
Tel. 01938 552525/556212
www.cprw.org.uk

Countryside Council for Wales
Maes-y-Ffynnon,
Penrhosgarnedd,
Bangor
LL57 2DW
Tel. 08451 30 6229
www.ccw.gov.uk

Forestry Commission Wales
Welsh Assembly Government,
Rhodfa Padarn,
Llanbadarn Fawr,
Aberystwyth
SY23 3UR
Tel. 0300 068 0300
www.forestry.gov.uk

National Trust
Membership and general enquiries:
Tel. 0844 800 1895
Wales Regional Office
Trinity Square,
Llandudno
LL30 2DE
Tel. 01492 860123
www.nationaltrust.org.uk

Ordnance Survey
Romsey Road,
Maybush,
Southampton
SO16 4GU
Tel. 08456 05 05 05
www.ordnancesurvey.co.uk

Ramblers' Association (Wales)
3 Coopers Yard,
Curran Road,
Cardiff,
CF10 5NB
Tel. 0292 064 4308
www.ramblers.org.uk/wales

Tourist Information
Visit Wales
www.visitwales.co.uk
Tel. 08708 300306
*Local tourist information offices
(*not open all year):*
Abergavenny: 01873 857588
Brecon: 01874 622485
Bridgend: 01656 654906
Caerphilly: 029 2088 0011
Cardiff: 08701 211 258
*Llandeilo: 01558 824226
Merthyr Tydfil: 01685 379884
*Penarth: 029 2070 8849
Pontypridd: 01443 490748
Porthcawl: 01656 786639

 ## Ordnance Survey maps for Brecon Beacons

The Brecon Beacons is covered by Ordnance
Survey 1:50 000 scale (1¼ inches to 1 mile
or 2cm to 1 km) Landranger map sheets
159, 160 and 161. These all-purpose maps
are packed with information to help you
explore the area. Viewpoints, picnic sites,
places of interest, and caravan and camping
sites are shown, as well as public rights of
way information such as footpaths and
bridleways.

To examine the area in more detail, and
especially if you are planning walks,
Ordnance Survey Explorer maps at
1:25 000 scale (2½ inches to 1 mile or 4cm
to 1km) are ideal:

OL12   (Brecon Beacons National
         Park – Western area)
OL13   (Brecon Beacons National
         Park – Eastern area)

To get to the Brecon Beacons, use the
Ordnance Survey Great Britain OS Travel
Map-Route, at 1:625 000 scale (1 inch to 10
miles or 4cm to 25km), or the OS Travel
Map-Road 6 (Wales and West Midlands)
and OS Travel Map-Road 7 (South West
England and South Wales) at 1:250 000
scale (1 inch to 4 miles or 1cm to 2.5km).

Ordnance Survey maps and guides are
available from most booksellers, stationers
and newsagents.

Further Information

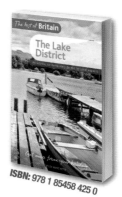

SEIZED

Teresa McLean

Also by Teresa McLean

Metal Jam
Medieval English Gardens
The English at Play
The Men in White Coats

SEIZED

My Life with Epilepsy

TERESA McLEAN

RICHARD COHEN BOOKS · London

Illustration Acknowledgements

Camera Press: 23; Patrick Eagar: 20, 21; Fogg Art Museum, Harvard/Bridgeman Art Library: 19; Hulton Deutsch: 6, 8, 11,12, 13, 15; Mansell Collection: 16, 17, 18; Popperfoto: 7, 9, 22; Private Collection/Bridgeman; Art Library: 14; Science Photo Library: 4, 5; Vatican Museums & Galleries, Rome/Bridgeman Art Library: 10

British Library Cataloguing in Publication Data:
A catalogue record for this book is
available from the British Library

Copyright © 1996 Teresa McLean

ISBN 1 86066 013 4

First published in Great Britain in 1996 by
Richard Cohen Books
7 Manchester Square
London W1M 5RE

Typeset in Linotron 202 Baskerville by
Rowland Phototypesetting Ltd,
Bury St Edmunds, Suffolk

Printed in Great Britain by
Mackays of Chatham plc

Contents

Introduction

I did not enjoy writing this book. Every time I started a new chapter, I launched myself into a new bad mood, laced with horror of the past and fear of the future. Epilepsy has always filled me with repugnance and now that I suffer from it the repugnance is personal. I am terrified, not just of having fits but of becoming a foul animal while I am having them. Thank God I am unconscious while I convulse, but it makes writing about convulsions difficult.

Last time I wrote a book about what it is like living with an illness, it was much easier. Indeed, it was positively fun. But then I was writing about diabetes, which did not rob me of consciousness. It stopped just short of that, robbing my brain of the sugar it feeds on, so that it did all sorts of extra-ordinary, undernourished things which I could describe with ease, if not relish: taking off my clothes while teaching; dismounting from my bike and lying beside it on a busy road; using a horse needle, borrowed from a crofter, to inject myself with insulin when I lost my syringe in the Highlands of Scotland. There were countless examples.

Eventually my diabetes went past such minor mishaps and gave me epilepsy, which is why I have written this book. A frightening condition that affects many thousands of people needs describing from the inside, however impressionistic the description in places, to stop the condition becoming an unknown darkness in those people's lives. I believe that the devil you know is never as bad as the devil you fear. So even if the book is grim in places, I hope the grimness will not be as bad as the dread that grows inside epileptics left in ignorance about their troubles.

In the past people's reactions to epilepsy have reflected the wild nature of the darkness that has always surrounded this strange disease. Research for the chapter on the history of epilepsy and its treatment was never dull. The main problem was that most of the extravagant records of epileptic history were impossible to check. For example, one sixteenth-century chronicler reports the old Scottish custom of gelding epileptic men and burying alive pregnant epileptic women. He does not cite examples of either practice; he may not have seen one.

Epileptic history is elaborately and uncertainly written around the unchanging theme of fear. I was following this tradition of fear when just two years ago I went to look round the St Piers Hospital School in Lingfield, the Surrey village where I grew up. St Piers is a school for chronic epileptics, I had always been frightened of it, but I learnt a lot by talking to its staff and pupils, and if I was not exactly comforted I was calmed and I am glad I went.

Maybe that trip helped me look at myself the way I looked at the St Piers children with a touch of outside, clinical interest. I got into the habit of sizing up my epilepsy and reading about it in official leaflets, medical publications, writings of all sorts, including diaries and the lives of famous epileptics.

Autobiographical writing by epileptics through the ages is heart-breaking, a tradition from which I would like to escape. There has never been any reason to smile and the condition has never before been as well treated as it is now. You would still have to be mad to smile with delight at having epilepsy, but you would not be mad to be more hopeful that it might be kept under control. So far, mine has been too active to leave me in peace, but as I said I don't intend to let the grimness get too bad and I certainly don't intend to let it get the better of me.

When it comes to reading about epilepsy in works of fiction, I found an unexpected saving grace in a sense of humour.

Even though it seldom made me laugh, literary epilepsy always inspired me with a sense of the ridiculous; it is such a daft way for an author to escape a dead-end. By the time I had finished reading all the literary mentions I could find of epilepsy I felt almost high on 'the dire disease', 'the temptation of carnal frailty' and 'the demon force'. Life without such interruptions is a lovely, flat old procedure for which I am homesick nowadays.

I can't write about this sense of nostalgia. I may have learnt to think about epilepsy clinically, but not psychologically. The weak link in this story of my life with epilepsy is the psychological one, for the simple reason that I am not interested in psychology. I have tried to say something about what epilepsy has done to my character, but I don't trust myself to have got that right, or even taken it seriously. This is a narrative, not an analytical account of the epileptic years of my life.

However, I have tried to explain how religion has helped me over the years and through the confusions of living with fits. I have a friend who is a friar and he has helped me to believe that it is worthwhile praying, whatever happens. I find him easier to talk to than the eminent consultant and professor of neurology who looks after me at the hospital.

I fear this book may have been too hard on this consultant, who still sees me, after years of limited success. We speak briefly and not very happily, but I am grateful to him and realise what a distinguished neurologist he is. All I can do if this book seems rude to Professor C is apologise. My cry is one of anguish, not anger.

I could not see much point in giving a long, detailed description of my life before it was changed by epilepsy; it would depress me and probably bore the reader. The only lead-in to this book is a description of the diabetic background that caused my epilepsy. Nor can I pretend that I want to share my epilepsy with readers, because that is not true. I would rather protect people from epilepsy, but the fact of my epileptic life is that the beastly thing is better explained. Apart from earning some money, my reason for writing this account was

to give an insight into what it is like when life becomes a
string of time lags in between fits, for the sake of the person
seized by fits and the people who have to live with the one
who is seized.

Before I became epileptic, my only practice at living against
the odds of ill health was derived from my diabetes, which
came upon me over twenty years ago. I have always found it
easy to avoid sugary foods, although I like them, and I quickly
got used to injecting myself with insulin every time I had a
meal, because there was no alternative. If I don't inject, I
don't eat.

Now, over twenty years after becoming diabetic and some
ten years after writing about it, I am well woken up to the
challenge of carrying on with life when I feel like death. I
only know about this from a personal view point and cannot
answer medical questions with any expertise, only from my
experience of the treatment I have received from doctors. It
is because of that treatment, for both my diabetes and my
epilepsy, that I am still alive today.

It has been a happy life to look back on. When I left my
convent school in 1968 I applied to both Oxford and
Cambridge Universities to see if I could get a place to read
history, which had been splendidly taught at my school by a
stately nun who talked about historical characters as if they
were personal friends.

Both Oxford and Cambridge asked me for interviews and
I was delighted when both of them offered me a place. My
only difficulty was in deciding which one to accept. In the
end I preferred Oxford because the countryside around it was
more hilly and I thought it would feel less bleak than the flat
surroundings of Cambridge.

As well as enjoying the history I was taught at Oxford, I
played cricket for the University Women's Team, which had
welcomed me warmly when I presented myself at a practice
session on a rough old city ground. Oxford University

Women's Cricket Club provided me with many good games, against local and academic opposition, including Cambridge University. I managed to boast in a post-card home one week that I went to the races with one history tutor, then the next day went to the Test Match with another.

When I left Oxford I had no idea what I wanted to do, but thought I had better get on with something worthwhile. At Oxford I had spent several stretches of time during the vacation doing voluntary work in a mental hospital in Lancashire, which has long since been closed down. It was a huge, grim institution set in several square miles of walled Victorian grounds. It almost made me feel better that I was helping in a place where everyone looked so unhappy; though the help was only basic nursing and cleaning, I certainly felt help was needed.

Now that I was a graduate I could venture further afield. In a country too poor to have even the most basic hospitals, I reflected, the need must be desperate. What about working in India? Before long I was on my way out there − keen to help but not qualified to be of much use. I was hoping to work for Mother Teresa. Everything I had read about or by her in her early years had overawed me although I confess there was a element of curiosity in the way I presented myself at Bombay Airport, more of a burden than a benefit.

I was devastated by the poverty I saw all around me − in the streets, the building sites, everywhere I went. I was too childish to help this sort of people. The nearest I got to relief was becoming so ill with amoebic dysentry that all I could do was lie on my bed losing weight and feel sorry for myself and for all those who went through such misery all the time.

Nor did I fare much better when I was a teacher in an Indian convent school, to which I quickly went in the hope that I would be better able to cope there. I never felt the excitement I thought I would feel about trying to help people in a foreign country. I was too busy feeling ill and wishing I was at home. The sisters were obviously disappointed in my efforts and I did not blame them. I gave my apologies and escaped as soon as possible, though I was feeling so feeble that it was all I could do to reach the road out of town. That, however, is what I had to do as I had no money to buy an air ticket home: I had to hitch or work my way back towards England.

I went through northern India, Pakistan and Afghanistan, with ghastly memories of the Khyber pass, where I was rescued from one bus, full of Afghan louts, by an Iranian off another bus, who appointed himself my official escort. I often wonder what happened to that man after we finally separated. He saved my life and shared his bread and water with me, but he came from the kind of westernised family not popular with fundamentalist reformers of the Islamic revolution. I thanked him for his help, but not enough. With that help and the friendly hospitality of a kind family who picked me up off the streets in Tehran, I found enough tit-bits of work to earn myself the fare for the coach journey to Istanbul, where I first saw St Sophia's silhouetted against a sunset horizon.

On returning to England my main sense was one of failure, but I had learnt one valuable lesson: I realised how much more useful I was in surroundings that were familiar to me and took a job working with Mother Teresa's sisters in a house in London.

I was a different woman since returning from India, not just because I had grown up a bit but also because I had grown thinner and weaker, to the point where I woke up each morning with my knees and ankles rubbed raw with cracks and bruises. All my joints were sharp, and many of my bones protruded. The more sticky food I ate in an effort to put on weight the more weight I lost.

It was a relief when in spring 1973 a doctor at the Westminster Hospital, now closed, told me that I had diabetes. It meant there was a reason for my feeling so depleted. The doctor explained I would have to inject myself with insulin every time I ate, but that would make me feel better. I did indeed feel better when the insulin reduced my blood sugar to the normal level, without the non-stop pissing, drinking,

exhaustion, weight loss and, most dramatic of all, huge swellings around my bony ankles. These swellings got so big that
I could not get a pair of trousers over them. If I stuck a finger
in the bulges the finger left a hole which lasted for hours. I
felt finally persuaded to go to a doctor. The young medics at
the Westminster took turns in prodding the bulges and told
me they were accumulations of sugary water expelled by my
blood, which had nowhere else to put the sweet excess. As
my blood sugar fell, the swellings gradually disappeared.

I remember walking along the pavement of a busy street
near the hospital, rejoicing in my reduced ankles and the
outdoor air. Using a little plastic lancet the hospital had given
me to prick my finger, I put a drop of blood on a pad at the
end of a stiff paper strip, wiped it off after half a minute and
scrutinised the result. I could tell from the colour of the pad
that my blood sugar was about eight. What I had not understood was that eight is fine; it is the level of blood sugar I aim
for nowadays. However, it was my first day out of hospital
and I had been told that the ideal blood sugar level was four.
Without realising that four could be liberally measured, I
thought eight was double the desired level and that I was in
dire need of some insulin. I quickly took some – and within
minutes crashed down into my first 'hypo', critically short of
sugar.

I tripped and lay on the pavement, shivering and sweating,
but was rescued by someone who saw my hospital wrist-band
and helped me to my feet. They took me to the Westminster,
where I was better as soon as the nurse gave me a sugary
drink. 'Hypers' (being hyperglycaemic) are the most common
diabetic problem: having too much sugar in the blood. 'Hypos'
(being hypoglycaemic) are the opposite problem: not having
enough sugar in the blood. 'Hypos' are the result of not eating
enough carbohydrate to counteract the injected insulin and
ease its passage.

Both extremes are easy to put right, but I find the ideal
balance between them hard to maintain. I have always been
more inclined to go 'hypo' than 'hyper' and I never realised,

until I got epilepsy, how seriously hypoglycaemic sugar starvation can damage the brain. Had I done so, I might have
left myself more sugary over the years and suffered from problems of too much rather than too little sugar: gangrene, heart
disease, blindness and kidney failure rather than brain damage caused by my brain being repeatedly starved of the sugar
on which it feeds. It is not much of a choice. And twenty years
of increasingly severe 'hypo' attacks have finally caught up
on me.

I quickly got fed up with the fume-filled dead-ends of living in
London and moved down to Gloucestershire, where I taught
history at Cheltenham Ladies College. I was much happier
living in a country town and enjoyed this one's cricket, races
and second-hand bookshops, with the early years of the
Cheltenham Literary Festival.

In 1976, when I was twenty-five, I left to study for a doctor-
ate in medieval history at Trinity College, Cambridge, the
first year that college took women. I thought I might meet
more people to whom I could talk about history, poetry, life
– at any rate, it would make a change. Though researching
a thesis turned out to be a solitary business, with little opportunity for deep discussions, I did meet some interesting people
in my three years and was generously treated by Trinity.

My diabetes was looked after in Cambridge at Addenbrookes Hospital, where I am lucky enough still to be in the
care of the same doctor today. I used to be afraid of his smart,
well-spoken manner and found him a distant figure. He
seemed unwilling to try the new methods of treatment suggested by my GP when the people in the flat upstairs called
him out to rescue me from wild 'hypos' with falls and convulsions that had woken them up in the middle of the night.

Experience has taught me how wise the hospital doctor was
to be cautious. At the time I thought he was a bit depressing,
but I did what he told me, trying to avoid too many dramatic
'hypos', if only because they left me feeling drained afterwards

and liable to react from low to high blood sugar on a self-perpetuating shuttle of low-high-low-high.

The hospital doctor is now a consultant, which seems to have relaxed him. Power suits him, making him easy and humorous to talk to. I think of him as an ally.

After my three years of historical research, I returned to Oxford and taught history at Oxford High School for Girls. My diabetes was looked after at the John Radcliffe Hospital. I could hardly have been luckier in living near two such good hospitals where I have had regular and conscientious treatment – not always effective, but always expert.

In Oxford I lived in a small house by the river in Osney, next to an enchanting couple who owned my house and rented it out to me at a modest rent. They were friends as well as landlords.

Night-time 'hypos' were a particular danger when I lived alone because if they left me paralysed, as they were doing with growing frequency, there was no way I could reach the sugar I kept by my bed in case of need. The only other hope was to attract people's attention by screaming – reasonably easy if there was someone staying with me, harder if the nearest people were my next door neighbours. Several times I found myself alone, unable to move, my helpful Osney neighbours away or my attempts to scream amounting to no more than choking or vomiting. The only answer then was time, as I waited for the paralysis to wear off.

I enjoyed teaching, which is just as well as there was not much else I could do, with an inconsequential load of arts degrees to my credit. My favourite pastimes have always been reading and writing, but they are not safe ways to earn a profitable living. I made some radio programmes, but at £30 a time they were for pleasure rather than profit. I had to teach in order to live, adding bits of broadcasting and writing as diversions. I was lucky to get my High School job, which offered bright girls, friendly staff and long holidays.

While I was teaching one day, my diabetes contrived to give me a gruesome 'hypo' during a history lesson. My brain lost control of my actions and I started taking off my clothes. I daresay it made an interesting change from Gladstone's foreign policy, but it must have been disconcerting for the girls and it certainly frightened the headmistress.

One the girls ran and told a friend of mine on the staff, who came to my rescue with a sugary drink, draping her cardigan round me as protective cover. Later that morning, the headmistress called me to her room and said she thought it would be better for the school and for me if I stopped working there. I did not mind being given an excuse to try something else. I agreed to leave at the end of term.

As it happened, a term's notice suited me well. There was a note pinned up in the staff-room telling us that the mother of one of the 'O' level girls, Catherine, had just died. Catherine was in school as usual, before and after her mother's death. I could only hope that her work might help to keep her busy and distract her from her sadness, and therefore carried on with my usual tactic of being rather hard on Catherine, to overcome her tendency to work enthusiastically then lose interest part way through. I was surprised when after school one day she asked me if I would like to go to dinner at her home.

Normally I would have said no, not liking to mix work and social life, but in the circumstances I thought it would be kind to say yes. I was treated to an epic fish pie, cooked by Catherine's father, Mark, in the uncompromising masculine manner that makes the kitchen more of a battlefield than a workplace. There was no question of fish-stock cubes to help make the sauce; it was simmered fish bones and herbs added to sauce in a double boiler, slowly, determinedly. The sauce was perfect. The fish was delicious. By the time I left, it was very late and I cycled back to Osney with extravagent care.

It took quite a while to get to know Mark well enough to share my diabetic troubles with him. He was in the odd position of living in Oxford but working in Cambridge. His first wife had worked in Oxford and they had kept their home there, where Catherine and her two brothers were still at

school, even when in 1978 Mark got a job as a don at the
new Cambridge college of Robinson. Mark lived in a college
flat during the week and came back to Oxford at weekends. When Catherine's mother died, Catherine and her
brothers, Mat and Jack, looked after themselves during the
week.

When I got to know Mark, Catherine was studying for her
'O' levels, including history, Mat and Jack for their 'A' levels.
It was probably just as well they were so busy, as it was a
forlorn time, without their mother. It was soon to have the
added strain of getting used to living with someone else. In
the summer of 1984 I married Mark, who is tall, pale, dark-
haired and blessed with the kind of active metabolism that
burns prodigious numbers of calories, leaving him thin whatever he eats. The only disadvantage of this system is that it
leaves Mark only lightly asleep, so that if I start to move
quickly at night he instantly wakes up, afraid it might be the
start of a night-time 'hypo', which he seeks to forestall by
giving me biscuits to eat.

Despite the labours of preventive feeding, Mark looks
young for his age, and when we met, eleven years ago, it was
hard to believe he had children in the adult age range. A great
friend of Mark's gave us the lovely wedding present of an
outdoor celebratory lunch, complete with salmon, cham-
pagne, strawberries and a small contingent of close friends
and family, with Catherine, Mat and Jack, and my parents,
who were overjoyed that I had found someone to look after
me.

Mark is a perfectionist and when I married him I acquired
an overseer in taking scrupulous care of my diabetes. As I got
to know him, I tried to warn him of the nuisance value of
diabetes, but only flesh and blood experience of diabetic problems can show how many and inescapable they are. From my
point of view, it was marvellous to feel less alone with the
condition, especially its dreaded 'hypos', which had dogged
me from the start.

Catherine took the most approving and protective view of

the marriage, which she felt, reasonably enough, was a result of her work.

When I met Mark's children, they were all old enough to want Mark to do as he wished. I think it was something of a relief to have him kept busy during the holidays, as long as he was still a support when advice was needed. Mat and Jack soon got places at Cambridge University, to read medicine and law respectively. Catherine eventually qualified as a nurse but did not practise consistently. I had always liked Catherine at school and expected her brothers to be keen to free themselves of a vulnerable father. It never occurred to me that I might feel jealous of them if they were slow to do that or Mark slow to let them go.

In fact, when the boys left school, Mat aged nineteen and Jack eighteen, I felt not so much jealous as overcrowded. I am inclined to be impatient and must have been more of an intrusion on them, arriving in their family house in North Oxford, than they were a disruption for me.

Acquiring three grown-up step-children was a daunting prospect but it has worked out well. One potential area of discord in the family was religion as I am a Catholic and Mark, Mat and Jack are Protestants, but we are prepared to leave each other room to be different. The important thing is that we share a fundamental belief in the divinity of Christ and I usually find this best clung to without too much analysis of the different traditions it has produced.

With Mark's support, I returned to writing on a full-time basis. It can be a lonesome occupation so the daily trip to my local market provides a welcome break, being sociable as well as useful. I look forward to chatting about life with the stall-holders and shopkeepers who greet me as a regular. It was the moustached man in the butcher's who noticed one day about six years ago that my fingers were too flimsy to pick up the bits of warm sausage on sticks with which he tempts me, successfully, in the mornings. Only a few hours earlier, I had emerged from a set of deep 'hypos', of the sort that took a long time to wear off and left me immobile for hours on end, paralysed down one side of my body. There did not seem to be anything I could do about that, even if Mark gave me supplies of biscuits, so I just waited for the paralysis to wear off gradually. I became accustomed to this process and it never occurred to me that my diabetes was working its way towards doing dramatic damage to my brain.

My 'hypos' had been developing a change in my condition for some time, but when my epilepsy erupted it came to me like a bolt from the blue.

PART ONE

My Epilepsy

CHAPTER ONE

My Baptism into Epilepsy

My son Peter was born in 1985, just under a year after my marriage to Mark, well into my second decade of diabetes. We were pretty damn lucky. He is what is known as a normal, healthy child and all the time he was growing inside me his chances of survival were slight; his chances of normal, healthy survival were minimal.

But in the end, after a rough ride in advance of birth, the nearest Peter got to medical problems as a baby was being tongue-tied. That was put right by a snip of scissors under local anaesthetic in the hospital one afternoon, leaving him cheerfully garrulous, ready to return home later that day for a soothing, ice-cream supper. Providence has been benevolent with us, but frightening on the way.

It was obvious that my extremes of high and low sugar levels might affect the baby's development. However, I was warned more of the dangers of high blood sugar in pregnancy than the damage that low blood sugar might do, to me or the foetus inside me. We were living in both Oxford and Cambridge for most of that time, commuting between the Oxford house we were trying to sell and the Cambridge college flat we all had to use as a base, also between the John Radcliffe and Addenbrookes hospitals. We went back and forth. My sugars went up and down.

Maybe this acted as an immunisation period for Peter, getting him used to life with unstable sugar levels; he is none the worse for it now. But I would not recommend the system for any mothers curious to see what hypoglycaemia can do for their child. It is too hair-raising.

By the time we sold the Oxford house I was glad to be
centred on the attentions of my endocrinologist at Addenbrookes. Perhaps it is just that I was older, I don't know; but
I found him more confident and easy-going in his manner and
it was infectious. I trusted his advice, even though he had to
deal with difficulties which were sometimes too spectacular
for comfort.

One Saturday morning, the aftermath of some recurring
'hypos' with paralytic side-effects, I found myself stuck in
Addenbrookes after I was better. Mark had called our GP
because he could not stop my sugar plunging down; even if
he gave me sweet drinks and biscuits, the sugar kept on falling.
I rolled and thrashed around, despite his efforts to hold me
down and then, suddenly, the only part of my body I could
still move was my neck and face. Mark and the GP dragged
me down our miles of stairs and dumped me on the back seat
of the doctor's car, like a sack. The doctor then drove me to
the hospital himself and negotiated with the wards for a spare
bed, despite my protests that I would rather be at home. I
could not move to resist the decision.

By the middle of the following morning, I could organise
my movements again and was sitting on my bed, having had
my morning insulin and breakfast and a long series of x-rays
of the baby, to make sure it was all right. I had fallen out of
bed several times during my contortions, which were happening more often nowadays. My body was beyond my control,
and it was frightening me.

My kind consultant appeared and sat on the edge of the
bed, next to me, looking as if he had been hauled in from a
morning in the garden. It is the only time I have seen the
doctor in a polo-neck; it was a lightly bracken-brown-coloured
jersey, I remember, but I was alarmed at his presence and
indescribably relieved when he said, 'First things first: the
baby's fine.'

By that time I was about five months pregnant and he
explained in detail why we had to try to steady my sugar
levels; if we left them as chaotic as they were, the baby had

little chance of surviving and growing normally, in body or brain. I had grasped this principle some time ago; it was the means of putting it into practice that eluded me. The doctor took time to explain how much better long-term carbohydrate works than its short-time equivalent; for instance, how much better bread works than chocolate at keeping up blood sugar it has restored to normal. Biscuits or bread act slowly and last longer; sugar or chocolate act fast but can wear off fast. The more stodgy the food the better.

When I was eight months pregnant, Mark and I went up to Lindisfarne for a few days' holiday. Lindisfarne is remote and windswept, an outcrop of land that becomes an island at high tide, when the North Sea covers the causeway joining it to the mainland. As we left to drive home, we misjudged the speed of the incoming tide on the causeway and the vehicle was quickly knee-deep in the sea washing against it, deepening as it came. The engine of the car cut out and we were stranded. Mark steered, I pushed and the baby inside me offered lively encouragement, kicking and rolling as I strained to get the car back to the mainland.

Shortly after we got home, the hospital induced the birth about a month early because they thought the risks of waiting for the full term were greater than the possible benefits. I was connected up to tubes dripping insulin and sugar into my veins and wires measuring the heart-beats of me and the baby. The birth was pleasantly anti-climactic. A baby boy was born, rather small but safe and sound.

My blood sugars were fine and I brought Peter home the day after his birth in a spare cardboard box the hospital had used for storing nappies. My pregnancy had been so risky that I had not believed it would produce a healthy baby. When it did conjure one, I had neither clothes nor container for it. The name-band that was put round its wrist by the nurses only identified its bearer as 'BABY BENTLEY', as I was not confident enough to have a name ready. We only decided on the name Peter later on, in memory of an impulsive apostle.

I look back on 1985 as a year of miraculously good fortune. Peter was born alive and well and we found an empty house with five bedrooms in Cambridge, which we bought.

Until I met Mark, the men I had known were either practical or academic; he was the first one who was both. After eleven years of living with him, I am still in shock at the sensation of someone repairing the house, mending the car and the bike, and making book-cases to hold the books we both relish.

In a way, my husband's practical skills are bad for me. I used to be reasonably capable of looking after myself, not skilled but able to tighten locks, mend lights, re-fit insides of ovens and survive on my own. Now, as a result of living with help at hand for so long, I have grown dependent on it and am pretty well useless, scarcely able to change a light bulb. This dependence extends to my health as well as the mechanical small change of daily life. After ten years of handling diabetes on my own and ten years of handling it with a partner, I have become so dependent on Mark's help that now I don't like to contemplate it on my own, let alone handle it. I have become more cowardly.

I was interested, in an inconsequential sort of way, about six years ago when Mark told me that often my night-time 'hypos' were characterised by stiffenings of my body, holding it stretched and taut. I could not eat or drink while in that state because I was not conscious. When my body relaxed again, I had a drink or ate the biscuits Mark gave me and got better as usual. The following morning I remembered nothing about the attacks.

I began to have these strange night-time 'hypos' regularly, either going stiff or sometimes hurling myself wildly about, bruising Mark by thumping him in the face, or sometimes throwing myself out of bed. These 'fitting hypos' had seized hold of me a few times in the past when I was on my own, but never as often as they were doing now.

Years before, in Oxford, a doctor had warned me ominously but obscurely once, when I was taken up to the John

1. With Peter, shortly before finding out that I was developing epilepsy.
2. Winning the mothers' race at Peter's school last year.
3. The Marquis of Hereford's XI, which I captained in a match against the University library last summer. The Marquis' sad defeat was not due to ill health, or even ill leadership, but ill play. This year will be a different story.

Radcliffe hospital there, that 'fitting' such as I had been doing on admission was bad news. I was conscious but so exhausted that once I had stopped thrashing about I lay without much reaction. The doctor leant over me and said loudly, as if frustrated, 'You don't seem to understand. They're not good for you, these attacks.' I nodded weakly. He kept me in hospital overnight and I went home after breakfast the next day, frightened at my body going mad with my brain powerless. Thank God it did not happen too often at that stage.

When I married Mark, I married night-time help in the form of preventive and salvationary biscuits. Even that did not stop me stretching and fitting. Then, about six years ago, I made a disastrous mistake. I was stupid enough to let myself be influenced by some newspaper article about the marvels of artificial human insulin. Injecting myself with a dead pig's digestive hormones is not a romantic performance and somehow this new invention sounded less depressing. I was having a nasty patch of 'hypos' at the time and as my local doctor patched up my injuries after one of them, he asked me if I thought it might be worth trying human insulin instead of the animal kind. If it did not help, I could always switch back.

What a fool I was! The diabetic consultant at Addenbrookes advised me against trying human insulin, but I had not yet learnt what a valuable quality his caution is. Surely it was worth giving my insulin a change. Also, it would look less like using my GP just to repair me when my hospital-prescribed course of treatment went wrong.

I changed to human insulin and immediately not only got far more 'hypos' but far more dramatic ones. Before long I hardly ever got through a night without some sort of sugarless drama, either stiffening or convulsing. One night I threw myself out of bed, smashing my head through the glass front of a book-case beside the bed. The first I knew of it was when I woke to find Mark kneeling beside me on the floor with a sugary drink. I could move normally by then and drank what was left in the cup. The first half had been poured down my throat, leaving a sticky circle of overflow all over my hair and shoulders and the carpet.

Also on the floor were slices of glass, from the panel I had broken with my head. I was looking at them when Mark said, 'You need some stitches. Come on. Put your dressing-gown on and we'll go to the hospital.'

We went to the casualty department of Addenbrookes. My forehead was deeply cut down the middle and had opened in two separate halves. I couldn't feel it at all; it did not hurt and it did not bleed. My mouth had a much smaller cut at the edge, where my lips joined, and that was messier because it tore and poured with blood every time I opened the lips. You can only drink a certain amount of blood before feeling sick and I was feeling very sick by the time we reached Casualty, where I was 'laid out', as the jovial porter put it, and wheeled into a little compartment behind curtains, leaving Mark and Peter outside.

Laid out and curtained off, all I could do was wait and see what would happen next. A doctor came and sewed the top of my mouth back in touch with the bottom, then my forehead back together again, this last with a long line of large stitches. They were well placed, so when they were taken out a few days later, they left only the line of the cut permanently visible; the stitch-marks quickly faded.

While she stitched me up, the doctor and I exchanged funny stories about our convent educations. Mark heard roars of laughter and wondered what was going on. I think he was glad when the doctor left and was replaced by a nurse carrying with her a set of questions which she said the casualty staff always had to ask people with head wounds, to make sure they were not concussed. I did not distinguish myself.

Question 1: What year is it?

Answer: 1989

Verdict: Wrong. It was only a few days into 1990 and I was not yet used to the new year.

Question 2: What is your name?

Answer 2: Teresa Bentley.

Verdict: Wrong. I love using my married name. The hospital, however, had me registered under my maiden name, McLean, from the years I had lived in Cambridge before I was married.

Question 3: How many children do you have?

Answer 3: Hard to say. In fact, one; in law, maybe four.

Question 4: How many children does the Queen have?

I had a long think, remembering Prince Charles and Princess Anne and feeling pretty certain that there was at least one more I had seen in newspapers and magazines.

Answer 4, doubtfully: Three.

The nurse went and fetched the doctor again, as nought out of four is not a high score. The doctor reckoned I was all right and let me go, thank goodness. When we got home I drank my coffee using only the right side of my mouth, away from the stitches on the left. The next day was a Sunday. Mark gave Peter and me a lift to mass at Blackfriars and I hobbled in like an actress aspiring to be one of the war wounded. Nevertheless, I was pleased that I could still walk, albeit slowly. When Mark came to collect us after mass I felt wearily embarrassed by the teasing he got from one hearty member of the congregation about beating up his wife.

'What weapon do you use, old chap? I prefer a baseball bat, myself.'

I already felt a burden, all the more so with this growing number of uncontrollable 'hypos', of which the human insulin did not give me the advance warning the animal insulin had given me. I was getting tired of it and did not mind at all that I soon had to go back to the hospital for the regular diabetic clinic. Maybe they could help me improve my control.

I am used to hospitals. I am familiar with every kind, from the corrugated iron huts of countryside outposts to the multi-storey blocks of London teaching hospitals. I even managed to land myself in a hospital on the night I got married. It was in Worcestershire. The doctor on duty gave me a dose of glucose and discharged me with a smile, telling me that it was sometimes a good idea to eat a bit of chocolate if I was likely to lower my blood sugar with extra physical activity. The next day, as I sat with Mark in the sun, watching Worcestershire play cricket on their beautiful ground under the cathedral walls, I remember thinking that even though I would rather keep clear of hospitals, they were basically benevolent.

Despite Mark helping to fend off many hospital visits since then, the number had risen in the last few months, mostly visits to casualty departments in the middle of the night. An outpatients clinic would make a calm change.

On the day of my Addenbrookes appointment, once Peter was in school, I cycled to the hospital, taking with me a few flashy magazines to cheer up the clinic's dismal heaps of ancient offerings. I was weighed, had my eyes examined and gave a sample of urine to be tested for sugar. Routine stuff. I'm even getting used to being weighed in kilos now, though I can't say I'm resigned to it. It takes longer to lose a kilo than a pound and that morning I had chosen tiny ear-rings and a thin jersey to make the least of my troubles. I sat waiting to ask the doctor's advice about 'hypos', trying not to look at the jolly posters of modern medical propaganda plastered around the walls.

'Enjoy what you eat!' commanded one brightly coloured sticker resplendent with wholemeal recommendations. Next to it was one of the injecting diabetic, showing nice sharp needles on syringes held by smiling patients, promoting the triumph of stabs over bruises.

Nowadays the clinic has a drinks and biscuits machine, to ensure patients do not have their brains sinking into oblivion when they see doctors. In those days there was no such machine. It seemed a long wait. I knew it was going to be a bad day when they told me that the consultant was not there. I saw one of his senior registrars instead. I had met him once before but hardly knew him.

'I've been looking through your notes,' he began. That is always an alarming beginning. In my experience it is a doctors' favourite preface to announcing new solutions to old insoluble problems. I kept quiet. In this case it turned out to be worse than that: a new problem with no certain solution. The doctor turned the pages in the folder before him.

'All this paralysis down one side of your body when you run out of sugar; taut and uncontrolled movements; increasing numbers of fitting 'hypos' . . . I'm sure you've got epilepsy. We'd better start you on anti-convulsants straight away.'

He gave me a piece of paper to hand in when I left, then checked up on my diabetes. It was wobbly, with the worst of the wobbles at night. We decided to go back to the old animal insulin and worked out a few modifications to the doses. I was stunned by the news he had given me. He closed the folder of my notes.

'Come back in three months.'

I nodded. He looked over the top of his specs, with a slight puzzled expression on his face.

'Have you taken in what I've told you?'

'Yes,' I said.

He shook his head. 'If I'd just been told I had epilepsy, that's not how I would be behaving.'

I asked him what I was supposed to do.

He shrugged.

'I don't know.'

When I left his room, all I felt like doing was crying. Or, if not crying, I might bite my lip in heroic style, to let people know I was being brave in the face of suffering. In fact, all I did was hand in my appointments slip to the girl at the desk, who directed me to the neighbouring clinic, labelled neurology. They were no more pleased to see me than I was to be there.

I sat down where they told me and looked around at the patients. A few were the stuff of nightmares, like the epileptic children I remembered from the epileptic hospital school near my childhood home. I recognised their rubber helmets, worn to protect their skulls during convulsions, their blubbering, mis-shapen mouths, their struggles to co-ordinate their battered limbs.

Most of the patients, though, looked normal. The lady next

to me kept gazing at her watch. She smiled suspiciously at me, nervous that I might lengthen her time of waiting. But she looked in good health, not too bad an advertisement for her affliction and its treatment. After the grotesque finishing touches of the diabetic clinic – amputated feet and white sticks – neurology looked almost like a soft option.

Even so, I could not have read a cricket or a fashion magazine if there had been one there. I was too appalled at being in the clinic. In my mind I kept going over my earliest nighmare memory, of an epileptic girl from the hospital school in my home village, Lingfield, having a fit during mass. She was in the back row of the Catholic Church, with some other children from the hospital school, or colony, as it was then called. Children from the colony always sat at the back during mass, so they would cause less disturbance if they had fits during mass, and could be taken out easily by the nurses who accompanied them. I used to stare at them, fascinated with horror.

I was sitting with my family one Sunday when there was a loud crash at the back of the church and I turned to see a girl about ten years old, in the grim grey uniform worn by colony inmates in those days, knocking a chair across the floor as she fell to the ground. She then smashed her head, body, arms and legs on the floor, harder and harder, chaotically. A nurse shoved a jacket under her head. The girl carried on smashing herself against the floor, with loud cries that sounded as if she was trying to swallow them as she uttered them. I could hear her making bubbling noises as she shrieked. I whispered to my mother, in terror, 'Look! Look!'

My mother told me not to stare, but I could not help it. After what seemed like ages but was probably only a couple of minutes, the tumult stopped and the girl's body collapsed into a coma. They left her lying on the floor until the end of mass when someone took her back to the colony in a car. I was surprised she was still alive after what she had done to herself, but neither the nurses nor the other colony inmates looked very upset. An elderly man gave me a knowing smile on the way out of church.

'Don't waste time looking at her, dear. She won't be moving for a while now!'

. All those years later, when I was called in to see the consultant neurologist for the first time, having just discovered I was epileptic, I found myself telling him about the girl at mass and my great fear of epilepsy, which the colony had deeply embedded in me. The consultant, like the nurses at the time of the girl's fit, did not rate such things too highly.

'I wouldn't take too much notice of images like that. Children at hospital schools like the one you are talking about usually have other brain diseases, such as cerebral palsy, which make their epilepsy far worse than yours. What we have to handle here is the result of years of 'hypos', running short of sugar. You have probably given your brain a superficial scarring, but you're nothing like the girl you've been describing.'

I studied him as he spoke. He was, indeed is a professor as well as a consultant, a distinguished and highly respected neurologist.* He looks clever, with closely cropped hair giving the impression that it had been cut to allow his brain more room. His face only just fits inside his head. He has a keen, dark air and stares at his patients. I had been shoved into the end of his clinic, when he must have been exhausted. It was about 12:30. I saw him in a little room of his own, crammed with books and papers, set apart from his consulting room. It suited him. He talked intently. I did not believe him.

'I see you have quite a long history of seizures during 'hypos'. How long have you been having full-scale convulsions?'

'I don't know, but my husband says they have been getting more frequent recently and I have them most nights now.'

'Always at night?'

'Yes.'

* Mat worked with him for a while at Addenbrookes and says he is brilliant.

'Nocturnal epilepsy. Most epileptics who have convulsions have them at night.'

I sniffed a faint whiff of hope.

'Does it matter then? I don't know anything about the fits while I'm having them, so can't I just take some pain-killers if I pull a muscle and leave it at that?'

He looked tired.

'Of course you can't. These convulsions are very bad for you. The more you have, the more they generate. We must try to peg them back straight away.'

I too felt tired. I gave up trying to be hopeful and asked what exactly a fit is. He explained that it is a random discharge of electricity in the brain. His secretary brought him a cup of tea and he pointed at her.

'I could induce an epileptic fit in anyone in the room by disturbing the balance of electricity in their brain.'

His secretary smiled obligingly and left.

'What I'll do with you, though, is give you some anti-convulsants to slow up the electricity in your brain. I won't tell you what the side-effects are or you'll get them all. Come back and see me in a few days' time.'

My only distraction from thinking about my epilepsy was thinking about the anti-convulsant drug he gave me and what its side-effects might be. If these matched up to the worst side-effects of insulin, they would be horrifying. I did not like the way he had avoided talking about them. But maybe it would be better to be left in the dark.

CHAPTER TWO

False Impulses: What Causes Epilepsy?

It is extraordinary to think of the brain stuffed full of innumerable tiny nerve cells, each of them highly active, busy sending messages to its highly active neighbour. These minute nerve cells are called neurones and they spend their time transmitting minute electrical discharges to each other. Even when I am flopping lazily around, thinking or doing nothing at all, my neurones are hard at it.

If I had to look for a positive side to what Professor C. told me about the neurones in my brain and their teeming, ultra-sensitive, misguided electrical life, I suppose it would be in the sense of awe the idea inspired, despite my misery. The brain is always the home of activity that defies description, even when the activity has gone wrong.

Perhaps that is why I find it uncomfortable that my French cookery book takes brains in its stride, along with every other part of animals' bodies. Though I eat pretty well anything, I have always stopped short of eating brains, like tripe – something to do with texture, I think. Add to that the thought of brains containing millions of dead neurones and I could hardly bear to read the instructions on repeatedly soaking them to remove the blood from them, before frying them in black butter. Worst of all, the opening sentence is easily misread into a soothingly soporific one: 'First put them to steep in plenty of cold water.'

Presumably a few of the lambs' and calves' brains favoured by French cooks once held disorganised neurones, just as most held normal, well organised ones. As brains are one of the few things I would not like to eat, I refrain from thinking about the possible differences in flavour between eating normal and epileptic brains.

Nevertheless, I can see why neurologists regard their branch of medicine as far the most interesting one. The brain is such a complicated and intense organ, consisting of so many parts and capable of so many actions, that learning even a few facts about it makes one wonder why it does not go wrong all the time.

In fact few brains go epileptically wrong. Apparently at least one in every two hundred, perhaps one in every one hundred people, has epilepsy, which makes it one of the most common medical conditions, but still a rare one. There are 300,000 known epileptics in Britain, but probably there are many more unknown ones as well, who do not recognise their occasional blank patches, or 'absences', as epileptic attacks, and suffer little damage from them.

All epileptic attacks, even the weakest and rarest, start when the brain's neurones send out random electrical impulses instead of the planned and co-ordinated ones they should be sending out. How many, long and widespread these false impulses are determines the type of epilepsy in the brain.

Like most people diagnosed as having epilepsy, I was sent for an electroencephalogram, EEG for short, to find out what sort of epilepsy mine was by measuring its false impulses. I had heard of EEGs and knew they were brain tests, just as I knew ECGs were heart tests, but I knew no more than that. In my innocence, I washed my hair on the morning of my EEG.

The test took about half an hour, did not hurt and no-one has ever told me exactly what results it produced. It was messy because it required about 20 small metal pads to be stuck onto the scalp at one end, connected by long cords to a roll of revolving graph paper at the other end. An ominously jolly nurse appeared, with rubber gloves on her hands, clutching a bouquet of tiny metal blobs.

She said, 'I hope you haven't washed your hair recently.'

'Yes, I have, this morning.'

She roared with laughter. 'Bad luck.'

She put patches of sticky jelly all over my head, then pressed the blobs into them, testing their sticking power with an experimental pull here and there. Satisfied, she unwound the cords attached to the blobs, ending up behind a glass screen where she connected the cord ends to the measuring machine and where I could hear but not see her. Nor could I see the lines which the cord ends drew onto the graph paper when the machine got going. All I could do was obey instructions.

'Look at the bright light in front of you . . . Open your eyes . . . Close your eyes . . . Sit still . . . Hold your breath . . .'

When it was finished, the nurse offered me a plastic shower cap to cover my sticky tangle of hair on the bike journey home, but I thought it was the worse of two grotty options. The cap had little pink flowers on it. I cycled home and washed my hair with vinegar as well as shampoo, to try to dissolve the mess in it. There were little tufts of cut-off hair where there had been no other way of removing the metal blobs.

About a quarter of epileptics have normal EEG results and about five per cent of non-epileptics have abnormal ones, so the results are what the nurse called 'of limited use'. Most of their use is in finding the 'epileptic focus' of attacks, especially 'partial attacks', which only affect part of the brain and body. This focus, or starting point, of partial attacks is usually identified by an EEG in the form of sudden peaks, curves or distortions in the steady brainwaves of activity it records.

Partial attacks can take all sorts of forms, from relatively mild ones like absences, sudden limb jerks or twitches, sudden attacks of vertigo, numbness or stiffness, to more dramatic ones involving convulsions of one part or one side of the body. Most epileptics remain conscious during these partial attacks, though not able to control their bodies during them. I used to have partial convulsions when I went hypo and lost control of both brain and body; I was conscious and powerless at the same time.

Epilepsy, like all conditions, springs up everywhere as soon as you've got it. I don't talk about my epilepsy much,

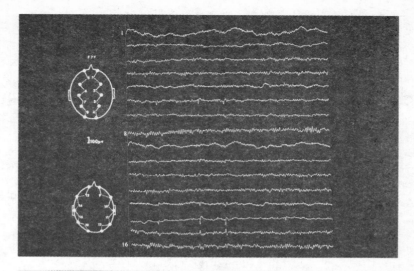

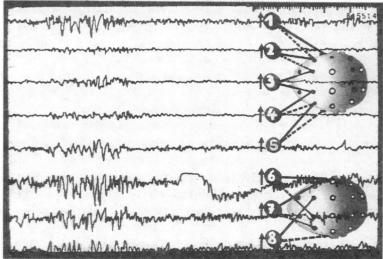

4. Focal epilepsy: electroencephalogram (EEG) showing focal epileptic spikes over the left mid-temporal region of the brain. The EEG records electrical activity within the brain through a series of electrodes taped over the subject's head. The traces (numbered 1–16) refer to locations over the brain as indicated on the diagrams at left. The epileptic spikes are most apparent on trace 14 (less so on 13 and 15) and trace 6. Focal or symptomatic epilepsy is a symptom of organic brain disease; location determines the nature of the fit or symptoms.

5. Electroencephalogram of an epileptic seizure. The traces show electrical activity in the brain picked up by electrodes placed on different parts of the patient's head. The positions of the electrodes are shown on the head diagrams at right. During an epileptic seizure a chaotic and unregulated electrical discharge passes through the brain, causing symptoms such as physical fits or loss of consciousness. The sudden onset of the attack is shown here by the abrupt increase in activity on the traces.

except to my husband and good friends if they really want to know about it, but somehow or other I seem to keep meeting people who only want to talk about epilepsy. Bus queues, hairdressers, market places, public lavatories – nowhere is safe. But everyone is sympathetic if they are speaking from experience.

Three years ago I met a cleaning lady at a monastery where I had gone for an Easter retreat. The lady had found me lying on the floor in my room, covered in blood, unconscious. When some hapless doctor who was also supposed to be on retreat was called up and decided I had been having fits, the cleaning lady helped him drag me on to the bed and then, when I was awake, told me about her daughter's 'turns'.

They were much more discreet than fits. Her daughter suffered from a very common form of epilepsy: absence attacks, little blobs of oblivion which did not develop into fits. The lady, if not her daughter, could tell when they were coming on. If her daughter started smacking her lips, wandering round as if she was drunk, making faces or plucking at her clothes, her mother told her, 'Diane, you're going to have a turn.'

It is hard to know what her daughter was supposed to reply, in the unlikely event of her feeling well enough to understand the warning, but that was no worry because her mother had the floor covered with cushions in a matter of moments, ready for her daughter to fall to the ground without breaking any bones. Diane did not convulse; she just lay limp and still for about a minute, then slept deeply for hours.

The kind cleaning lady was glad when I laughed at one or two of the more bizarre aspects of these attacks. She reckoned she was cheering me up and I reckoned it was probably cheering her up to talk about her daughter's epilepsy, which had obviously upset her horribly at first. She was used to it now and knew what she could do to help. That was not much, but over the years she had come to realise that the turns were not all that much either. They left her daughter unharmed afterwards. Best of all, they were fewer than they had been, with the help of a different drug.

I lay in bed while the cleaning lady scrubbed away at the floor by the basin, which I had splattered with blood when I'd bitten my tongue during one of the fits. I was embarrassed at seeing her cleaning up my mess for me, not knowing quite what to say except how glad I was that Diane was getting better. I could not help with the cleaning, much though I wanted to. Every inch of me hurt and any movement made me wince. I had wrenched my neck, stomach and thigh muscles. It hurt when I turned my head and when I swallowed. The inside of my mouth was torn to bits and I had chewed a chunk out of my tongue, which was agony, especially if I tried to speak.

Even so, it was worth the pain to join in the lady's laughter at her accounts of poor Diane's 'automatic behaviour', the term for strange actions that often precede and sometimes pre-empt partial attacks. I trumped her ace about clothes plucking with my account of my clothes-chucking in public when I was a teacher – half my clothes anyway – though I was not sure whether that counted as an epileptic or a diabetic reaction to a shortage of sugar.

I was growing used to the idea that the distinction was often a false one and also that as the reactions had grown more severe they had become more likely to skip the partial-attack phase and go straight into the generalised-attack phase, giving me no awareness of them and no memory of them afterwards. I lay listening to the cleaning lady's stories and realised in a wave of shame that I felt superior to Diane, her daughter, because my attacks were more serious than hers. She was an epileptic but she was only a mild one.

Competition for the worst symptoms is grotesque but it can have its funny side. This shows when the symptoms are invisible, relying on verbal elaboration to stake their claim to the worst spot. Outpatient clinics are the ideal place for this, where it grows into a sort of pinball game of affliction, contestants adding more and more grisly details to their descriptions of what they have been through. It helps to pass the time.

Any neurology clinic can treat patients to a good game of epileptic pinball.

A big, round woman is cheerful to announce: 'Mine are the real devils of fits, all over the place, lasting for ages. With the latest lot they could hear me screaming right down at the end of the street, they said.'

A gaunt woman replies in a faint voice: 'Yes, mine used to be like that. Now they throw me out of bed and I knock myself out, so I'm out on two counts, fits and knocks. I'm too far gone to scream.'

The stout lady takes up the challenge. 'Not to mention the time when I swallowed my tongue. My husband had to pull it out of my throat and I bit him so hard he's still got the marks.'

The gaunt lady, triumphant:'I haven't got the teeth to bite anyone with. Knocked them all out years ago.'

At this point only the arrival of the refreshments trolley or of a distressingly damaged patient, too far gone to be a rival, can break into the exchanges. Those who don't wish to take part in the contest have to sit quietly, reading a magazine with looks of disapproval at the competitors, or walk about looking as if they have great secrets they would rather not inflict on others.

I usually go for the second of these two pacifist tactics, but I never leave the clinic with the same look of satisfaction, not infrequently of success, that adorns the faces of those who have been publicly discussing their misfortunes. Still, it is always a good idea to see the silly side of something terrifying like epilepsy, just as it is vital to make sure it does not become a sympathy-sucker.

It is not just patients but innocent bystanders as well who seek sympathy in the top stakes of epileptic terror, and it is hard to blame them. High temperatures can cause small children to convulse; it is a harmless means the young body devises of lowering its temperature. These febrile convulsions happen to quite a lot of babies and do not constitute a true epilepsy, rather an epileptic tendency in extreme circumstances, which nine out of ten such children grow out of at an early age. But they happen out of the blue and parents often become hysterical at the sight.

Mark told me of the time he carried his baby daughter Catherine, who had turned blue and was convulsing furiously, through the endless corridors of an empty ship, in search of a doctor. They were on their way to England from New Zealand, the ship had docked and everyone had gone ashore. They had no clue what was wrong with Catherine and Mark was extremely relieved, first to find a stand-by doctor deep in the bowels of the ship and second to be told that the convulsions were transitory and were not a cause for alarm.

Less dramatic strains on the system, such as menstruation and lack of sleep, are capable of provoking epilepsy, as are strong drugs and strong drink. Some people respond with attacks of reflex epilepsy to sharp stimuli – most commonly flashing lights, but also loud or sudden sounds or touch. Church bells, whistling kettles, unexpected embraces and chess boards are but a small selection of the many stimuli that can induce reflex epilepsy.

Shakespeare's Othello is described as 'fallen into an epilepsy' when he believes Iago's lies about Desdemona. The emotional strain brings on a seizure that can, Iago tells us, be either an absence or a convulsion.

> The lethargy must have his quiet course:
> If not, he foams at mouth, and by and by
> Breaks out to savage madness.

The reflex epilepsies I have come across can't compete with that, but in a patients' pinball session at the clinic recently I did hear one young man make mincemeat of his competitors with his tales of light and dark lino squares zapping him blank in his girlfriend's kitchen. I suspected him of foul play and dislike of housework until he went on to his story of cycling along a street of tall buildings. The sun shone above the tops of some buildings and was hidden behind other buildings. He woke up on the road with his arm cut open by one of his elaborate speed-cycling pedals and his face cut and bruised all over. It was still cut and bruised as he spoke a week later.

He was not sure what sort of reflex attack it had been but it had been enough to knock him off his bike and he was frightened by it – the more so as it had made his friends edgy and uncertain how to treat him; was he normal or not? I hope he was going to see a sympathetic and practical doctor.

I have read several reports recently of an epilepsy that sounds half-way between reflex and hypnosis, with people doing repeated auto-actions, such as sucking or swallowing, after watching screens for long hours: all day in front of a video machine followed by hours of rocking backwards and forwards, eating one's mouth. There seems to be some debate about whether this is a genuine form of epilepsy, but it is said to have been reported increasingly often among young people who spend a lot of time in front of screen lights; some neurologists are taking it seriously as the latest malignant bequest of contemporary life to the sensitive brain. If not a cause of epilepsy, succumbing to screens may at least be an aggravation of existing epilepsy. Whatever its medical status, it is depressing.

I think it helps me that I know precise details about my epilepsy, including its cause. It removes some of the mystique that surrounds the condition. One of the aspects that most upset the cleaning lady about her daughter's epilepsy was that no-one could find a reason for it. It overhung Diane as a hidden danger.

I suppose that also means that Diane's epilepsy may go as inexplicably as it came. That is always a source of hope and epilepsy quite often does disappear of its own accord, particularly as the patient grows old, as if the brain no longer has the energy to muck up the body.

Though my epilepsy started with a clear trigger, in the form of hypoglycaemia, it has developed into a condition in its own right. More often than not these days I start convulsing when my blood sugar is all right, as well as the convulsing I always do when it is too low. I don't know whether or not my epilepsy will ease with age, though presumably I will never be free of the hypo-triggered attacks. I don't think much about whether I will live long enough to be old, nor do I think much about my epilepsy in the future. When I do, I drift into a cloud of fear-filled dread, so I am glad that I have never had much sense of the future.

About 60% of epileptics have no known cause for their attacks, but they can allow themselves some optimism for the future. Most convulsive attacks are at night and most cannot be explained, except perhaps by a low epileptic threshold, a tendency for the brain to release electric discharges too loosely, and that is more of a description than an explanation. Whether those convulsions are partial or generalised, they usually disappear gradually with age, sometimes with the help of drugs, sometimes without.

Mine are generalised attacks and are among the 40% that do have a known cause – in my case, repeatedly starving my brain of the sugar it needs to live. A drastic lack of calcium or vitamins can occasionally cause epilepsy, but far the most common starvation leading to the condition is that of oxygen. Before the brain can think about feeding, it needs to breathe. Oxygen-starved epilepsy is a severe disorder, associated with profound brain damage.

It used to be frequently seen in the neonatal seizures of babies deprived of oxygen during a difficult birth. With more sophisticated maternity care, this sort of violent epilepsy has become much more unusual, though the outlook for the few who have it is still grim. About a quarter die in the first year of life; a half are badly spastic or mentally retarded, suffering severe convulsions all their lives; only a quarter recover.

The thought of starting life in an epileptic convulsion is desperate, for mother and child alike. West's Syndrome is an epilepsy of early childhood with an anguished desperation all its own. It is named after the man who first diagnosed it, in 1841. He was a doctor who watched the epilepsy of his six-month-old son carefully, then described it in detail. He knew there was nothing he could do to cure it, so he sat and took notes on the sudden, massive jerks, the head-bends forward, knee-bends and arm-flexes of his baby son who, like most small children with this epilepsy, was badly mentally retarded by it. Such epilepsies do not respond to drugs. There are masses of different epilepsies, several of them named after the people who first identified them, but I have never heard of a more painfully named one than that one.

Brain damage, as a cause or a result of epilepsy, is usually easier to map than it was for Dr West. Strokes often produce epilepsy in older people, but only partial attacks, easily controlled by tablets. A few years ago my father had a bad stroke, during which he convulsed. He has made a remarkable recovery and the only remaining trace of the stroke is the anticonvulsants he still takes. He has not had any further convulsions.

Brain tumours are another kind of brain damage and they often have epileptic repercussions. We have an Italian friend, Ferdinando, who had a large tumour removed from the outside of his brain about a year ago. It was a benign tumour and the epilepsy it caused gradually disappeared once the tumour was removed. He is well again now, but he is different.

His epilepsy never convulsed him; it gave him short absence attacks, with no memory of them afterwards. For a year or more his memory also failed for long periods, without warning. He did not recognise people. He wrote letters and when he came to sign them did not know what they were about or why he had written them.

Last time he was in England, Ferdinando sat in our kitchen while I cooked dinner and made a few cryptic remarks about how much that had scared him. He is a man at home in the world, tough, capable and cool, but I have seldom heard him talk personally. He did that evening, also asking me how I was and seeming upset when I said I was all right at the time but had battered myself in some fits a few days before. He would be embarrassed to read this and would not thank me for writing it, but I think the devastating ordeal he went through has given him an extra layer of gentleness beneath his successful layers.

There is such a range of epileptic causes and classifications that if one goes through them all they start to sound like a repertoire. Perhaps it is better to overlook the abundance of medical groupings – the generalised and partial attacks, known and unknown causes, in childhood and adulthood – in favour of the simple, old, popular classification of epilepsy into the sort with convulsions (*grand mal*) and the sort without convulsions (*petit mal*).

That is the obvious dividing line. The cleaning lady at the monastery was extra-specially kind to me because I was on the wrong side of the line, the side with fits. Her daughter was on the right side of the line, the side with anything from absences to strange performances that looked almost like being possessed, but were not fits. Anything rather than fits.

CHAPTER THREE

While I Lie Sleeping

There is a void at the centre of this book because I am unconscious during the fits that dominate my epilepsy. The first I know of them is waking up the next day in pain, after tearing my muscles during the contractions.

The fits themselves I know nothing about. However much I mutilate myself, it does not hurt at the time, I only feel the results of it afterwards. It is a strange sensation, the more so as I know how violent fits can be – such fearsome shocks of force wracking body and brain, while I lie sleeping.

Above all, this sensation is a relief. I and everyone else who has generalised, double-sided fits – tonic-clonic is their official title – is spared the experience of them. No pain, no stretching of the body until muscles tear and arteries bulge under the strain, no slamming back of the head against walls, through sheets of glass or whatever is in the way, leaving the neck wrenched and the head bleeding and throbbing; no biting like a mad animal, tearing the mouth to shreds.

The 'mouth' part of my fits is the one that upsets me most. I think it must be because it leaves its legacy inside my head, which feels like my deepest reservoir of consciousness. When my teeth are broken, with displaced fillings stuck under flaps of skin, and when my tongue has whole pieces bitten out of it, it is not just painful, it is depressing in a way that is hard to describe. I don't mind stitched-up limbs and black eyes nearly as much as I mind a lacerated mouth. There is too much hostility in an attack from within, destroying myself inside my own face.

I have never been at my best with dentists and I was

amazed at the understanding my dentist showed over the mess in my mouth after one of these attacks. Of course, he is the one person who looks right inside people's mouths. More than that, he spends his time servicing mouths. He has always prided himself on seeing the mouth as the most sensitive part of the body, the harbour of taste, home of the wine palate, deserving the most tender treatment. So he expressed dismay when I showed him my mouth soon after some fits.

'Jesus! What have you been doing? You've ground some of your teeth down to nearly nothing and the ones you haven't ground you've smashed to bits. Look at this!'

He showed me a fragment of tooth which he had picked out from where it had wedged itself between two broken fangs. It felt good to have sympathy from someone taking an inside view of the trouble. He went round my mouth, excavating broken bits of tooth and refilling emptied teeth. I agreed reluctantly when he said he should crown both my lower wisdom teeth, reminding him that I am the kind of neurotic dental patient who needs a general anaesthetic before having an inspection. He can be down-to-earth in Professor C.'s style when need be and explained that one of the reasons my gums were always sore and bleeding was that there was only a tiny level of tooth sticking up above them. I was pretty well eating with my gums.

I took his advice and agreed to have two of my teeth built up with crowns. Though the crowning was expensive and unpleasant, it has meant that some of the fits I have had since then have torn the back of my mouth less than before. Smooth crowns do less damage than jagged peaks.

The dentist is a rugby fan and also made me a plastic tooth guard in rugby style, to wear at night in case I have fits. It is a good idea but I'm afraid I hardly ever wear it; it feels too obtrusive and takes the spontaneous element out of night-time kissing.

It is well known that Fyodor Dostoevsky was an epileptic: he wrote about it in his letters, diaries and novels. But one of the most touching diary entries I found on his epilepsy was written by his wife, Anya. In Geneva on 17/18 October 1867 she wrote:

> I heard him cry out . . . I ran to him. He was in seizure, his eyes were terribly crossed and his teeth were grinding. I was afraid he might swallow his false teeth and choke.

Even the great Russian writer had epileptic problems with his teeth.

At least Dostoevsky seems to have had the vast majority of his fits at night, so usually he woke in the knowledge that both the fits and any lead-ups to them were confined to his bedroom. That is a considerable relief. Although my fits come in clusters nowadays, spread through day and night, the sequence always starts at night, when I am in bed.

It was about a year after I started seeing Professor C. that my fits extended from happening one at a time to happening in groups or even long chains of groups. Mark came with me to the clinic one day to give details of a recent string of sixteen fits that had started one night and gone on, with gaps in between the fits, all through the next day and the following night. Despite Professor C.'s attentions, my fits continue to generate each other in sequences of 'serial epilepsy', though not usually as prolifically as on that occasion. The first fit leaves me knocked out when the second fit happens, maybe only minutes later, maybe hours later. The second fit leaves me knocked out for the third, and so on, until I wake up, fighting through a crushing weight of exhaustion, anything up to twelve hours later than I should have done. By then it is night-time again and I have missed the day's insulin injection, so I am full of sugar, which makes me even more sleepy.

With help, I can limp to the lavatory and pee out some of the sticky mess that has accumulated inside my bladder. I take the anti-convulsants I should have taken for that day, together with those for the coming night and struggle back to bed, where I am asleep, or submerged, before my head hits the pillow.

The nastiest of the assorted adornments accompanying such fits are left to Mark to clean up. One of the stories that most frightened me as a child was being told that if I were ever near an epileptic having a fit I should try to put a key, or something hard and flat, between the epileptic's teeth, to stop him swallowing his tongue and choking on it. The thought of getting within range of those wild mouths with all their foam and blood was unbearable. The nurses from the colony always seemed to have huge rings of keys to put into their patients' mouths, seemingly without effort, but I was glad to hear Professor C. say that putting things in the mouth was out of favour nowadays.

The received wisdom now is that the epileptic is more likely to choke on the saving instrument than on his tongue and that putting anything in the mouth is more likely to aggravate than to calm seizures – as indeed is anything that restrains or interrupts the convulsive movements while they are releasing the excess of pressure sent from the brain. Generations of epileptics have been tied, bound and wrapped up tightly, in attempts to suppress the convulsions by brute force, but Western medicine now takes the view that this does more harm than good. Bodies and rampant mouths are best left alone to dissipate their fury.

'Tastings' are combined workings of the mouth and teeth on their way up to the furious stage, a well-known signal of approaching fits. Apparently they sound like chewings with too much saliva. I am already unconscious when they start and I am much more upset by hearing about them afterwards than Mark is by hearing them at the time. He treats them as a useful warning to get ready for preventive action.

Even without my mouth, Mark has a whole range of messy sites for his actions. Two of them are so humiliating that it embarrasses me to write about them, but I must, to give a full picture of life with this sort of epilepsy. One morning I woke up lying on clean sheets which had not been there the night before. I asked Mark how they had got there and he said I had let out a tiny bit of urine during a fit the night before, so he had whipped the sheets off, washed me and put me back into bed before I knew anything about it.

'Hardly anything,' he assured me. 'Took no more than two minutes.'

It took me longer than that to come to terms with myself. Many epileptics are incontinent, some doubly so, during fits, but my thread of hope is that I have only suffered from this indignity on two occasions.

The other occasion was so horrid that Mark could not pretend it was 'hardly anything'. Like many women, I am liable to have fits just before a period or after a day or two of bleeding. The last little cluster of fits I had were few but furious and left the bed covered in a mixture of blood and urine. Mark told me little about them, except that they were bad. But he had changed the sheets, cleaned me and stripped me of protective wear and all semblance of modesty.

One of the reasons I disagree with the arguments currently being put forward on behalf of euthanasia is the importance they attach to living and dying with dignity. People are just as important and valuable when they live and die without any dignity at all. I have a vested interest in that ugly belief, but I have always believed it and the only time I have found it hard was that time I lay there in bed, knowing that in five minutes I had forced five days' worth of blood out of myself. That meant a short menstrual period but a lot of shame. Mark was embarrassed and so was I, foul and messy as I was.

Waste blood is an unpredictable addition to fits, but the rear end of my messy misery does have a regular aspect, which is associated with its treatment. During a pause in a particularly violent sequence of fits, Mark phoned our GP, in case he could recommend anything to ease them. The doctor came straight round, though it was the middle of the night.

I was not aware of him until I regained consciousness, just as he was saying, 'Next time she has a bad set, shove one of these up her bottom.'

He gave Mark a yellow plastic tube about the size of a little finger, with a blob on the end. This holds liquid valium, which is squeezed into the system and calms the brain's emissions, perhaps easing the fit and sometimes even preventing a fit that is getting itself ready to erupt.

'An ignominious procedure,' said Professor C., when I told him later that we sometimes found this helpful, 'but if it helps and Mark doesn't mind doing it, go ahead with it.'

Mercifully, I only know about it after the event, when I wake up and there is a little yellow tube on the bedside table.

Once, not long ago, I found such close comfort heart-rending. It made me cry. Mark was having no luck trying to calm some of my fits. Valium did not help. So he tried to hug me during the worst one, to stop me jerking too badly. But the harder it became for my body to release my overdose of electricity, the harder I tried to do it through my mouth, which tore itself to bits. Mark was cross with himself for having made the violence worse, but his was an instinctive reaction to the fury, a helplessly loving gesture.

Being so dependent on my husband makes it impossible but at the same time vital to achieve some measure of self-sufficiency. If I had been alone in trying to manage these fits, I doubt if I would be alive and writing this today, though I'm sure I would have made greater efforts to look after myself. That is why I find the views given by one particular epileptic, the novelist Margiad Evans, when she was the same age as me, in her early forties, only part of the story. She pronounced all epileptics egoists because they need to cling to themselves. She backed this up with examples from her own life.

Though she only had two fits in her first year of epilepsy, she said she had months of uneasiness before each of them. Her life-long manic depression worsened. She felt far apart from everyone around her, in love with nature and at one with the universe. My heart sank as I read this; I longed for a thriller. But Ms Evans had much to say. Her nervous tension became so bad that she could not stop hurrying for a whole year before her epilepsy began. She could only write poetry, not prose.

Most impressive of all, in the time between the fits she grew

frightened of counting because it made her think that the time
before her next fit might be countable. Soon she could not
count the ingredients for making a cake or pudding. Her doctor told her not to worry about such mild epilepsy but she
was good at worrying. The fact that she had separated from
her husband and had to cope with her epilepsy alone must
have aggravated her feelings about egoism. Her only means
of surviving were to persuade her husband to come home at
weekends, which he heroically agreed to do, and to shroud
her epilepsy in a would-be mystical air.

Although I can't stand Ms Evans's gushings on the subject,
I know what she means by the 'probable darkness of death'
in epileptic fits of unconsciousness. No-one can describe it
because there is nothing to describe. When you wake up you
have to join in again with all around you, not telling but
listening to everything that has been going on while you were
gone in your lost patch of utter nothingness.

I suspect the fear of this was a greater weight upon Ms
Evans than the nothingness itself, which seldom befell her.
All she remembers of her first fit is waking up late one summer
night in the 1950s, in her cottage near Cheltenham. The time
was twenty minutes past midnight, she was on the floor
in front of the fire, covered with urine. The last thing she
had known before that was sitting down with a cup of tea at
11 p.m.

Time left no way of escape for Ms Evans, before, during
or after fits because she had a few minor 'absence' seizures as
well, which she thought about for a long time afterwards and
dreaded for ages beforehand. I have an advantage over her
in that, as I have explained, my fits start at night, out of
nothing, so I never have protracted forebodings closing over
me. I have never had to endure an aura or its more intense
form, a *furor epilepticus*.

By no means all epileptics go through these strange states,
which can result from fits as well as run up to them or even,
occasionally, take the place of a fit, in the form of a maniacal
spasm. They take a whole variety of forms: vertigo, delirious,

6. Fyodor Dostoevsky wrote frighteningly about his epilepsy in his diaries, letters and novels.

7. Edward Lear, author of comic verse, was always depressed by his 'terrible demon'.

8. Gustave Flaubert: his family and friends referred to his 'epileptiform' rather than epileptic attacks, hoping that sounded less cruel.

9. Margiad Evans, Welsh poet and novelist, suffered few epileptic attacks but felt they separated her from all around her.

even ecstatic drifting, or constant wandering about, with the person unable to settle down. Edward Lear was an epileptic whose 'terrible demon' kept him constantly on the move. He was so ashamed of his epilepsy that he kept it secret, even in his diaries, only giving it the briefest mention as he travelled far, wide and incessantly, in Britain, Europe and the Middle East. Lear had another characteristic often attributed to epileptics, which makes a suitable accompaniment to the urge to travel: the urge to collect. He never went anywhere without adding masses of photos, letters, cards and mementos to the vast stocks he already had at home.

I don't know how fully these sorts of mental states can be proved to exist or how widely they can be identified. I don't think doctors know for certain either. Violent and homicidal mania has long been recognised as an involuntary epileptic state of mind. Mindless automatism, such as making vegetable soup with custard powder and, in the succinct words of Sir William Gowers, a great clinical neurologist (1845–1915) 'undressing, which is occasionally very inconvenient'.

I heard a lady on a recent radio programme describing her mindlessly automatic, semi-conscious epilepsy. She said she very rarely had 'spells'. Her last one consisted of doing some routine chore of housework, as usual, then waking up, or coming round, about three hours later in the process of finishing off a big shopping spree in a supermarket on the edge of town. The most frightening thing about this was that she knew she must have driven to the shop, because it was some miles away and her car was in the car park. But she remembered nothing about that.

She was included in the programme as an item of encouragement. Having undergone extensive brain scans, which revealed a small point of scar tissue, she is going to have an operation to remove that; her doctors were pretty sure this operation would cure her epilepsy. She had started off dubious about the benefits of brain surgery, but now that it seems to be a new-wave success story, astutely performed, she will gladly use it to free herself of the long spells when her life goes on without her. As she is lucky enough to have a definite solution on offer, she wants to make the most of it.

Feelings of epileptic despondency and obsession with death have never troubled her as they troubled Margiad Evans and, apparently, trouble many epileptics of all sorts when there is no conceivable answer except ever increasing doses of vile drugs.

These are the suburbs of epilepsy, horribly frightening for all concerned, in a tangle of involuntary action, semi-consciousness and madness. Though I think it is all too easy to overdo Evans-style leanings towards epileptic despondency and obsession with death, I have no trouble understanding how epilepsy in its fullness can erode the happiness of those who live with it.

Gowers was proud of his pronouncements about epilepsy. He began by describing fits and attacks, then went on to describe their effects on those who have to live near them. Reading his descriptions almost made me wonder whether he was not in some way addicted to this painful subject. This description of a major fit and its effects on others (in his *Manual of Diseases of the Nervous System*) spared no detail. These are only snippets from it:

> . . . rigid, violent, muscular contraction, fixing the limbs in some strained position . . . deviation of the eyes and of the head towards one side, and this may amount to rotation involving the whole body . . . the colour of the face . . . pale, then flushed, and ultimately livid as the fixation of the chest by the spasm stops the movements of respiration . . . the pupils of the eyes dilate widely as the cyanosis comes on . . . The fixed tetanic contractions of the muscles can be felt to be vibratory . . . the stage of clonic spasm is reached, in which the limbs, head, face, and trunk are jerked in violence, and through similar spasms in the tongue and muscles of the jaws the former is often bitten . . . air is expelled, and saliva is frothed out between the lips . . . the patient may seem to be at the point of death . . . At last the spasm is at an end and the patient lies senseless and prostrate . . . Urine frequently, and faeces occasionally, are passed during the fit . . . The bloated, dusky aspect of the face, with features distorted by

the spasm, renders the appearance of the patient most alarming
to those unaccustomed to the disease.

One always gets one's money's worth with Gowers. He was
upset by the distress all this caused to people watching fits,
but was not one for locking epileptics up, out of sight. Besides
being unfair, it was impractical because even locked-up epileptics could be 'most alarming' to others while being stupid
and dull themselves. I found a monumentally morbid work
on the topic, written for the *Journal of Mental Science* in 1873
by Dr James C. Howden, Medical Superintendent of Montrose Royal Lunatic Asylum: a real period piece, but still
interesting. Dr Howden described an unusually high level of
religious keenness he said he had found in epileptics, a keenness which until then had been 'insufficiently reported'. He
made up for lost time with a vigorous description of epileptic
misery in this life.

As well as the usual epileptic characteristics which he noted
– suspicion, irritability, egoism, impulsiveness, violence and
strong homicidal propensities – he found three main causes
for epileptic religious enthusiasm.

First, epileptics always craved sympathy because they were
often ostracised by those around them and left out of amuse-
ments; they looked for divine comfort because they found little
on earth. The more I read Dr Howden's account of the forlorn
groups of epileptics standing together in the rain in the
asylum's recreation ground, surrounded by raving lunatics,
the more easily I could imagine other reasons the Montrose
epileptics craved sympathy.

The second religious trigger Dr Howden mentioned was
more surprising – hope, despite drugs usually failing to help
epileptics. I would have thought it was because of, not despite
the fact that drugs at that date failed to help epileptics that
they had nowhere else to go in their desperation but hope,
the only alternative to despair. Dr Howden did not fully eluci-
date his views on hope.

The third religious trigger he reported seemed to show his

attitude to the whole subject as a dispassionate one, looking
on epilepsy and religion alike as matters of scientific interest,
with quite a bit in common. He mentioned delusions of hope
or fantasy as common epileptic means of escaping a bleak life.
He said he often met epileptic patients who had turned to
God and interviewed the Almighty. At this stage his portrayal
of the Montrose Asylum's huddling, howling inmates,
speckled with epileptics, gave way to writings he had found
in all ages and cultures about 'religious maniacs' with feelings
'often epileptic or cataleptic', performing contorted dances
and hysterical convulsions in the Lord. Quiet religion did not
figure.

I am naturally sceptical about all such experiences and I
was wearily unhappy to hear a friend of ours, who always
spends Christmas with us, saying this year that she was fascinated by the subject of near-death experiences. She had seen
a television programme in which some patients who had been
in deep comas, with their pulses more or less stopped,
described their encounters with God, a screen-age version of
the interviews with the Almighty which Howden's patients
had described.

Most of the modern patients described their encounters as
going into a whirling force which centred on a light. All those
who had seen this central light became changed people, secure
in the knowledge of God's existence. Apparently only visual
excitements were worth investigating, inexpressive experiences were ignored, just as they had been in Dr Howden's
day.

I have never been able to take such marvels seriously and
these stories did nothing to help. When I go through 'the
probable darkness of death', it doesn't make me spiritually
anguished or spiritually peaceful, only estranged from life
when I return to it.

Nor am I any better at the purely inspirational forms of
pre-fit visions, without explicitly religious overtones. I don't
know any epileptics well and I am too English to go up to
people at outpatient clinics and ask them if they are familiar

with ecstatic auras such as Dostoevsky described. In the 1860s he wrote to his friend Ivan Yanshev:

> There was a sensation of life, of consciousness increased almost tenfold in those instants, which passed like lightning. Mind and heart were illuminated by unusual light ... a kind of higher calmness filled with clear, harmonious joy and hope, intelligence and ultimate reason.

After the fits, Dostoevsky dismissed this as 'illness, the very lowest form of being'. Heaven knows what such feelings could feel like. I have never felt like that. If I did have auras with a literary complexion they would be more likely to resemble Gustave Flaubert's sensation that he 'felt madness coming and was carried away in a sea of flame'. This was not inspirational. 'I clutched to my reason. I had to,' said Flaubert.

These sensations were coupled with dejection after attacks, when Flaubert was too battered and exhausted to do anything. After a fit only a few seconds long, during which he plunged his fingernails deep into the arm of his beloved companion, Louise Colet, gave rattling cries and vomited, she described him as 'broken'. When doctors had been at him, he lay half-conscious for days before declaring, 'I am purged and bled; they treat me with leeches. Good food and wine are kept away from me; I'm a dead man.'

It's the first time I have felt some understanding for Flaubert.

I won't go on about the after-effects of fits because once I am conscious again I have few effects to go on about. Also, every epileptic has his own, individual experiences, which will be different from mine. Reading Dostoevsky's epileptic memoirs, however, has reminded me of one common affliction which often follows fits, in one form or another. I have found it to be, in its own way, the most horrible of all the effects of epilepsy.

Loss of memory is hard for other people to take seriously because many people have trouble remembering certain things and think little of it. All writers make excuses for their barren patches, but Dostoevsky was honest about his epilepsy, never over-stating it. He did not want to lose his friends. In April 1876 he wrote bluntly to Pyotr Vasilievich:

> I can't write a biography because as a consequence of my epilepsy – which however hardly ever troubles me any longer – I have somewhat lost my memory. Would you believe it – I have forgotten (literally forgotten, without the slightest exaggeration) the plots of my novels and the characters I portrayed in them, even *Crime and Punishment*.

I forget less impressive items than Dostoevsky did, yet I have forgotten everything from my own signature when I needed to sign a cheque, to people I have met, arrangements I have made, rules of card games and pieces out of my life. I know everyone forgets faces and names, but I was shaken to find myself with no memory at all of a holiday I had in Greece with a friend, Kate, a few years ago. She was full of tit-bits from the holiday, many of them colourful and, I would have thought, hard to forget. The holiday was before I had epilepsy. But my only knowledge of it comes from what Kate told me about it the other day.

Forgetting is an ungenerous affliction, which stops one from responding to other people's memories. It upsets me, especially as I used to have such a good memory. I was not at all surprised to see, reading through a neurologist's report of his years of work on epilepsy, that of all the things his patients disliked about their condition, by far the most unpopular was loss of memory. My only surprise was *his* surprise at this.

And madness? The next step must be madness. Epilepsy has always been associated with lunacy, in the traditional, vague meaning of lunacy as a derangement under the influence of the moon. It is only in this century that Western Europe has discarded the moon as a force in medicine, distant and deliciously indefinite, there when needed to blame for inexplicable aberrations such as epilepsy.

There is an animal reaction deep in all of us, including me, when confronted with epilepsy that makes it feel as if it must come from a force beyond the ordinary world, maybe not a lunar force, but certainly an evil one. If this is not the devil in simple terms, to be cast out directly, then it is the evil force of madness. The history of this primitive feeling is a long one, even when epilepsy and madness began to be distinguished from each other scientifically, towards the end of the nineteenth century, madness was still acknowledged as a frequent companion and a possible result of epilepsy.

Henry Maudsley was an outstanding psychiatrist who had a brain hospital named after him. His work on epileptic insanity in the 1870s saved the lives of epileptic murderers about to be hanged, by arguing that epileptics could not be murderers when they did not know what they were doing. This juicy topic was written about by Maudsley not in an obscure medical journal but in the *Pall Mall Gazette*, of which successive editions were sold out at once. It had all the ingredients of popular reading: blood, sweat, tears, killing and madness bordering on possession.

Like his illustrious contemporary Howden, Maudsley gave examples of religious excess in long-term epileptics, featuring visions and talks with angels and prophets, though he stopped short of talks with the Almighty. Instead Maudsley described some killings committed by epileptics 'with the whole mind in a state of furious derangement' shortly before or after fits, or even during 'an epilepsy of mind' which took the place of convulsions. In these states epileptics who killed could not be found guilty of murder because they were not responsible for their actions. He cited the case of a thirty-year-old epileptic in an asylum at Avignon who stabbed the hospital superintendent through the heart with scissors the night before having an epileptic attack. It was one among many assaults the man had made over a long period. Although Maudsley argued powerfully that the patient was not responsible for these assaults, he did not make any suggestions about what should be done with him, for the safety of the public, the hospital or the man himself. Late-nineteenth-century medicine followed the old policy of locking people up, not the modern one of doping them out of action.

Maudsley's description of epileptics worn down by their repeated derangements, rather than epileptics homicidally possessed by them, upset me as a cruel, simple possibility:

> Confidence wanes as the attacks recur, the mind is slowly weakened at the storms of fury through which it passes, and patients sink finally into the apathy of dementia – a state of mere oblivion, in which they cease to hope or care more.

It was a dark November afternoon when I read this and I could not get it out of my mind. It was hard to persuade myself that there was something else beside madness or a 'state of mere oblivion' awaiting a long-term epileptic like myself. I find it all too easy to sink into a mire of general fear on behalf of my struggling brain, which will surely not stand the strain.

This is a kind of soggy thinking Professor C. is keen to dispel, but he has never told me clearly whether my epilepsy might exhaust or irreparably damage my brain. I have never asked him. Whatever he said, I would still be afraid.

I think loss of memory, paralysis and speech difficulties are probably more likely outcomes than madness to repeated epileptic attacks and there is no future in working out which would be worst. They are all uncertain and they all carry the same hallmark of horror: they go on and on.

So far in my life, bruises and scars have faded; lost movement has returned, though it feels lost forever at the time, the excruciating pain of torn muscles has lessened. Even the hideous rolling out of sockets which eyes somehow manage, hanging limp over the lids in watery inability to hold themselves in their place, has retreated in the end. The eyes, eventually, have closed.

The indefinite end is the one I fear. I have been comparatively softly treated by the short-term effects of fits. I have avoided breaking bones, which is lucky, surely too lucky to last. When I was having a fit once, early in my epileptic career

– or whatever it should be called – Mark phoned the doctor because he thought I might have broken my shoulder. The doctor tested it and said it had done no more than strain it. He said to Mark as he left, 'If it had been a really bad seizure, she would not just have broken her shoulder, she would have dislocated her neck as well.'

Remarks like that give one the full context in which to feel grateful and kill the worm of self-pity before it crawls silently into one's life.

PART TWO

Epilepsy in Society

CHAPTER FOUR

The History of Epilepsy and its Treatment

The temptation when looking at the history of epilepsy and its treatment is to write off human reactions to epilepsy as a bad joke. One recent writer on epilepsy, Henry Alden Bunker, went straight to the point when he said that 'the history of epilepsy might well be said to stand as a monument to human error.'

It is easy to see why this is so. Epilepsy is horrifying. It is common, mysterious and even today, after at least twenty-five centuries of human effort, has proved well nigh impossible to cure completely. The public at large and doctors in particular are frightened of epilepsy as something beyond their control. There is one pervading theme evident throughout the long, ghastly history of epilepsy and its treatment: the feeling that epilepsy shows the human body in the power of a force greater than itself.

Far more epileptics suffer from blank patches or dizziness than from the seizures which seem to have given the condition its name, rooted in the Ancient Greek verb *epilambanein* – to seize or take hold of. An epileptic is one who is seized. The seizures may be few, but they are the features of epilepsy which show people in the grip of a greater force.

At various times in history this force has been thought to be an undefined supernatural one, at times a form of personal religious possession, either malevolent or benevolent, that causes seizures because it is too much for a human frame. At times the force has been thought to be sexual, inspiring some of the most drastic and alarming methods of treatment to overcome it. Genius too has had some great moments – epilepsy as the force of inspiration at work is a recurring image in the history of the condition, especially among those who considered themselves to be touched with genius. Even eras of reaction against the supernatural interpretation of epilepsy still feared the force of nature in all its terrifying grandeur, thought to be playing with pathetic man.

Many writers about epilepsy did not waste time trying to define exactly what sort of force one was faced with if one was unlucky enough to see an epileptic seizure. The obvious fact was that it was beyond human endurance and this applied to the onlooker as well as the victim.

Back in the first century B C, Lucretius explained the nature of the world in a lengthy discourse, *De Rerum Naturae*. His poetic powers were not abashed by the sight of an epileptic having a fit. As an expounder of science and admirer of Epicurean philosophy, he found himself inspired to a poetic portrayal of details that would help to show the fit as man's soul in the grip of a mighty affliction:

> It often happens that before our eyes some wretch falls down,
> Struck as with lightning, so with disease,
> By the dread attack overpowered.
> He foams, he groans, he shudders and he faints;
> Now rigid, now convulsed, his labouring lungs
> Heave breath, and trembles each exhausted limb . . .
> Then madness follows on
> Since strength of mind and soul is out of tune and,
> As I've shown, torn all to bits by the same dire disease.

Though it would be against my interests to think Lucretius meant that fits are clear instances of the devil showing off his strength, I can see why Lucretius, like all the Ancients, Greek and Roman alike, found epilepsy so repellent. It is physically unclean, with its blood, spit, incontinence and the body contorted beyond human control; it is often accompanied by strange cries and facial distortions and followed by weird breakdowns of character. It looks more like the destruction of a person than the onset of an attack of illness.

The spectator as well as the seized epileptic was thought to be in danger. The obvious thing to do when faced with epilepsy was keep away from it and people were only too glad to do so. If Ancient doctors did try to treat epilepsy, there was little confidence in the treatments they recommended. They usually looked more like spells than drugs, supernatural cures to fight supernatural ills. One of the most common was the placing of an iron nail near the epileptic to prevent him having another attack.

Great emphasis has been put, rightly, on the medical breakthrough made by Hippocrates, or one of the Hippocratic school, in the book *On The Sacred Disease* in about 400 B C, which denied that epilepsy was an example of demonic possession. Hippocrates did not mind descriptions like the one Lucretius later gave, as long as they stopped short of calling epilepsy a supernatural illness:

> It is a hereditary disease with its cause in the brain when the brain is overflowing with too much phlegm. It is no more supernatural than any other disease.

Hippocrates decided epilepsy was a disorder of the humours. He described a complicated system of veins carrying air to the brain, whence they came back out to the heart. Epilepsy was a cold derangement of the humours, preventing them from keeping the brain well aired at the right temperature. To call it a sacred disease was an insult to medicine.

'Those who first referred the disease to the Gods appear to me now to have been just such persons as the conjurors, purificators, mountebanks and charlatans now are, who claim great piety and superior knowledge. Such persons use divinity as a pretext and a screen for their own inability to afford any assistance.'

Such persons did not let inability cramp their style. They took strict control of the diet of epileptics. Among recurrent forbidden foods were some familiar taboos such as onions (symbols of death) and the meat of the goat (an animal sacred to the moon goddess). More active prescriptions covered a vast spectrum in which the blood and bones of the dead were old favourites. These medicines might be eaten or drunk, sprinkled, rubbed or administered by some other means; the important thing was the magical power they might show.

Presumably the 'spell-binders' got away with such cures because no-one was offering any better cures. Indeed, the Hippocratic method of proving that epilepsy is a natural, not supernatural, disease is one that would incline me, *faute de mieux*, towards the supernatural option:

> If you cut open the head, you will find the brain humid, full of sweat and smelling badly. In this way you can see that it is not a God which injures the body, but a disease.

Should patients survive their operations, Hippocratic doctors prescribed curative diets and drugs, which often included some of the traditional remedies favoured by the magicians.

It was not until the second century AD that Galen took up the Hippocratic doctrine that the brain is the centre of consciousness. Even Galen, a model of progressive neurology in his emphasis on the pre-eminence of the brain, had only old superstitious medicines to offer when epilepsy took hold of the brain. He advised doctors prescribing burnt human bones as an anti-epileptic medicine not to tell their patients what it was they were about to drink, 'lest they become nauseated.'

At times, vomiting might be useful because a vital organ like the brain needed to be kept clean by being purged. When in doubt, flush it out. By the fourth century AD the Hippocratic notion of ridding the brain of trespassing humours had produced much literature about the best ways of cleaning out both body and brain. Blood-letting and the induction of vomiting after meals, drinking vinegar and sneezing at bedtime continued in favour for centuries, at least among those who could read about them.

I doubt if we will ever be able to know how often such medical schemes written up in textbooks were put into practice, any more than future generations will be able to know how many of us follow the medical instructions we are given today. But more of us today can read them.

The fact that blood-letting was mentioned so widely and seems to have lasted for so long suggests that it was a well-established method of trying to heal a variety of diseases, including epilepsy. Leeches made a change from emetics and for centuries they were actually used.

In 1824 when Byron had an epileptic fit in Missolonghi, Greece, it frightened his companions and left him pale and weak. He was carried up to bed where a doctor said he should be 'bled'. Byron was nervous about having his veins opened but the following day at noon he let the doctor put eight starving leeches on his temples. Once opened, the temples went on pouring out blood, even after the blood-bloated leeches had been removed, until 11 o'clock at night. Weakness from this loss of blood made Byron faint and lie in bed all the next day, unable to get up, even though a Greek expedition set out to capture a nearby Turkish brig-of-war, a sight that would have gladdened his heart. He had been sucked 'clean' until he dropped, as many an epileptic before him had been, through centuries of cleaning out.

I can't resist mentioning that this present decade has seen leeches make a bit of a come-back, though not for treating epilepsy. An American called Roy Sawyer deplored the abandoning of leeches late in the last century and, knowing that the animal in question is 'a living pharmacy', a few years ago he set up the world's only commercial leech farm in the Welsh countryside. Biopharm has gone from strength to strength and now has branches overseas. It seeks to extract proteins from the saliva of leeches, treating the little worms as givers, not takers, in order to cure. Heart attacks, strokes, embolisms, arthritis and glaucoma are said to respond to the riches of leech saliva, which Roy Sawyer is now trying to engineer genetically on a big scale.

But I must not let converted blood-suckers distract me. Despite the morbid cures Galen offered for epilepsy back in the second century, he was a clever anatomist and through

watching epileptic patients before and after as well as during
their seizures, he did realise that the brain was in control of
mind, sense and movement. He gave some accurate descriptions of localised epilepsy, instead of dismissing it as 'hysterical epilepsy', which is what many doctors of that period did.

Aretaeus of Cappadocia, soon after Galen, also described
some aspects of epilepsy accurately, in particular the facial distortions and swellings, the 'aurae' before fits and the disorders,
such as dementia, amnesia and depression, after fits. These left
the patient, in Aretaeus's words, 'spiritless and dejected, from
the sufferings and shame of the dreadful malady'.

Already by this time the malady was acquiring the popular
name 'the falling sickness', though the new name never
became fully recognised as a medical term. The falling sickness was widely used as a name for all conditions that could
be fittingly described like that, but it was mostly used as a
name for epilepsy, all over Europe, right up until the nineteenth century. At that point, other kinds of epilepsy – ones
that did not cause patients to fall and have fits – were accepted
as genuine forms of epilepsy and the term became out of date.

If Aretaeus knew the term 'the falling sickness' he did not
use it. He made his close observations on the disease, but on
the question of cures he could only come up with the old
faithfuls of purging, bleeding, trepanation (removal of a piece
of the skull) and, worst of all, cauterising and trepanation
combined so that the scorched bones could be removed from
the skull, 'letting out the animal spirits causing the trouble'.

It is no surprise at all that pharmacology thrived on the
weakness of medicine. Faced with doctors' cures such as that,
any alternative must have been welcome, even absurd drugs
'said to' bring healing. Dioscorides, an outstanding expounder
of ancient pharmacology, listed in his *De Materia Medica* forty-
five substances to help cure epilepsy, at least thirteen of them
only 'said to' help. I bet none of them did. This trio is an
example of Dioscorides' reputedly helpful substances: the liver
of a he-goat; storks' dung; an amulet of stones found in the
stomach of swallows at the waxing moon.

The phases of the moon were never out of it for long. The moon, like the sun, was a great force playing with the fate of epileptics. Origen was following a long pagan tradition when in 245 he declared epilepsy to be a disease of the moon, a kind of lunacy. This identification soon came to add madness to the evils of epilepsy. The debate continued, involving physicians, writers, scholars, religious teachers and doctors as to whether epilepsy was a religious or natural condition and whether nature included forces beyond all control, such as the moon. It is an easy move from phases of the moon to phases of spirits, and every culture has some room for the idea of illness as an evil spirit possessing a body. I am not going to try to discuss the ins and outs of demonic possession, but I have never been able to see why miraculous cures of possession, such as Jesus's cure of the epileptic boy after the Transfiguration, reported in Matthew, Mark and Luke, should be incompatible with medical practice.

Obviously, medicine had not helped this boy, whose frequent fits, according to his father, sometimes cast him into the fire and into water, endangering his life. In his father's words, when 'taken of a spirit' he cried out, gnashed his teeth 'and is torn apart, which is why he is bruised all over' (Luke, ix, 39). Jesus cast out the evil spirit and cured the boy.

Those who believe that this happened, do not have to believe that this is the only way miracles can happen or the only way illnesses can be cured. For me, the problem is deciding whether or not to pray for a cure, rather than finding room for religious and medical practice together and knowing where to draw the line between religion and superstition. That is as difficult now as it has ever been.

All through the Middle Ages, people found it easy to see epilepsy as direct possession by the devil, in the philosophical sense in which all illness and pain come from the force of evil, the devil. Trinkets and symbols were as popular in Christian religion and medicine as they had been in pagan religion and medicine, especially when dealing with such a graphically evil illness as epilepsy.

Church lights were symbols and focal points of communal prayer in church for delivery from epilepsy. Saints' relics were sometimes credited with being centres or sites of prayer with more obviously decisive roles. In the sixth century Gregory of Tours described how an epileptic boy, or at least a boy with a body 'possessed by devils', had been cured by visiting the grave of St Nicetius and praying for healing.

Amulets and rings were used for centuries in the battle against epilepsy, by priests, doctors, patients and friends. There were all sorts of medieval healing rings and legends attached to them, with particular reference to epilepsy. Vertuosi were talismanic rings inscribed with the names of the three kings, who were often regarded as patron saints of the healing of epilepsy: Caspar, Melchior, Balthazar.

There has never been a fixed patron saint of epilepsy, but different saints have been burdened with the task at different times and places. In Flanders there was a tradition that God punished St John with epilepsy because the saint once pertly asked God to show him thunder. In several countries St John was a popular saint with those seeking help with epilepsy because the worst disease called for the most powerful helper, close to God. Some old cures mention St John's name among the primitive medical aids they list: leaping over St John's fire; mixing wheat and flour with dew gathered on St John's day, to make a curative cake; St John's wort, worn as amulets or taken internally.

Some scholars think that because the German pronunciation of St Valentine's name, with a soft 'v', sounded like the affliction in need of curing: *fallende sucht* (falling sickness), he was probably the patron saint of epileptics in German-speaking countries. In the medieval Franciscan church of St Valentine in Wurzburg, Bavaria, epileptics kissed or touched his relics on his feast-day, in hope of a cure. Whether this was regarded as a worthwhile hope it is impossible to tell.

In the Arbuzzi district of Italy, St Donato has always been popular as a helper with epilepsy, though the reasons for this are not clear; in Holland, Belgium and some of south-west

Germany, St Cornelius; here and there in many Christian countries, St Christopher, because it must be part of his job as patron saint of travellers to stop people falling; in Wales, St Tecla. But the most popular saints for helping epileptics have nearly always been the three kings. The kings' closeness to God would calm an epileptic's spasms, and rings engraved with the kings' names were blessed and worn as anti-epileptic tokens.

In Plantagenet times other rings too were sometimes worn as protection against epilepsy, as were cramp-rings, blessed by the king on Good Friday. The power of the rings lay in the blessing given them at a special service, beseeching God that, among other things, 'no contraction of the nerves or any danger of the falling sickness may infest all such as wear them.'

The use of the word 'infect', is painfully accurate. The fear that it was not just infectious but contagious had been present in Antiquity, with different force at different times and places. A more down-to-earth name for epilepsy than the early Ancient Greek name 'the sacred sickness' was the popular Roman name 'the meeting-room sickness', which reflected the gruesome fact that an epileptic having a fit immediately emptied a room full of people because everyone ran away from the person convulsing.

Every step was to be taken against the evil effects of being touched by an epileptic in seizure, everything from wearing magic or miraculous rings to running away or another common resort, covering the face to prevent the sight of a fit contaminating the onlooker with its wicked power. Traditionally a dark covering-cloth or '*larvatio*' was put over the face of a convulsing epileptic. As late as 1867, the first reaction of Dostoevsky's wife Anya when she heard him having a fit was, she wrote in her diary, 'the fear that I would lose the child I was carrying if I saw the attack'. Moved by love and pity, she ran to him anyway and was overtaken by the fear that he might choke on his dislodged false teeth.

Cloths to cover the face of the epileptic in seizure, or those nearby, were mentioned as items of preventive medicine throughout long periods of history, especially for pregnant women. For all I know, they may still be used in some places today.

A while ago, I was talking to a friend who recalled being a fellow in the 1970s at Keele University. She said she was surprised when a young university fellow there, who was epileptic and pregnant, was excluded from all the meetings and social occasions the mothers-to-be organised for themselves.

One of them drew my friend aside and said, 'You do know what's wrong with her, don't you?'

My friend replied, 'Yes, she's an epileptic.'

It is sad but not hard to believe the following advice from the voice of modern medicine: 'The midwife told us to keep away from her, for the sake of ourselves and our babies.'

When medicine was at its most ignorant, it was not enough just to look the other way. The thirteenth-century preacher Berthold of Regensburg warned his congregations in spirited style against getting anywhere near a person who had been epileptic for more than twenty-four years:

> When he falls down, lies on the ground and froths, beware of him if you value your life! Let no-one go near him, for such a terrible breath comes out of his mouth that anyone breathing it in may get the same disease.

Just as well there was also some preaching on the Christian duty to take pity on the isolated. I do not know from reading medieval records how many epileptics were isolated; some may have been cast out to fight, or beg, for themselves. Some may have remained members of families, in homes, monasteries, households, with a job to do, prayed for and looked after when their health was bad. Epileptics are often mentioned without any particular background to go with them; their only constant features are fear and the pity they generate in all around them.

Though congenital epilepsy was incurable, at least it could not be caught. The belief in the contagious nature of epilepsy, especially by simple means like inhaling epileptic breath, was being dropped from medical thinking at the same time as its hereditary nature was being emphasised. In 1572 an enthusiastic pathologist named Johannes Fernelius, who influenced a whole school of followers in Frankfurt, published an important book, *Universa Medicina*, in which he said:

'A person who takes poison or has epilepsy cannot contaminate others, either by his breath or by contact. That is why these are not epidemic or contagious diseases.'

I have a lingering doubt about how many people believed that and how accurately we can judge what life was like for epileptics by reading books about their illness. Did people stop jumping back from a person having a fit because a doctor said there was no need to jump back? I doubt it. I doubt if I would have watched a fit with calm interest; more likely with fascinated horror, if at all.

Ignorance of the hereditary element has lasted all through the history of medicine. People have always asked about it. It was one of my first questions. I was not given a definite estimate of how likely my son is to inherit epilepsy from me. Doctors have told me the chances of this happening are 'increased' in our case, but apparently they remain 'small'. I had not developed epilepsy when I had Peter. In any case, I would rather be left with no more than an indefinite warning like that. As Peter is perfectly healthy now, I cannot see that statistics would affect the way we try to bring him up.

Hereditary epilepsy is a macabre fear. By the sixteenth century, the hereditary nature of epilepsy was taken for granted by many Arab and Christian writers. Fernelius described the way 'children follow their parents as heirs to their diseases no less than to their estates,' if the father was suffering from the disease at the time the child was begotten.

Hector Boece, who died in 1536, reported in his *Book of the Chronicles of Scotland* the Scottish tradition of gelding men who had 'the meeting-room sickness, madness, gout, leprosy or any other such dangerous disease easily propagated from father to son'.

Though Boece's references are often fictitious and he does

not say where he got this one, he is one of several who report the continuation of the old practice of castrating epileptics, as a cure as well as a way of stopping the disease being passed on. If nothing else, it must have discouraged malingerers.

According to Boece, women with such diseases were kept away from men; pregnant women were buried alive, complete with the foetus they bore. Melancholy though the Scots can be at times, I would like to know details of particular cases before I believed this latter claim.

Robert Burton, an incomparable melancholic, had no such hesitation. In his *Anatomy of Melancholy* (1676) he commented on the castration Boece had described: 'A severe doom you will say, and not to be used amongst Christians, yet more to be looked into than it is.'

Once into his stride on matters of misery, there is no stopping Burton, who ended this section of the *Anatomy* with the characteristic observation that as a result of being too lax with fierce measures of correction, the country now found 'no man almost free from some grievous infirmity or other'.

Good old Burton.

In fact, although epileptic life can only have been grim, by the seventeenth century it was inspiring quite a few pseudo-epileptics, who imitated it to attract sympathy and perhaps even, occasionally, awe that bordered on worship. Meric Casaubon, a scholar and divine living in Puritan England, was moved to write *A Treatise Concerning Enthusiasme, As It Is An Effect of Nature: but is mistaken by many for either Divine Inspiration, or diabolical possession.*

Casaubon believed in both divine inspiration and diabolical possession, but in their proper places, which should not be the playground of epileptic antics. The presence of God in a possessed human he found a no less frightening idea than the presence of a devil. It was too much. It could be neither cast out nor faced. Worst of all, it inspired frauds and undermined the faithful.

One of the cases he reported in his *Treatise* is that of a boy who, in about 1581, in trouble with the baker who employed him, 'had diverse terrible fits, and was 12 days speechless. . . . But then instead of them he fell into ecstasies, in which he continued 2,3,4 hours without sense or motion'. Afterwards the boy said 'he had been in heaven with his heavenly Father, having been carried thither by angels, and placed in a most pleasant green, where he had enjoyed excessive happiness and had seen things he could not express'.

This boy was one of a long line of epileptics and pseudo-epileptics all through history who claimed to have experienced interviews, encounters, visions and countless other recreations with Almighty God. When the doctor from the boy's town was called in, he said he had found many such cases, most of them women, often examined by divines as well as physicians to explain their heavenly excursions. The doctor thought the boy looked as if he suffered from a melancholic disease 'occasioned by the epilepsy'.

It was the boy's prophesies of paradise that made the doctor suspect 'art and imposture; The boy had always been an arrant rogue (for his age) and very subtle and cunning'. The doctor recommended the boy be moved to a different house and watched, whereupon both prophesies and ecstasies stopped. Casaubon was glad to do his duty in warning his readers against false religious possession, which was quite often accompanied by false epilepsy.

Even the miserable epileptics who spent their lives as social outcasts on the street, alongside beggars, were imitated by 'crank(e)s' in the sixteenth and seventeenth centuries. The word 'crank' soon passed from official language, where its meaning was a general one: a rogue feigning (with no description of what was being feigned), to thieves' slang, where its meaning was more specific: a rogue feigning sickness in order to move compassion and get money.

Thomas Harman published an illustrated booklet, *A Caveat or Warning* about a 'monstrous disembler, a crank all about', whom he had met in 1566. The crank in question claimed to have had the falling sickness for eight years and said, 'I can get no remedy for the same.' His father and friends had been epileptics before him and he had been reduced to begging in London for the last two years, though he was a Leicestershire man by birth.

All too easy to believe, especially with the man's tattered clothes and bruised and bleeding face, shown in the booklet's pictures. But his statement that he had been in the St Mary Hospital of Bethlehem for a year and a half surprised Harman, who asked if he had been out of his wits, checked with the hospital and found that the man had never been there. Convulsions did not automatically mean madness, any more than they automatically meant supernatural possession, by good or bad powers, but people still found it easy to believe that they did.

After vigorous early discussion in the west, the question of Mohammed's possession by divine power or, as some Christians maintained, by the power of the devil, went through a quiet patch. By the nineteenth century, however, Mohammed had again become a favourite subject of examination for doctors and psychiatrists interested in the nature of religious visions and the relationship between fits, hallucinations and religious visions. Dostoevsky was keen to claim Mohammed into the privileged minority of inspired epileptics.

While the power of the moon to influence epilepsy was finally beginning to be questioned, though only tentatively, by the seventeenth century, all sorts of religious associations with the condition continued to be reported, claimed and investigated.

In the late seventeenth century some new, fundamental discoveries were made about the role of the brain in epilepsy. Sir Thomas Willis recognised the forebrain as the origin of nervous impulses. Though vague on the subject, he placed the factor that excited epileptic attacks in the forebrain, rather than outside the brain in the humours and irritating forces that for centuries had been thought to be responsible. Though Willis was accurate in this respect, he still declared that 'the devils can't show miracles by any better witch than by assaults of this monstrous disease'.

Not surprisingly, the eighteenth century saw the development of a 'natural and healthy' school of approach to epilepsy, tired of the shortcomings of official medicine. Naturopaths such as Thomas Beddoes (1760-1808) had plenty to fight. They concentrated on epilepsy as a nervous disorder like any other, better prevented than treated. Living an idyllic pastoral life would get 'our middling and affluent classes' back to the earth, where they belonged.

One remedy which Beddoes supplied for 'swooning fits and other semi-epileptic qualms' was gardening. One evil to avoid was too much reading, especially of novels. The need to read his books of healing was an irony not mentioned. The real devil was introverted hypochondria, best defeated by an outdoor life.

Support for the outdoor life was plentiful, but where epilepsy was concerned, that life did not offer cures if the illness succeeded in striking someone down. Cures were always in short supply. John Andrée, for instance, was a doctor from the Royal College of Physicians in London, but did not belong to any clear school of medical thought. His 1753 book *Cases of the Epilepsy, Hysteric Fits, and St Vitus's Dance, with the Process of Cure: Interspersed with Practical Observations. To Which are added Cases of the Bite of a mad Dog, And a Method that has been found successful* could only offer the primitive cures of blisters, purges, cathartics and bleeding.

Andrée's report of case no. XI begins: 'The title of this case would not improperly be Fits from the drinking of Dorchester Beer.' However, he thought that looked a bit romantic, so he simply reported the facts, leaving the readers to draw their own conclusions. An eighteen-year-old serving girl had such violent fits that men couldn't hold or bleed her. Feathers were burnt under her nostrils and she was splashed with cold water, but the fits went on, intermittently, for eight hours. Then she was bled and took tinct. She had not had a fit since then. The only traceable cause of her fits was the Burton's Ale she had drunk while bottling it in the afternoon, 'its volatile and acrimonious particles stimulating the nervous system'. Andrée was always more fulsome on the causes than the cures of fits.

By the nineteenth century, interest was growing in the connection between epilepsy and genius, reacting against too much pastoral resting of the brain and the standard medical failure to control epilepsy. Cesare Lombroso's book *The Epileptoid Nature of Genius* was a best-seller in this country. Lombroso was Professor of Legal Medicine at the University of Turin and wrote with authority, putting the emphasis on genius before epilepsy: 'Inspiration often produces convulsing.'

He went on to list some examples of unusual characteristics common to both men of genius and epileptics. Such people are 'subject to curious spasmodic and choreic movements'; they have heads too big or too small; they are sexually or intellectually precocious; they are somnambulists; they have amnesia; they have religious feelings, even if they are atheists; they have a passion for wandering around. Mohammed, said Lombroso, told us proudly that he used to visit all the abodes of Allah in less time than it would take to empty his water-jar.

Lombroso welcomed a long list of celebrities into his family of those possessed by epileptoid genius. Some were better qualified for membership than others. Newton and Swift, for example, were described by Lombroso as suffering from vertigo, but no more than that. Even he did not try to produce evidence that they were epileptic; their genius was their distinction. Molière, like Swift, was only qualified for the 'epileptoid genius' list by his talent as a writer; the nearest he got to epileptic fits was fits of rage which he described himself as having at times. When his friendship with Racine broke up in 1665 he was bad-tempered and struck a servant, then wrinkled his face and sat in his room. Hardly a case of epilepsy. Nor was the composer Handel, with his bouts of psychosomatic worry when work was going badly.

A few on Lombroso's list do seem to have had some kind of seizures at times. Boswell described his friend Dr Johnson as having 'convulsive contractions' now and then. Pascal as a child had 'weaknesses followed by sleep for days at a time'.

There were none Lombroso loved so much as those who

convulsed when they were at the height of inspiration. He was delighted with Paganini, not so much for his brilliant violin playing as for his musical convulsions as he worked his way up to it. Liszt, who heard and watched Paganini play on his concert tour of Italy, had already written in 1808 along the lines that Lombroso was to develop later in the century.

'The excitement he created was so unusual, the magic he practised upon the imagination of his hearers so powerful, that they would not be satisfied with a natural explanation. Old tales of witches and ghost stories came into their minds; they attempted to explain the miracle of his playing by delving into his past, to interpret the wonder of his genius in a supernatural way; they even hinted that he had devoted his spirit to the Evil One, and that the fourth string of his violin was made from his wife's intestines, which he himself cut out.'

Lombroso's fascination with genius in connection with a number of neurotic conditions, ranging from epilepsy to insanity, was one which the late nineteenth century enjoyed. His books on the nature of genius went through one edition after another in England, where people delighted in his discussion of weird, genius-stricken epileptics, deformed with melancholy, maddened by inspiration. For most of his life Lombroso was a passionate enemy of religion and found in genius the uncontrollable force that others found in God. One example of the strangeness of genius was its association with epilepsy. Another was its association with gloom: 'the great majority of thinkers are melancholic.'

This line of thinking would not have upset the previous generation of naturalists at all. The only difference would have lain in their regarding the melancholy as a mental disturbance, whereas Lombroso believed it should be regarded with awe, not pity. For him genius was puzzling, frightening and compelling.

By the late nineteenth century, there was growing interest in the psychological problems which the world and the epileptic, with or without inspiration, made for each other. There was also a revival of interest in the relationship between epilepsy and sex, a topic that had always attracted attention.

Epilepsy and sex had always been associated with each other in the same instinctive, indefinite way in which epilepsy and religious possession were associated with each other. There does sometimes seem to be a hormonal dimension to epilepsy, which some early writers noticed but could not analyse with significant results. It is a condition which is often most active at the time of puberty and, if that is so, can calm down later.

In women, epilepsy is at its most menacing just before having a period. I know from personal experience that this is true. John Andrée, who wrote about fits and the drinking of Dorchester beer, wrote in the same book about several cases of 'menses spasms' of epilepsy. He prescribed cleansing as a cure. He gave one lady who suffered from fits at the time of her periods 'a strong purge', but the fits continued and were 'commonly worse after the changes of the moon'. Dr Andrée only abandoned his attempts to cut open a vein in this lady's neck during the most fierce of her fits because he thought he was in danger of cutting her throat and killing her.

Epilepsy caused by sexual forces was usually to be cured symbolically, either by cleansing the patient or dominating the sexual power upsetting the patient. Cleansing meant purging or castrating – getting rid of the problem. Dominating meant cutting off the sexual organs or eating the sexual organs of another – the testicles of a hippo or the genitals of a seal, for example, though these sound to me like prescriptions of fantasy.

One of the dreariest sections of research I undertook for this book was the one on epilepsy and sex – centuries of warnings by physicians, churchmen, scientists and wise men of folklore against too much or too little epileptic sex, performed in any but the most unadventurous ways. Just as an inspired man might reasonably expect to have fits, so too might a man having intercourse with his wife too tempestuously.

Masturbation as well as menstruation was a dangerous channel of the uncontrollable. In 1881 Sir William Gowers, one of England's prime neurologists, carried on a long tradition when he denounced masturbation as a prime cause of epilepsy.

If evil practices causing epilepsy could not be stopped and the epilepsy could not be overcome or purified, there was one last alternative: surgery. This ranged from the removal of the sexual organ associated with the trouble to drilling a hole in the head or trepanation.

It is no surprise that medical care of epileptics was feeling sorry for itself by the mid nineteenth century. It had made little progress. England did not have an epileptic hospital until 1860, when the National Hospital for the Paralysed and Epileptic opened in Queen Square, London. It soon became the foremost neurological hospital in the country and was known as 'Queen Square'.

Before Queen Square was opened, English epileptics who went into hospital went into lunatic asylums. One of the reasons epileptics were eventually separated from lunatics was the bad effect that epileptic fits might have on the lunatics: epileptic fits might terrify the weaker-minded into some sort of hysterical fits. This was pointed out with more alarm than the danger of the poor epileptics being driven mad by living with madmen.

There was also the added factor that the mid nineteenth century was the age of statistics-gathering in medicine. Statistics were easier to gather from a large number of epileptics gathered together in one place than from the same number scattered about and keeping quiet about their condition.

The French psychiatrist Jean Etienne Dominique Esquirol organised huge research projects into the statistics of heredity in epilepsy and into the thesis that confidence in remedies is more important than the remedies themselves. As well as the 'old faithfuls' of epileptic treatment – bloodletting, cold baths and cathartics – Esquirol prescribed 'secret medicines' which, he claimed, gave thirty of his patients at the Saltpiêtre Hospital short spells of remission from fits.

10. Raphael's *Transfiguration* is one of the few famous pictures featuring an epileptic. The man is in the bottom right-hand corner, being healed of his convulsive affliction by the Lord's transfigured glory.

11. In the fourth century BC Hippocrates denounced those who called epilepsy a supernatural disease; he declared it to be a natural brain disturbance. The cures he offered for it were not encouraging.
12. Dr Johnson was described by his friend, James Boswell, as sometimes shaking with convulsions. They may have been St Vitus's dance or epilepsy.
13. Byron enjoyed claiming that his 'convulsive mental energy' emptied itself in rhyme. 14. Paganini played the violin so magically that Liszt described him as being possessed by supernatural powers. This led to rumours that he was epileptic. 15. Cesare Lombroso's writings on the connection between epilepsy and inspiration were fashionable for a while in late nineteenth century England.

The prospect of a life full of fits, locked up in the cellar out of the way, or in a lunatic asylum or, just possibly, in a hospital for epileptics, human fodder for psychiatrists and students of the convulsing brain, would be every reason to announce confidence in recovery, whatever the medicines offered. Mind over matter, against all odds.

Although John Hughlings Jackson published some papers in 1861 which gave final proof that epilepsy is a primary disorder in the nervous tissue of the brain cortex, few thought this would transform the nightmare lives of epileptics. It did not provide a way of healing the disorder.

Nowhere to go but experimental drugs. William Gowers, fellow student of epilepsy with Jackson and author of the most important book on epilepsy in the late nineteenth century, *Epilepsy and Other Chronic Diseases*, included nitroglycerine as one of the more surprising in the wide range of drugs he suggested for use on epileptic patients. Others of a calmer nature were coal-tar derivatives, codeine, opium, chloroform and the bromides.

By this time, the bromides were being taken seriously as effective ways of stopping convulsions. In 1857 Sir Charles Locock told a medical discussion in London that he had tried using bromide of potassium to cure some patients' fits at times of menstrual periods, having read German medical reports of how useful this drug could be in producing temporary impotence in men. Sir Charles said he too had found it useful at damping down the old enemy of what Gowers called 'deleterious sexual excess'.

Sir Charles had then used bromide against 'hysteria' in epileptic young women at times of sexual strain and to cure 'hysterical' epilepsy. In thirteen out of fourteen epileptic cases, bromide had cured his patients of their fits.

This was, at last, a small breakthrough in treatment, but bromide had its drawbacks. Samuel Wilks doubted the theory behind the use of bromide but was impressed by the drug's results and did much to make it popular in a medical world that had learnt, rightly, to have little faith in new cures for epilepsy.

The New World was more willing than the Old to try to have faith. In New York, William Hammond gave a lecture on bromide of potassium which showed its effects, good and bad, when taken in large quantities. He paraded a fourteen-year-old boy who took 120 gm of bromide a day, which had cured him of his epilepsy:

> As a result you see he is broken down in appearance, has large abscesses on his neck and is altogether in a bad condition. But this is better than to have epilepsy.

By the mid 1870s, bromide was all the rage, on both sides of the Atlantic. No less than two and a half tons of it were used every year at Queen Square as sedatives became the order of the day. Dangerous drugs, including silver, belladonna and turpentine, were discarded and drug research concentrated on looking for more comfortable sedatives than the bromides. Unpleasant though some side-effects of modern sedatives are, they do not compare with the effects of bromide on Hammond's boy, horribly helped by his wonder drug.

In the late nineteenth century, both pharmacology and neurosurgery began to make some progress in the treatment of epilepsy and they did not necessarily see each other as incompatible, though neurosurgery, understandably, saw itself as the underdog, because its range was limited and it was risky.

Surgery was greatly helped by Joseph Lister's discovery of antiseptics in 1867. This lessened the danger of what William MacEwen, intrepid pioneer of neurosurgery, spurned in 1870 as one of 'the main inhibiting factors for brain surgeons in the past': inflammation during and after operations.

There was another danger, now past, which MacEwen mentioned: the fact that 'the brain was a dark continent' until Paul Broca and Jackson and MacEwen himself, along with other brain specialists of the 1860s and 70s, often working from experiments on animals' brains, proved that different parts of the brain controlled different bodily functions.

This was a major breakthrough for brain surgeons. For the first time they could try to identify the faulty area of the brain and operate on that area exactly, rather than operating on the whole brain in the hope of letting out whatever might be causing the fault. In theory at any rate, an epileptic patient might have his epilepsy pinpointed.

There was still a flavour of 'releasing the evil vapours' about the reports on his operations which MacEwen wrote in the 1880s, but at least these reports did start from the knowledge that the brain worked in separate sections, not as an unknown whole.

In 1888, the *British Medical Journal* published MacEwen's account of a sad case of epilepsy, an example of public reluctance to give the new neurosurgery a try. A young man suffering from bad convulsions and paralysis of one side of the body was brought to MacEwen, who decided that these troubles were caused by an abscess on the left-hand side of the frontal lobe. This is one of the four brain lobes, frontal, parietal, temporal and occipital, which were still having their functions more clearly defined at the time.

It had already been established that the left-hand side of the brain controlled the right-hand side of the body and MacEwen wanted to expose the left-hand side of this boy's frontal brain lobe and remove the abscess putting pressure on it. The boy's parents refused permission for the operation, his convulsions worsened and he died. The operation was performed postmortem, to help neurological research.

MacEwen described in detail the trepanation of the skull to expose the brain, then the insertion of a sharp instrument into the third convolution of the frontal lobe, to a depth of half an inch. Pus flowed out and MacEwen wrote wistfully about the sight of an abscess 'about the size of a pigeon's egg', which it was too late to remove. He did admit that 'the unfortunate refusal to allow the operation to take place during life leaves uncertain the ultimate issue'.

I have every sympathy with the boy's parents. Such operations were desperate measures. One of the methods

MacEwen used to help him confirm which bit of the brain needed the operation was the artificial stimulation of an attack of epilepsy, once the patient was under anaesthetic. This stimulation might be achieved by pressing or pricking the brain with instruments or by releasing short bursts of electrical current into the brain. The stimulation provoked epilepsy and MacEwen watched the effects which the epilepsy had on the different sections of the body.

Despite the skill and dedication with which MacEwen and his associate, Victor Horsley, used this and other brave techniques in their operations, MacEwen recorded grimly at the end of his August 1888 article that he had asked many chronic epileptics whether they would let him operate on them, 'but none have expressed their willingness to undergo such a cure'.

Although there was more medical interest in epilepsy by the beginning of the twentieth century, there was limited progress in the best ways of managing the condition and there was no absolute cure for it, any more than there is today. The medical research into the nature of epilepsy, hysteria and 'state-of-mind' diseases made epilepsy almost trendy among turn-of-the-century thinkers. Nietzsche was intrigued by epilepsy and diagnosed himself as having 'convulsions of ideas', just as in the nineteenth century Maudsley had talked of his psychiatric patients and Jackson of his epileptic patients being possessed by 'great mental energy', over which the brain had no control. Echoes of Lombroso.

Except for the introduction of less harmful sedatives, such as phenobarbital (Luminal), which came into use in 1912, there was no significant improvement in the treatment of epilepsy until the 1930s, when the medical development of the EEG made it possible to differentiate more clearly between different kinds of epilepsy and also between epilepsy and other diseases, especially hysterical diseases, which can cause convulsions.

At least, by the late 1930s, an epileptic in this country could probably have his condition accurately diagnosed. Milder forms of epilepsy could be recognised as such and contained, to some extent, by sedatives. Convulsive epileptics were unlikely to be shut up in lunatic asylums.

St Piers, Lingfield, now a hospital school for children with acute mental illnesses and learning difficulties and/or epilepsy, was originally founded as a 'colony' to train unemployed men as farm labourers, before exporting them to Canada and Australia, where farm labour was much in demand. The Colony's governors toured workhouses all over the country to find suitable candidates for such training. They were shocked to find many epileptic boys, often intelligent and very young, living wretchedly in workhouse imbecile wards, unwanted.

In 1899 Mrs Ruston of Lincolnshire provided the money, and the noble Julie Sutter, a German lady, provided the impetus to include epileptics in the Colony. Miss Sutter had seen some epileptics looked after alongside non-epileptic poor people in a 'Colony of Mercy' in Westphalia, West Germany, where they were trained for more rewarding jobs and lives. She decided to found a similar Colony in England.

It was hard to persuade The Lingfield Colony's Board of Guardians to include epileptics among its charges, but as the Colony had originally been inspired by Miss Sutter's book on the German Colony of Mercy, it was also hard for the Guardians to refuse her when she told them all to imitate her book and not leave epileptics out in the cold.

The 1902 *Education Act* then gave County Councils the duty of educating 'defective' children, including those who were epileptic, blind or deaf. In the early 1900s a growing number of epileptics found places at Lingfield, where Kate Carston was probably the country's first qualified teacher of children with epilepsy.

Sedatives were the main treatment for epilepsy, as they are today. Brain surgery was rare, as it is today. Outside the Colony, epileptics were frightening freaks. They still are today. I don't blame people for that. Fits are as frightening a sight as they always have been because the onlooker can do nothing to stop them; they are beyond control.

We may be more used to strange-looking people 'living in the community', because there are fewer institutions to house them now than there used to be, but I am not aware of there being more chronic epileptics wandering around, having fits everywhere. I have not seen any. Maybe modern drugs are suppressing more epileptic street theatre than I realise. It would be nice to believe that.

The only aspect of neurology that has attracted any public attention recently, apart from the general poor state of the whole science, is a kind of neurosurgery in which, in the words of John Duncan, the neurologist responsible for it, 'a whole new world of research and treatment is opening up'.

In March 1994 Dr Duncan cut a piece of brain 1 cm square out of the brain of a twenty-two-year-old Metropolitan Police clerk called Emma Downes and stored it in frozen nitrogen. Ms Downes lost two per cent of her brain in the operation and feels a lot better without it. She has not had a convulsion since, and is delighted that since then she has been free of her life-long epilepsy.

Dr Duncan had used an ultra-sensitive brain-scanner to find the tiny patch of brain damage that was causing Ms Downes's convulsions, so he could remove it. Despite some of the extravagances of early neurosurgery, the drama in epilepsy has more often lain in the condition than its treatment, but this recent genetic research may help to break into the hitherto impenetrable bastions of exactly what it is that sets off epileptic fits. Now that this fragment of defective brain is in cold storage, Dr Duncan hopes that by putting it through close genetic tests, he may be able to identify the trigger causing brain tissues to release the chemicals responsible for convulsions. When I asked him how important this might be for the genetic de-coding and perhaps, eventually, cure of epilepsies like that of Ms Downes, which had their original cause in a clearly limited area of brain damage, he was cautious.

'The work is at a very early stage and we don't have any published results so I think the best thing would be to just mention it as work that is in progress.'

Still, it is comforting to have some work in progress to be cautious about, after a history of neurosurgical failures. Whatever the results of this piece of work, I know an operation like that one would never be of any use to me. I have dispersed, superficial damage over my brain, not a single patch that could be the target for accurate treatment or accurate surgery to remove it. Even if I could have the damaged area of my brain taken away, the periodic sugar shortages that gave rise to my epilepsy would start causing more damage to my brain, and with it more epilepsy.

Thank God, I don't think I will ever have to make the decision about whether or not to have an operation on my epileptic brain, because my diabetes means that I carry within myself the seeds of my own decay.

CHAPTER FIVE

Epilepsy in Literature and Drama

This chapter offers no more than a sprinkling of epileptic snippets from literature and drama because epilepsy only appears when the author cannot think of an alternative. It is not popular in its own right, but it is useful for plunging characters into fury, madness, despair or helplessness at the mercy of the elements. Shakespeare torments King Lear with all of these, knowing that, as Lear put it with elegant simplicity:

> . . . we are not ourselves
> When nature, being oppressed, commands the mind
> To suffer with the body.

Shakespeare stops short of naming Lear's condition as epilepsy, but mentions him suffering a fit and, eventually, an unnaturally deep sleep. Lear's illness portrays the destruction of an old man by the harshness of life.

That is how writers of fiction almost always write about epilepsy. If a character is to be ruined but not quite killed, epilepsy is ideal. It frightens the reader at the same time as evoking pity, and the temporary collapses it can give a character in hard times remain just about credible. The danger is that it can become too grimly convenient and lose its dramatic power. When Othello hears of his wife's infidelity, he 'is fallen into an epilepsy' and Iago goes on to remark conversationally that, 'This is his second fit; he had one yesterday.'

Only Shakespeare's brilliance keeps the fit in its subsidiary place in this play, where it is not badly devalued.

To make too much of epilepsy would be a mistake because

at the heart of it is oblivion, which does not have much to say
for itself. That is why epilepsy is most useful as a device for
removing characters under too much strain. It acts in masculine parallel to fainting, decorated with uglier details but subject to the same limitations.

In Dante's *Inferno* it is not clear whether it is fainting or
fitting he is describing in Canto 24, which leads him to marvel
at 'the power of God, which in revenge does deal such blows
as these'. The blows are devil-sent and they befall a man, so
I am inclined to think they may be epileptic blows, in the
widest sense of epilepsy as an emotional and nervous as well
as a mechanical illness destroying the brain. I have only ever
seen epilepsy in fiction applied to men, though there is no
scientific connection between epilepsy and masculinity;
research seems to show that about 60% of epileptics are
female. Epilepsy is attributed to men because it is rough and
ugly, just as fainting is attributed to women because it is quiet
and restrained.

> And as is he who falls, not knowing how,
> by demon force which pulls him to the ground,
> or by some other obstruction binding man,
> and who, on getting up again, looks round
> bewildered by the great distress
> which he has felt, and as he looks, heaves sighs.

The sighs Dante gives his man in hell must have been partly
sighs of regret but I expect they were also partly sighs of
humiliation. If I had to describe in one word the worst thing
about epilepsy, I would choose the word humiliation. That
probably says more about me than it does about epilepsy and
means I am overdue to read the early thirteenth century *Ancren
Riwle* (*The Old Rule*), written for three ladies who decided to
exchange the tumult and traffic of their lives for lives of daily
meditation and prayer. The reason I mention the *Rule* written
for them is that the section on 'moral lessons and examples'
has a curious little passage on 'the falling sickness', using it
as an image of humiliation; not destructively, but in the sense
of something that humbles helpfully.

It is uncertain who was the author of the *Ancren Riwle*, probably a bishop, writing in response to the requests of these ladies of good family. One possible candidate is Bishop Poor of Tarente in Dorsetshire, who would have been familiar with the author's west-country dialect of semi-Saxon language, here translated into modern English:

> Be always chirping your prayers, as the sparrow does that is alone . . . The sparrow hath yet another property, which is very good for an anchoress, although it is hated: that is, the falling sickness. I do not mean the falling sickness which is so called; but that which I call falling sickness is an infirmity of the body, or temptation of carnal frailty, by which she seems to herself to fall down from her holy and exalted piety. She would otherwise grow presumptuous or have too good an opinion of herself.

There is a little more on the external evils and spiritual disorders likely to befall a woman living this life, then the author ends with a reference to the falling sickness 'said to be the sparrow's infirmity'. He thinks God has designed it like that so that an anchoress will 'fall to earth, lest she become proud'.

Though his spiritual point regarding pride is plain, ornithologically he is on shakier ground: sparrows may sometimes flit, but they do not suddenly fall or dive in flight. I don't remember seeing epilepsy referred to elsewhere as 'the sparrow's infirmity', though I have seen 'a little bird of the Indies' called 'the bird of epilepsy', in Bartolemeus Ambrosinus' *History of Monsters*, in 1642. That reference is because the bird's burnt body is said to have been taken as a cure for epilepsy. The whole book is devoted to spectacular fantasy.

In a roundabout sort of way, Chinese tradition does connect sparrows and the falling sickness: slaves were hired to bang gongs, so that the noise would put sparrows away from coming to ground and eating the seeds. The birds would then die of exhaustion, falling in their final sickness to earth. This policy was abandoned when it led to a surfeit of caterpillars, which ate the seeds.

It may be, however, that in the thirteenth century 'the sparrow's infirmity' was a term used in spoken, not written English, lost to us with the passing of time. Maybe it was a local nickname; maybe the author made it up to give his readers a striking but homely image to contemplate. Whatever the truth, it does make a pleasant change to see the falling sickness reduced a little in the writing and given a useful instead of melodramatic complexion.

More often, epilepsy has been a chance to introduce drama, albeit of a limited variety, into writing. In the first century BC, when Lucretius felt his mammoth work on the nature of the world was flagging a bit, he rejuvenated it with a lurid account of 'the dire disease':

> There follows a groan because his limbs are racked
> With pain, and the voice-producing seeds
> Are driven forth and through the mouth are borne
> In one great mass, the road they know so well,
> The path that's paved.

A more reticent approach, however, more like the one used in the *Ancren Riwle*, was not altogether unknown, even at that time. A little later than Lucretius, about 25 BC, a man called Aulus Cornelius Celsus also wrote a large and informative treatise, of no less than eight parts, not quite covering the entire world, but touching on everything from agriculture and the military arts to philosophy and jurisprudence. The second volume, on medicine, is written in Celsus's distinct, tight style.

He writes about epilepsy briefly, but with shafts of piquant detail which are unusual and show him to be a better writer than doctor. Avoiding the Greek name *epilēpsia*, meaning 'the illness of the seized', with its connotations of devilish possession, he calls epilepsy by its Latin name, *comitialis morbus*, 'the meeting-room illness', the illness which would break up the political assembly. Celsus admits that 'while there may be some hope from nature, there is scarcely any from the art of medicine'. He writes tersely about this hopelessness, with a talent for unlikely combinations. When an epileptic has fits, according to Celsus, 'he should avoid sunshine, the bath, a fire and all heating agents, cold, wine, greenery, overlooking a precipice, everything terrifying, vomiting, exhaustion, anxiety and all business.'

However, Celsus was not typical of medical writing, any more than the author of the *Riwle* hundreds of years later was typical of religious writing.

The *Riwle* is not the only incident of an author using the falling sickness to illustrate falls following pride. The most spectacular of such references that I have found is in Ambrosinus' masterpiece on monsters, which is illustrated in the grand manner. Ambrosinus is not interested in reticence. It does not suit his subject.

The illustrator has had a marvellous time doing full-page pictures of some of Ambrosinus' monsters: a woman with a face thickly thatched with long hair; a man with a neck several yards long, looping round itself before reaching its fulfilment in a hugely beaked head; giants; three-eyed people with hooves; a cyclops; a man with three arms and huge, horse's ears, a woman with a monkey's head. Those are at the polite end of things. The serpentine monsters are better not described.

I didn't expect the epileptic references to compete with these fantasies and there were only two of them, neither of them illustrated. One reference was to a traditional sort of folk recipe for making destroyed and pulverised animals into cures. The other, in the chapter on human morals, was more unusual, similar in spirit to the *Riwle*'s reference to the falling sickness 'stopping anyone having too high an opinion of herself'. Ambrosinus says:

> Epilepsy is a disease to do with the upper parts of people, the thinking parts. But when an epileptic falls, he becomes an animal . . . therefore epilepsy has been compared to pride leading to a fall.

Writers did not commonly use the falling sickness as a moral symbol. When they did, it was usually humorously, as a symbol for the evil condition that pulls woman down until she is a fallen woman. John Heywood, the sixteenth-century English playwright, sought to convey the falling sickness in this way, in purposely ambiguous language, to titillate his audiences. In his play *The Foure PP*, a palmer, pardoner, 'pothecary and pedlar compete to see which of them can tell the best lie.

The 'pothecary tells with bawdy delight how he managed to cure 'a woman young and so fair', who needed help because:

> This wanton had the falling sickness,
> Which by descent came lineally,
> For her mother had it naturally.

He saves himself the need to report this woman's many falls and frustrations in detail by saying simply:

> 'Down would she fall even by and by.'

The time and space this brevity left him was filled with crude anatomical titbits of the cure he provided, which he thought would be more entertaining for his listeners. For the cure is a 'revel', consisting of double entendres between instruments of firepower and sexual organs:

> 'Sir, at the last I gave her a glister [purge]:
> I thrust a tampion [plug] in her tewell [pipe],
> And bade her keep it for a jewel.

The revel goes on with painful predictability from one stage of sexual intercourse to the next, culminating in the final triumph of a castle ten miles away being blown up by the cannon fired at it:

> And she delivered with such violence
> Of all her inconvenience,
> I left her in good health and lust;
> And so she does continue, I trust.

The only comfort for the reader is that the other three lies are no better. This one is best treated as a deterrent, to save one reading the others.

Straightforward writing about epilepsy, free of symbolism

or excess, is a rare relief. The only time I have found it is when Dostoevsky writes from experience, not imagination, about the affliction; he does not play on the popular idea of epileptic deformities. I felt sympathy when I should have felt disgust for Smerdyakov, the dismal epileptic in *The Brothers Karamazov* whose troubles ended up giving him several fits at a stretch, like mine. His tongue hung out and impaired his speech, and 'Throughout the interview, which lasted 20 minutes, he kept complaining of headache and of pain in all his limbs.'

I was not surprised when Smerdyakov hanged himself in the end. Statistically, people with epilepsy are five times more likely than people without it to kill themselves; it is a fitting end, almost a relief, to find Smerdyakov doing it. Before that final stage, his hideous life on the sofa accentuates his horror.

Taking to the sofa is a time-honoured way of developing an aura around a character and if the aura is an epileptic one, so much the better for terror. It is when writers feel they must exactly portray the terror, in terms that seek to describe the indescribable, that they falter.

When Emile Zola became obsessed with physiological man, 'the successor of metaphysical man, who is now dead', he wrote novels exploring the idea that criminals are pre-destined by heredity to their lot in life; they are driven by physiological forces more powerful than themselves. It was no surprise to find that Zola was impressed by Lombroso's *L'Homme Criminel*, 1887, with its theory that criminals, like men of genius, are psychologically distinct from normal men, born to be what they are, like it or not.

That theory suited Zola fine. He considered humans primitive creatures driven by 'love and death, possessing and killing, the dark foundations of the human soul'. His job was to turn them into good fiction. He tried.

In *The Human Beast* Zola described the hero, Jacques Lantier, as a psychopathic murderer, living in a tortured state of mind that might have been epileptic, at least in part, and was certainly dangerous:

He was moving like a sleepwalker, with no recollection of the
past, no concern for the future . . . His body moved along but
his personality was not there . . . Then everything had subsided
into a black chasm, a void where neither time nor space counted
any more and he lay inert, for centuries, perhaps . . . He came
out of a deep sleep with a shock at suddenly finding himself in
full possession of his faculties, as one does after a dead faint. He
might have slept for three hours or it might have been three days.

There is an abundance of this in Zola, not just in *The Human
Beast*, but in many of his novels on the mental traumas of
man. I have never liked this kind of writing and am a harsh
judge of it, peppered as it is with psychological pits. I find
few things more futile and unconvincing to read than guesses
at what unconsciousness might be like.

I was glad to see that Dostoevsky did not like Zola any
better than I do. He wrote from Ems in July 1876:

I signed up at the lending library (a pathetic library) and took
out Zola because I've terribly neglected European literature in
recent years. Just imagine: I can scarcely read it, it's such revolt-
ing stuff. And in Russia people carry on about Zola as about a
celebrity, a leading light of realism!

Whatever one's view of Zola's kind of writing, the interesting fact for us here is that both he and Dostoevsky, each in
his own way, sought to be 'a leading light of realism' about
epilepsy by going beyond its surface and writing about the
problems behind it. The key to a good novel lies in the telling
of the problems; the more perplexing the answers, the better.

I can only read little bits of Zola and the French naturalists
before drowning in their vast depression, vaguely flavoured
with epilepsy and evil possession. So I seized on Rudyard
Kipling's extraordinary departmental ditty about the antics
of a pseudo-epileptic, 'The Post That Fitted', as light relief.
It is a strange piece. In its hard-hearted way, it is a love song.
It makes a change after the long lines of epileptics who twitch
their way in and out of literature all through history as hall-

marks of horror and symbols of psychic forces, but it is still off-putting. It looks cynical.

Writing in Betjemanesque couplets, Kipling describes a young man called Sleary whose 'pay was very modest'. Sleary went out to India, and:

> Long he pondered o'er the question in his scantly furnished
> quarters,
> Then proposed to Minnie Boffkin, eldest of Judge Boffkin's
> daughters,

in order to obtain whatever money he could from the Boffkin family. So ugly was Miss Boffkin that, knowing she would not get another offer, she accepted Sleary's proposal at once, her family got him promoted and he set about putting her off, by pretending to have epileptic fits of an appalling kind.

> (Of his modus operandi only this much I could gather:
> Pears' shaving sticks will give you little taste and lots of lather.)

Kipling has not left letters and diaries which might show whether Pears sponsored him to write the poem, in which Miss Boffkin returns the ring and Sleary returns to England with a much better income, enough to marry the girl, 'my little Carrie', whom he had always loved but was once too poor to marry.

> Year by year, in pious patience, vengeful Miss Boffkin sits
> Waiting for the Sleary babies to develop Sleary's fits.

Kipling gives the reader a neat little lesson to be learnt from this strange poem:

> Though tangled and twisted the course of true love
> This ditty explains
> No tangle's so tangled it cannot improve
> If the lover has brains.

Counterfeiting fits is an unusual device to put at the centre of a romantic poem. Why it is that foaming at the mouth is so popular with people describing epileptic convulsions I am not certain. I suppose foamings invigorate the horror, along with writhings and anguished cries.

My husband says I start my fits with a cry that sounds like
'an anguished yawn'. It would seem automatic for the fits
themselves to be as frothy as they are anguished. If a patient
groans and rolls, surely he also foams . . . . Thank God,
though I have leaked from my bottom end, I have not leaked
from my mouth. Nor do many epileptics; but it adds a bit of
lurid horror to Kipling's ditty, a challenge with new dimen-
sions for a brave reader or actor.

A much lighter literary reference to epilepsy can be found
in this passage from Richmal Crompton's 1925 classic, *Still –
William*, where the characters display a combination of fascination, ignorance and fear which is all too common. William
is trying to get his sister, Ethel, out of an awkward social
engagement:

> William thought over all the complaints he knew. None of them
> seemed quite serious enough. She might as well have something
> *really* serious while he was about it. Then he suddenly
> remembered hearing the gardener talking to the housemaid the
> day before. He'd been talking about his brother who'd got – what
> was it? Epi- epi-
> 'Epilepsy!' said William suddenly.
> '*What?*' screamed Mrs. Morrison.
> William, having committed himself to epilepsy, meant to stick
> to it.
> 'Epilepsy, the doctor says,' he said firmly.
> 'Good heavens!' said Mrs. Morrison. 'When did you find out!
> Will he be able to cure it? Is the poor girl in bed? How does it
> affect her? What a dreadful thing!"

Humour is a much needed commodity in writing about
epilepsy. It is an unattractive subject, probably best left as
most authors and dramatists have left it, off the page. Failing
that, epilepsy can be an alternative to fainting, an embodiment
of a blank patch. After all, that is what epilepsy is in real life,
which means that short of it being decorated as a gruesome
showpiece, it deserves obscurity.

CHAPTER SIX

Famous Epileptics

Such is the repulsive potential of epilepsy that it is often attributed to unattractive celebrities who cannot be proved to have suffered from it. A good dollop of epilepsy makes everyone more disgusting.

If the opposite effect is required, epilepsy is kept secret, so as not to tarnish the image of people in the public eye or frighten those who have to deal with them. There is no middle ground with epilepsy, especially convulsive epilepsy. Either it crops up all over the place or it is wrapped in secrecy.

Neither makes it easy to find out the truth about well-known epileptics, their epilepsy being the one thing about them that is seldom well known. Alas, that does not seem to have changed much as the centuries have passed, but a cure for epilepsy is still a mirage for most people and control, as I have come across it, is a hit-and-miss affair, more of a dream than a hope and, if it is achieved, it is by a heavy dependence on obnoxious drugs.

The famous people I have discovered who did or do have epilepsy are looked at in this chapter according to type rather than time. For instance, I have grouped together epileptics who had or have a religious side to their condition, or a political or a sporting side, not epileptics as the centuries pass by. Either way of writing is tricky; all ways have to be based on the individual character of each person concerned, with the only consistent feature being a smog of secrecy that is hard to penetrate.

I remember being puzzled at the newspaper reports of Tony

Greig's collapse from fatigue after a plane journey back from a short family holiday in South Africa in 1975. I was sympathetic, particularly as he collapsed at Heathrow Airport, but puzzled that his fatigue should be so desperate after a holiday. In fact he had put his anti-convulsants in his suitcase, which ended up in the plane's luggage compartment out of his reach. He had missed his regular doses and that caused a fit. No-one was told about it.

Greig's epilepsy is mild. He has stretches a year or two long between his fits, which never stop him playing or organising professional cricket. The most interesting thing about his epilepsy is the way it used to be hushed up. His family in South Africa in the 1960s kept it secret and, as soon as he developed it at the age of fourteen, kept him away from all activities they thought might be risky, such as bike-riding, swimming without adult company and doing anything at all near the edge of a cliff.

As a South African, he was brought up near some spectacular natural dangers and ignored the family restrictions, with no ill effects. Even so, he continued to keep his epilepsy secret after his marriage and when he had his fit at Heathrow Airport in 1975, his young daughter Samantha watched it in amazement through a glass screen, not knowing what was happening.

Eighteen centuries earlier, Galen had written to the father of an epileptic boy, telling him that epilepsy, like every kind of illness, was an affair of the humours, best cured by self-control, body-rubbing, a strict, wholesome diet and tough work in the gym. Bleeding had also been shown to be a powerful way of relieving blocked-up humours and, if all else failed, evacuating phlegmatic humours. With tension thus relieved, the priority – to prevent fits – might be achieved. If the fits could not be prevented, concealing them from the boy who suffered them might keep him in a good mood through the awkward years of puberty.

The fog of concealment is easy to understand in the history of epilepsy, not just as a reaction to the horrors of the condition but also as a defence against the vile treatments recommended to heal it. There was little point broadcasting one's epilepsy if it was only likely to attract gladiators' blood by way of a cure.

However, in theory at least, eminent epileptics who admitted their condition were less likely to become objects of public horror. Like pleading guilty in court, pleading epilepsy in life might deflate hostile reactions. Even so, a celebrity's account of his own epilepsy, though an invaluable source of evidence, is never an easy one to unearth, often only existing in diaries and letters which are hard to find or understand.

Julius Caesar, for instance, is three times described in Plutarch's *Lives* as suffering from 'the falling sickness'. Plutarch does not make it clear where he got the information about the epilepsy. He says that in Thapascus, in the African campaign against Pompey's son:

> Caesar felt this sickness coming on before he was overcome by it. So he was carried into a nearby castle and rested there until the worst of the disease had left him.

Caesar does not mention the falling sickness in his own writings, but most of those are reports of wars and all of them were written to further Caesar's political ambitions. In neither case would epilepsy be positive propaganda.

Negative weaknesses like nightmares or the headaches and fainting fits Caesar was said to suffer in later years were often attributed to tyrants by ancient historians. The attribution of such symptoms to Caesar is unimportant, except for its possible connection with epilepsy. Writing later than Plutarch, Suetonius, who as secretary to the Emperor Hadrian had access to the Imperial archives, says in his *Lives of the Caesars* that 'Julius Caesar was twice attacked by the falling sickness during his campaigns', but that is all he says on the subject.

On the whole, Caesar emerges from the pens of the press relatively unscathed, considering they had hints of such a juicy topic as the falling sickness. It sounds to me as if Caesar may have had a variety of *petit mal*, but that is only judging from a sketchy look at the documents concerned.

The British Epilepsy Association sent me a list of famous
people with epilepsy, on which Caesar was one in a little
group of Ancients; others were Alexander the Great and
Pythagoras. I read biographies of both along with as many of
their own writings as I could find, only in translation because
I cannot read the Ancient Greek required. I could find no
record of either man showing exact symptoms of epilepsy.

Alexander's temperament was prone to furious rages at
times if his vast enterprises left him exhausted or – not often
– defeated. But these fits of temper cannot be proved to be
fits of epilepsy; they may or may not have been and I have
read many biographies of military leaders, including
Napoleon, which declare them to have been epileptics but
offer no substantial proof of this.

In a sense, it is not so much the fact of someone having
epilepsy, at any stage of history, that is important, but what
their epilepsy can show us about the world in which they
lived. If Julius Caesar had epilepsy, he thought it best to keep
quiet about it, lest it inspire confidence in his opponents.

The easiest time to attach the smear of epilepsy to someone
famous is after their death. It is impossible to refute totally and
posthumous rumours can quickly become legends or street
traditions. Joan of Arc, another celebrity on the BEA list,
appears only to be there because the Middle Ages are under-
represented. Being burnt to death provides just the right frantic atmosphere for convulsions and who could begrudge a
martyr a spasm or two on the way to eternity?

Several religions, including Christianity and Islam, have
had traditions of religious possession and these have always
been open to cynical interpretation by opponents. Islam has
been more consistently proud than Christianity of the idea
that people in a high stage of holiness can be taken up into a
sort of mystical trance, sometimes accompanied by seizures.
When nineth century Christian writers wanted to undermine
Mohammed's growing popularity, they declared him to have
been an epileptic, while ninth century Arab writers declared
him to have been visited by God.

Contemporaries of Mohammed, such as Ibn Ishaq the chronicler, wrote about the prophet's short periods of revelation and recitation in the hands of God, 'when Mohammed sweated and lay unconscious for an hour as though drunk'. One crucial revelation in about 610 AD was the occasion of Mohammed's visitation by the Angel Gabriel on Mount Hira, when the Angel told him that he was to be the messenger of God. This visitation gave Mohammed his role in life and gave the Arabs a new religious leader.

Ninth century Christian writers stressed the probability that such visions were features of epileptic seizures; ninth century Mohammedan writers stressed the visions' divine inspiration, though the two views did not have to be at odds.

We can do no more than admit ignorance about Mohammed's fervours, fits and visions. I doubt if he was epileptic, but if he was he would not have considered it important; the important thing was, in his own words, 'the true visions coming to him like the light breaking through the darkness'.

Non-convulsive epilepsy does not have the same fascination. It does not add to the charisma of the person in question to have momentary blank patches which disappear after a short sit down. Plenty of people with humiliating illnesses like epilepsy, of course, would settle for that. They would prefer an indirect sense of spiritual power invisible to anyone else, not a charismatic seizure.

I was surprised to find a mention of this by Tony Greig in his autobiography.

It sounds odd, I know, but being an epileptic might just have done my life a lot of good. It has taught me, for example, to be grateful that I am *only* an epileptic . . . God has granted me the serenity to accept the things I cannot change and to live with my condition.

Greig says he has become less shy and scared about his epilepsy, which has shown itself to be of a relatively gentle sort. He writes almost nostalgically of the only time he ever had a *grand mal* seizure on a cricket ground.

In 1970 Greig played his debut game for Eastern Province against their rivals Transvaal. The game starred his cricketing heroes the Pollock Brothers and the night before it Greig went out to celebrate his selection. On the day of the game he got up and keeled over. He ignored his doctor's warnings not to play and took two slip catches off Peter Pollock, feeling dizzy in between the catches, then collapsed. Great occasions merit great seizures, not small, polite ones and on this occasion he gave as good as he got.

Pollock had been told about Greig's epilepsy and got Dr Ali Bacher to inject him, presumably with sedatives to relax him. After an abundance of hospital tests, he was welcomed back to play in the next game for Eastern Province. Greig describes his attack in detail; one might nearly say with relish; it was a big-time seizure.

Peter the Great of Russia felt a similar nostalgia for the big time, a sense of lost panache, after his rare and ferocious seizures, though these sound to me as likely to have been seizures of misery as epilepsy. He was an emotional man, prone to bad moods all through his life, sometimes resulting in fits of melodramatically bad temper. His letters refer to his depressions leaving him too weak to walk, but every so often he does clearly mention convulsions. In 1711 the Tsar lay on his couch in Lutzk, South Poland, for three weeks and his wife Catherine was with him as 'the life was almost shaken out of me with convulsions'.

He sweated much, but recovered slowly and those who were with him did not write about another fit until the last few months of his life. In September 1724, when he was afflicted with all his customary ills: fevers, aches, pains, v.d., 'stoppages and gravel', he suffered a terrible fit which so upset him that apparently he drove the doctors out of the house with a cudgel. He felt weak and in the end, in January 1725, 'his bloodshot and palsied face contorted itself', but that seems only natural as 'his bladder was so inflamed that he shrieked for sixteen hours from the pain'.

Peter the Great was often ill. If he was epileptic, he had

hard but only occasional trouble from it, though it may have been one of the reasons he was so inclined to plunge into deep glooms.

Pope Pius IX, who started life as Giovanni Mastai-Ferretti, ninth child of a local noble family in Sinigaglia, near Ancona, Italy in 1792, was depressed by his epilepsy, but in a simpler way. Medicine had little to offer in the way of helpful treatment and local society nothing but fear and shame. His '*malattia di nervi*' was diagnosed as epilepsy by a local doctor, following a number of convulsions. During one of these Ferretti is said to have been saved from drowning by a shepherd lad, Guido, after he had fallen into a pond where the boys were trying to catch some small fish.

His epilepsy seems to have been a slightly extended version of a type of epilepsy found in both sexes but most common in males, stretching from puberty to young adulthood. In 1814, when he was twenty-two, Ferretti had one of his last attacks, a severe one which left him feeling feeble, miserable and uncertain for a long time afterwards. It was a time of comprehensive uncertainty for him, while he tried to decide what to do with his life.

Two years later, he wrote to a friend starkly: 'My health has made me more fully aware that there is no happiness in this world.'

In 1817, after working at a hostel for the homeless near the Tiber, Ferretti decided to become a priest. One of his superiors in Rome, Cardinal Testaferratta, was not at all worried by the epilepsy of his new young recruit and helped him rise quickly to become a sub-deacon, then a deacon. Pope Pius VII, by contrast, was frightened in case Ferretti had a fit in action and only allowed him to say mass if he had another priest or deacon with him on the altar. This restriction was later removed, but then so, of course, was his epilepsy.

Ferretti rose through the complicated power structures of mid-nineteenth-century Vatican and Italian politics, leaving his convulsions and lack of confidence behind him as he went. By the time he became Pope he was free of his epilepsy.

16. Julius Caesar, reputed by his early biographers to have 'the falling sickness', did not mention it in his own writings.   17. Peter the Great of Russia was subject to fits, furies and depressions; he may have been epileptic.   18. Pope Pius IX had grown out of his occasional convulsions by his mid-twenties.
19. Van Gogh hoped briefly that his wild attacks were due to epilepsy, not madness.

20. Tony Greig was a high profile figure in 1970s English cricket, a crypto-epileptic. 21. After bowling for England at Headingley in 1899, Johnny Briggs had a fierce fit which led to him spending several months in Cheadle Asylum. 22. Jonty Rhodes, one of South Africa's brilliant present-day fielders, makes no secret of his minor, non-convulsive epilepsy. 23. Rabbi Lionel Blue is happy to discuss his epilepsy publicly.

Whatever else he was when he published the *Syllabus of Errors* and declared Papal Infallibility in 1870, he was fighting fit.

It was a relief to find the facts of Pope Pius IX's epileptic life, few though they are, verified by contemporary documents. More often celebrities said to be epileptic turn out to have had no more than some sort of interest in or connection with it, perhaps knowing an epileptic, for instance. The artist William Morris is on the BEA list of famous epileptics, but it was, in fact, his daughter Jenny who developed epilepsy and as a result was always kept at home. The nearest Morris himself got to fits, as far as I can tell, was his fits of uncontrollable rage. There is no proof that an epileptic cause can be found for episodes like his standing up at breakfast one day, shouting out, 'These six eggs are bad!' and throwing them out of the window.

Neurotic, grumpy, worried or epileptic, there was nothing wrong with Morris's appetite.

Artist Morris in the 1890s was still keen to hide his daughter's epilepsy. Just a few years earlier, artist, illustrator, travel writer and producer of 'queer songs and sketches' Edward Lear kept his epilepsy so secret that hardly anyone knew about it until after his death. In a way he kept it secret from himself. He never really accepted it, though his sister Harriett taught him when he was a child to forestall the attacks, which were short black-outs, by using a mixture of relaxation and willpower. Lear would lie down and try to stay calm as soon as he felt he was drifting into an aura. His attacks were many and mild. Even if he managed to ease or prevent them, he dwelt on them all the time and much of his childhood was spent in a cycle of unhappiness centred on his blackouts.

Later, he wrote in his diaries about his life as a young child:

This demon oppressed me then, I not knowing its wrong and misery . . . a sorrow so inborn and ingrained, so to speak, was evidently part of what I had been born to suffer.

Lear took up outdoor painting to help him escape his gruesome destiny. This did distract him somewhat from his ills, which included asthma and bronchitis as well as his 'terrible demon', epilepsy.

Lear was a peculiar and troublesome man, easy to offend. Painting and the writing of limericks were refuges from the evils overhanging him. When he was twenty-five he went to Europe with his sister Ann and stayed in Italy for two years. The sunshine seemed to help his lungs and he was happier there. When he came back to England he published drawings and lithographs of his stay in Italy, which sold well.

As the years passed, his epileptic attacks became less frequent and more fierce. Ann was one of the very few family members with whom he kept in touch and he was extremely upset when she died in 1861. He had lost a confidante. His incessant travels may have acted as some sort of a let-out for his worries, which were always many and usually highly strung and gloomy. On the subject of his epileptic fears Lear wrote little.

By the 1860s some of his epileptic attacks were taking the form of fits. They left him senseless for hours afterwards. He described himself simply as 'coming to awful grief' at these times. It seems extra cruel that the man best known for his delightful nonsense rhymes, like 'The Dong With the Luminous Nose', should have been living a life of such haunted unhappiness while he wrote.

Nevertheless, there has often been a contrast between public imagination and the facts of epileptic life.

I do not want to damage cricket's public image, but the sad truth is that the only epileptic sportsmen I have been able to discover despite searching through the ranks of all sports, are cricketers. One of them shows with poignant perfection the public fear of his condition and the damage that did to him.

Johnny Briggs, late nineteenth century toast of Lancashire cricket, was one popular public figure with a demon tracking his later life, driving it on from fit to fit, or rather from despair to despair following fits. In his later years, his epilepsy was known to the public, who loved 'Boy Briggs', only 5'5 tall, for his craftily flighted left-arm bowling that made batsmen look such fools, his dynamic fielding, scuttling about in the covers with unusual zip, and his whole-hearted, middle-order batting, often worth half a century or more. An all-round enthusiast against the odds of health, with special distinction in bowling.

In 1899 they poured into the Headingley Test to watch Briggs, but all they saw by way of a spectacle was Briggs taking three wickets on the first day. That night he had an epileptic fit in the music-hall where he went with some other players. He never got over this incident. It was the *pièce de résistance* of his epilepsy and it started him on a downward slope of dread and madness.

At least I think that is what happened. There is no clear writing about Briggs' decline. His epilepsy and his madness were often mentioned, but with no clear distinction between the two or explanation of cause and effect. Briggs' captain, MacLaren, wrote grimly and unhelpfully that 'the excitement proved too much for him and sent him off his head'.

The 1900 *Wisden* report on that Headingley Test mentioned the seizure slightly more fully but no more specifically than did MacLaren: 'the popular player being seized on the Thursday evening with illness of so serious a character as to prevent him playing any more during the season and rendering necessary his detention in the Cheadle Asylum'.

In fact, Briggs seems to have got the train home to Manchester the day after his fit, which would be fair enough. He was said to have been met by a man from Cheadle Asylum, where he was taken and kept until the following March. Released in time for the 1900 season, he did his best ever for Lancashire that year, taking 105 wickets and scoring 761 runs, but was back in Cheadle Asylum by March 1901. He died there in January 1902, almost certainly killing himself.

The third of the trio of cricketing epileptics I have found is, I trust a less desperate case. Jonty Rhodes is a fielder in the best tradition of South African vigour. He is energetic and athletic, obviously taking the view that the more a fielder moves the better his chances of avoiding fast-flying balls of the kind that may aggravate an epileptic brain. He did avoid them until he ducked into a phenomenally fast bouncer from Devon Malcolm at the Oval in the summer of 1994.

Rhodes regained consciousness well enough to be escorted from the field, was kept in hospital for the night with concussion and was well, brave or mad enough to come out and lose his wicket to Malcolm again in the second innings. Thank goodness he still plays. I could easily imagine myself settling into a nervous aura of anticipatory panic at the sight of a bowler such as Malcolm, not noted for his control and accuracy, working up his momentum towards me from the other end, little red weapon in hand. In the circumstances, reflex epilepsy might look more like a deliverance than a handicap. It is more than a legitimate means of withdrawal from the contest; it is a positively overwhelming means.

Rhodes was sensible enough to give only measured bulletins of personal publicity to the predatory press who flock round every cricketing accident in England, baying for blood. He played down his epilepsy and emphasised the benefits it has brought him, in evangelical Christian terms. He sees his epilepsy as one of the divine instruments manipulating his life, with immeasurable benevolence, in tune with God's mysterious plans.

Reading Jonty Rhodes' brief comments on his epilepsy as the whiplash of divine destiny reminds me what a sharp dividing line convulsions make between the bearable and the unbearable, especially in sport. Non-convulsive epilepsy may be as physically troublesome, but it is not as demoralising.

Algernon Charles Swinburne, poet and critic, pre-Raphaelite hectic and alchoholic, was demoralised by epilepsy which hovered on the border between convulsions and blank patches. At moments of high excitement he sometimes worked himself up to suffering what looks like a kind of hysterical epilepsy. As a child he used to have occasional black-outs, some of them with convulsive movements, which his doctor diagnosed as connected with his cerebral excitement.

Swinburne's mother seems to have been more upset by these
sessions than the poet himself, but they remained with him
as he grew older.

By the 1870s he was drinking heavily and experiencing
periodic fits. He recovered quickly from these fits and continued writing and publishing his work. But in 1879 he
collapsed, a wreck, and was rescued by his friend Walter
Theodore Watts, who took him back to Putney and kept him
there under a benevolent dictatorship, without drink and with
few fits, for no less than thirty years, writing. Swinburne was
a complicated collage of emotions, in which it is hard to place
epileptoid nervousness or epilepsy exactly.

Byron had already taken Swinburne's line of disinterested
silence about his epilepsy some years before and done it with
his customary humour, all the more pointed because in
Byron's case it was concerned with convulsions, not intermittently convulsive blank patches. Byron had few seizures but
those he had were severe.

In February 1824 he wrote from Missolonghi in Greece:

'On Sunday (the 15th I believe) I had a strong and sudden
convulsive attack, which left me speechless, though not
motionless; but whether it was epilepsy, catalepsy, cachexy,
or apoplexy, or what other exy or epsy, the doctors have not
decided; or whether it was spasmodic or nervous, etc.; but
it was very unpleasant, and nearly carried me off, and all
that. . . .'

Byron's life can provide us with another, more oblique
glimpse of the general uncertainty in the last century about
the nature of fits. His affair with Lady Caroline Lamb is well
known. It has a finishing touch seldom mentioned – when
Caroline Lamb received a letter marked with Lady Oxford's
coronet and initials, telling her of Byron's attachment to
another, she went into a fit 'which involved leeching, bleeding
and bed for a week.' Never one to be outdone, Lady Caroline.

Prolonged rests in bed have always been the basic treatment
for fits and it is easy to see why. I lie in bed after my fits, for
the simple reason that I cannot do anything else. I would

have thought that epileptic fits have a taut strength more destructive than any other kind of fits, but I don't know; I speak only from experience of epilepsy with a physical cause, never from experience of nervous, emotional or psychosomatic fits. I found a dreary satisfaction in reading Fyodor Dostoevsky's descriptions of being battered into bed by his epileptic fits. It made me feel one of a community, though it is one that I, like everyone else, would rather have avoided.

In 1873 Dostoevsky told his friend Mikhail Petrovich that he needed at least five days in bed to come back to normal after his monthly attacks, instead of the three days that had sufficed for many years. Another friend had earlier described these three days in dire terms, after seeing Dostoevsky 'lying almost unconscious for three or four days after a terrible attack of epilepsy.

Dostoevsky showed a few signs of epilepsy early in his life, but it was in middle age that he wrote more and more often about it, as indeed he wrote about all his health problems. His ill health was one of his favourite topics; the only other thing that he wrote about so much in the last twenty years of his life was his love for his wife and family. In March 1857, after his wedding, he wrote a letter to let his brother Mikhail know about both subjects.

'On the journey back (through Barnaul) I stopped over at Barnaul at the home of a certain good acquaintance of mine. There a misfortune befell me: completely unexpectedly I had an epileptic attack that scared my wife to death and filled me with grief and despondency. The doctor (learned and sensible) told me, contrary to all doctors' previous opinions, that I have genuine falling sickness and that I should expect that during one of these attacks I will die precisely from that . . . If I had known for certain that I had genuine falling sickness I would not have married.'

Though Dostoevsky wrote prolifically and vividly about his epilepsy, it is not easy reading; it is too sad. The only saving grace is his description of the momentary auras he sometimes felt before attacks. He is not the only epileptic who has described a strange moment of feeling something that sounds like inspiration or moving onto a different level of consciousness, in the same mode as religious epileptics. Mohammed wrote simply:

'Not once did I receive a revelation without thinking that my soul had been torn away from me.'

Dostoevsky wrote in more detail.

'If the attack comes when I am awake, suddenly, amidst the depression, the psychic darkness, the anxiety, for some instants my brain seems to flame up and all at once my vital forces were intently exerted. My sensation of life, my consciousness increased almost tenfold in those instants which passed like lightning. My mind, my heart, are illuminated by an unusual light, all my agitations, my doubts, all uneasiness are instantly tranquilized, resolved in a kind of higher calmness filled with clear, harmonious joy and hope, filled with intelligence and ultimate reason.'

I have never felt anything like this. The few times I have gone from being awake to having a fit I felt agonisingly exhausted, longing to stop being aware of anything. I am afraid I find the extraordinary auras too much to imagine or believe, even when Dostoevsky described them more bluntly as 'mystical terrors'. I felt more at home reading Dostoevsky's bitter remark after a fit once that, looking back on these moments, they were no more than 'illness, the very lowest form of being'.

As the years went by, the fits played the very lowest form of tricks they could find on a writer, depriving him of his memory.

'What a horrible memory I have as the consequence of my fits of epilepsy. I even forget the faces of people I have met, and when meeting them later don't recognise them and thus (would you believe?) even make enemies.'

Dostoevsky has left us in his letters a blow-by-blow account of his obsession and destruction by the assorted aspects of 'blackness in the soul' which ravaged him, everything from gambling to epilepsy and the mental weaknesses he attributed to it. He indulged himself in a horribly detailed description of the epileptic attacks which his wife Anya missed, challenging her to accept them and what they did to him. He was lucky to have her.

Others were less lucky. Vincent Van Gogh sounds more like a madman than an epileptic and the women in his life found the effects of his fits intolerable. On Christmas day 1888 he was treated for a break-down in the hospital at Arles, during which he had what his doctor, Rey, described as a fit. He cut off his ear and gave it as a present to his girl-friend Rachel, who had been kind to him in the last few months of what Gaugin had called 'strange and threatening' behaviour. Whether the ear-cutting was a part of or a result of the fit is unclear.

After being released from hospital, he returned of his own free will and was taken to the nearby asylum, St Pierre de Mausole, a converted monastic building. He wrote to his brother Theodore:

'Little by little I shall come to consider madness as an illness like any other . . . As far as I know, the doctor here, Dr Peyron, is inclined to think that my attack was of an epileptic kind.'

Van Gogh found madness and epilepsy equally hard to take and he painted frantically out in the fields when he could persuade the doctors to let him out of his padded cell, between attacks. One of these attacks was described by the doctor as being 'fierce pressure in the head which sent the body rigid and he uttered a cry. He was confused for three weeks afterwards'.

If Van Gogh was epileptic, he was not a good advertisement for it. His suicide in 1890 came after long stretches locked away, with frequent attacks. There is a horror surrounding convulsions which has always terrified onlookers so that they, in a way, share the suffering of the one convulsing. Even nowadays, with many epileptics suffering fewer convulsions, many epileptics still keep quiet about them. Those who only suffer absence attacks have less excuse for secrecy.

The more that people in the public eye admit their epilepsy and show that they can still do their jobs, epilepsy notwithstanding, the less daunting the condition will be for those newly in its grasp, filled with terror. I could not help laughing when I saw that Rabbi Lionel Blue has 'come out' about his epilepsy as well as his homosexuality. He obviously considers they are both important, challenging parts of his high-profile personality. He has the confidence to be honest, indeed to do well out of his honesty.

But I do not blame the many more people in the public eye who I'm sure lack that confidence and are keeping quiet about their epilepsy. It is perfect fodder for panic reporting and it is not always clear whether announcing it is likely to make more alarm or to remove it. I suppose it is best in the end to trust people's wish to be brave – when in doubt, come out.

PART THREE

Coping with Epilepsy

CHAPTER SEVEN

Care of my Epilepsy

There is a lot to be said for modern life, even if it cannot cure me of epilepsy. At least I don't go to the hospital to be given my next batch of gladiator's blood, which is what Pliny the Elder described in his first-century *Natural History* as epileptics' favourite medicine. 'By Hercules, they think it most efficacious to suck the blood as it foams warm from the man himself.'

Whatever else was wrong with medicine at this early date, it can't have been dull.

Many hair-raising cures persisted all through epilepsy's superstitious history, though how many were put into practice as often as they were described and prescribed is an open question. Freshly dead and foaming gladiators, for instance, cannot have been on hand near every epileptic's home. Still, we must have gained as much by getting rid of some of the old cures, however rare they were in practice, as by introducing the new ones we use today, which are often feeble. Free of old horrors, I reckon that even the intermittent protection I get from my anti-convulsants makes them worthwhile.

These drugs aim to stop convulsions by slowing down my brain's rate of activity, which means I sometimes find it hard to remember whether I've taken them or not. The secret to being epileptic is to be painstaking as well as resilient come-what-may, free of regrets and built with bones which are hard to break. But I am better at drinking coffee than being painstaking or resilient first thing in the morning. I always remember to carry my pills around with me, just as I always carry my insulin and syringes around. I am used to medical bits

and pieces being part of the baggage of life and anti-
convulsants have quickly become a habit. My problem is
remembering whether or not I have taken them.

On the whole, insulin injections are sharp enough to remind
me where I have put the needle in and usually, but not always,
I remember doing them. If I forget an injection, I feel bad
enough a couple of hours later to realise my mistake and put
it right. The anti-convulsants, by contrast, need no equipment, only a cup of liquid to wash them down. The nearest
I get to the horrible sugary feeling I experience if I have
forgotten my insulin is feeling well if I have forgotten my
anti-convulsants. If I start feeling well, with the smog of
exhaustion and double vision clearing, I check to see whether
I have forgotten to take my pill, because that is not how I
should be feeling nowadays.

Remembering when you have forgotten is a fine art, at
which I am no more than an apprentice. Recently I took a
pill, sure that I had forgotten the one due first thing that
morning and soon had to get off my bike because I was too
heavy to make the pedals go round. I must have taken a
second one by mistake and fallen victim to their knock-out
effect.

More often I forget to take them, especially at lunch, which
is a recent addition to the meals when I have to take the pills
and which I often eat on my own, with no-one to remind me
about pills.

Mark made me a little wooden panel, divided into seven
lines, each named after a day of the week. Each day has four
pills in four holes – one for breakfast, one for lunch and two
for dinner. To check whether I have taken a pill, I look and
see if it is still in its allotted hole; if it is still there when it
should have been taken, I take it at once.

This timetable of supplies is the same size as my small
diary and easy to carry around with me in my handbag.

To stop the pills falling out, Mark covered it in the nearest
piece of cardboard, which was bright orange check in colour,
like a crazed brick.

Plastic 'drug wallets' with holes for scheduled drugs can be bought at chemists. Recently my local chemist gave me my drugs in tinfoil sheets punched with holes, instead of loose in bottles. The drug sheets are thin enough to carry in an evening bag and are most welcome. I have yet to find out whether there are sheets big enough for six pills, eight pills or however many pills I may soon have to take every day. At present I take four pills a day and have drug sheets with lines of four holes in them.

Fortunately, my diabetes means I get all my prescriptions free of charge, so the only remembering I need to do in that respect is to order in good time everything I need. Usually I manage that. Getting my ever-increasing load of medical goods is all right; paying for it is a non-event; it's swallowing the pills that I need to perfect.

At first the pills I took were Phenytoin, which is a sedative, like all anti-convulsants. It produced uneven results, sometimes not bad at preventing my fits, sometimes pretty well useless. Professor C. had not told me the side-effects I was likely to feel because, he said, 'if I tell, you'll just go and get them all.' I can see his point, but I think it is a patronising approach and, if anything, I found myself imagining more, not fewer, unusual feelings. In fact, the only side-effects which I felt were sickness and exhaustion.

If that had been at the same time as having fewer fits, I would not have minded, but most weeks I still had two or three fits. The fits became more numerous until my long-suffering GP, tired of patching me up after the worst of them, suggested I increase the dose. When that did not help, he wrote a letter to Professor C. and made me an appointment at the Professor's next clinic.

I used to think that novelists writing books to do with education exaggerated staff-room politics for the sake of a good plot or a dramatic setting. Then I became a school-teacher and revised my opinion. When I married a Cambridge don, I realised that the only distortion on page or screen is in the direction of understatement. College plots and power struggles are deep and refined to infinitesimal degrees of complexity. So, I have come to suspect, are the politics, plots and power struggles of medical life, though of course I can only judge that from the outside looking in. Or perhaps it is better described as 'from the receiving end'.

When I made my extra visit to Professor C.'s clinic, he greeted me in a cold voice, holding in his hand the letter my GP had written.

'I have received a letter,' he said, evidently not pleased to have his treatment of my epilepsy questioned. I said it was my fault because I had asked my GP whether this was the best I could expect or whether there might be a chance of a different drug producing better results.

The Professor stared at me. 'I sense unease.'

I stared back at him. 'Yes. That's why I came.' I also sought refuge. 'Professor, this is my husband.'

This was another idea of my GP, who thought it would help if I had a witness to answer the questions I could not answer about my fits, especially since the fits had taken to arriving in groups. How long did each fit last? How long was the gap between them? Were they all over my body or only over half of it? Were they all of the same ferocity? How many in each batch?

There was a litany of questions which Mark answered for me, without any comment from Professor C. or any answer to the simple question I kept trying to ask him about changing the drugs. I've never known Professor C. like he was that day, unhappy with intruders into the forum he usually held with me, insulted by the double intrusion of my GP and my husband. If I hadn't known that he is an eminent professor I would have said that he was feeling threatened.

I am used to seeing Professor C. for about ninety seconds, every one of the seconds taken up with his pointed questions and instructions. That day we drifted round the edges of argument for about twenty minutes, most of them spent with Mark and Professor C. sparring, the rest of them with Professor C. talking about epilepsy in general, not specifically.

It only ended when I butted in and demanded desperately, 'What would you do if you were me?'

'I would change drugs.'

'What to?'

He recommended tegretol, which I have since found out is more quick-acting than Phenytoin – and gave me a prescription for it and a date for my next appointment.

'Give it time, to see how it works. It may take a while and it doesn't do to be impatient, you know.'

This was Professor C. as I knew him and I was glad to return to the flinty expert. It had been a mistake taking Mark and I have not taken him since. The relationship between Professor C. and my GP soon returned to its customary state of remote silence, the GP taking care of me if the Professor's efforts produce results too dangerous to be managed by Mark at home.

Thank God, that seldom happens. Mark is an old hand at mopping me up and an increased dose of drugs means he has to do it less often nowadays. I seldom see either my GP or Professor C., which is a relief for all of us. Except for that one unscheduled visit, my hospital appointments for epilepsy settled down to one every six months, the same as my diabetic appointments.

I have made rather a lot of my GP's unusual intervention in the relationship between himself and Professor C., which on the whole is peaceful. It follows an understood pattern, with Professor C. the deciding force and my GP the agent of action on the spot.

The last three times I went to see the Professor, he was away giving lectures or attending conferences abroad and I saw one of his senior registrars, who was friendly but did not feel he could change the treatment prescribed by the Professor. 'That's the trouble with seeing the top chap,' he said. 'He's interested in your epilepsy because of its connection with your diabetes, but he's not often here.'

It would be nice to feel I was an exhibit of success if things improved, rather than an object of interest when things go wrong.

I can't pretend I am over-impressed by what Professor C. has done because I am not. I am happier than I used to be and I can only hope that the arrangement between hospital and local practice will not be upset, with an unwonted weight put on my GP, now that I am no longer going to make automatic appointments at the hospital's neurology clinic.

I was amazed last time I was there to hear Professor C. say, as I was leaving, 'Don't make an appointment for next time. We don't do that any more. I'll let you know when I think it's time to see you.'

How will he know if trouble has made it time, except through a worried GP? I am nervous at the idea of being given a clinic appointment a long time after the clinic, instead of immediately afterwards on the basis of what has just been seen and heard.

I disapprove of every change that has been made to the medical service in the last few years and if this one is an attempt to transfer the burden of care from hospital to family doctors it is misguided. A complicated neurological problem left to a willing GP without specialist knowledge is likely to result in the patient ending up in hospital, probably as an emergency admission. That saves no-one time, money or trouble.

In fact I think the difficulties of neurology probably leave specialists and GPs alike in the dark most of the time. In my case at least, I know the GP would rather not be left with the responsibility of making important decisions about the best treatment to give. That would worry him. It is noticeable that when he was unhappy about my treatment he did not change it himself; he wrote to Professor C.

As I was leaving the Professor on that occasion, he broke into an unexpected account of the possible superiority of mind over medicine, willpower over drugs. He said he had one patient who could feel a seizure coming on and, when she did, sat in front of a mirror and said to herself: 'This is not going to happen.' In that way she talked herself out of her fits. The Professor looked at his notes on me and added, 'But I can see that's not much good if the seizures begin when you're asleep.'

Even so, the story impressed me. I have since read several similar newspaper accounts of epileptics helping themselves in that way, including some written by the epileptics themselves and published in *Epilepsy Today*, the magazine of the British Epilepsy Association, giving the bad as well as triumphant details of their efforts. Even the slightest achievement of this psychological sort is a big one.

The key to all such successes, Professor C. said, is willpower, and I admire it. If people manage to control their frantic little neurones without drugging their brains into a stupor, how marvellous for them. Epileptoid fits with nervous, psychological or hysterical elements and epileptic fits with warning patches beforehand are the most responsive to this sort of treatment. Preventive thought-waves last thing at night, just in case a fit comes while I am asleep, do not seem to have the same effect.

I have learnt from decades of using assorted medical weapons against diabetes that it is a mistake to change weapons just because you don't like the present one; there has to be a positive reason. Where there is doubt, stay put. Even so, I changed anti-convulsants because Phenytoin was not just failing to help me but, gradually, letting my epilepsy slide back to a free-range policy of profligate fits. On the positive side, all I had was my GP's advice to change drugs and Professor C.'s reluctant acquiescence in the idea, painfully drawn from him like a bad tooth.

Things have improved. It was a slow start, with a fit-free fortnight a rarity. Then Professor C. increased the dose of tegretol, after a blood test showed I only had a low level of it in my system. Now I take more and feel extinct all the time but a short while ago I had no less than six weeks of extinction without a fit, the longest stretch I have experienced since being epileptic. I knew I would be a fool to trust it, so I settled for hope instead of faith and was horribly depressed but not surprised when I woke up the other day with my head feeling as if it were full of spikes, the result of a fit during the night.

When I managed to put on a dressing-gown and make
my tentative way downstairs, I found Mat, my neurologist
step-son, entertaining the household with some accounts of
the bizarre brain behaviour he has come across in his work.
Driving over instead of round a roundabout, then sleeping,
unwakeable, for three days was one of the many episodes Mat
had encountered from a brain out of tune. A nice friend of
his, who has stayed with us before, appeared at breakfast the
following morning and told me about the research he will soon
be doing into diabetes and endocrinology. I congratulated
myself on acquiring family and friends to my own advantage.

My only mistake was that because I had been unconscious
for a day, the shopping had not been done and all I could say
when it came to breakfast, after apologetic searches in the
kitchen, was,'No bread, no bacon, no eggs . . . but always
welcome.'

If I am going to keep a good stock of human experts on hand,
I must have an extra good stock of edible resources, to keep the
experts well fed for whatever action may prove necessary.

Professor C. would find it hard to believe if my epilepsy
made such action necessary. When he increased my dose of
tegretol, he said it should bring me to 'a new frontier of control'. The 'new frontier' has something of the mirage about it
and I was not inclined to believe him, but the new regime
has so far given me this intoxicating spell of one delicious
week after another without trouble from fits.

One of the main threats to these fit-free spells is the pills'
weakness for being neutralised by alcohol, especially wine. If
I drink red wine, the pills fail to work. This is the one side-
effect I would like to have known about before taking the pills.
We paid dearly for not knowing last summer when our holiday
in Burgundy was full of wine and fits. The hotels where I
made a mess of our stay, covering the sheets with blood and
broken teeth and staying in bed for days on end, were kind and
sympathetic. One particularly kind place brought up meals on
trays and, once, a glass of wine, which I was stupid enough
to drink.

I had suspected for some time that wine was hostile to the pills I take. Now I only drink it when we have people to dinner or go out to eat and then in very small quantities. I can absorb about a glass, but if I have more than that I have a fit. Last summer we had our tenth wedding anniversary, went out to dinner and shared a bottle of wine. We both knew it was risky, but I had been having a lot of fits in the previous few weeks and thought that as I was having them anyway I might as well go down celebrating. I also decided to try to rise above it all with a dose of willpower, not letting routine concerns suffocate a special occasion. I was a fool. I had savage fits that night and all through the following day.

When I asked Professor C. if it was possible that the drugs were adversely affected by drink, he said yes, it was easily possible and the thing to do was to find my own safe level of drink. Experiment would show me excess. What I have found by this cruel means is that my level seems to be, alas, less than one glass of wine.

Still, small and weak drinks are extra-welcome these days. The only time I find it hard not being able to drink much is when people make it hard by pressing me to drink more. A few weeks ago we had dinner with some people we barely knew who insisted that I drink three glasses of wine. When we got home, I thrashed around in bed, wondering whether it would be better to go to sleep, a policy advocated by doctors as a calming resource against convulsions, or to stay awake since my convulsions invariably start when I am asleep.

In the end, I did the worst of both, staying awake in a sweaty mess of anxiety until just before dawn, when I finally fell asleep and started the heavy breathing and 'tastings' that are signs of imminent fits. Michael gave me a dose of Valium and I woke up hours later, safe after being within a hair's breadth of an attack.

Next time I shall be ruthless in my refusal of drink and give those who don't know me a temperate first impression, so they will always offer me orange juice. I never thought the day would come.

The only warning I have ever been given about these pills was not concerned with drink, but pregnancy. It was given to me by my local chemist when I went to get a new load of anti-convulsants from him.

As he handed them to me, he said, 'You do know that these make contraceptive pills much less reliable, don't you? It is low-dose contraceptives like yours that call for the most care.'

I did not know, but I was not surprised to hear the chemist telling me. It may be largely by contrast with my Professor of few words, but I have got the impression that chemists in recent years have become more keen to give advice and warnings. Even our local chemist, with his small circle of familiar customers, is more inclined to treat them not just as customers but as clients, recommending suitable medicines to buy and warning about many possible hazards and side-effects of drugs.

Warnings about minor side-effects are sometimes printed on the labels of pill bottles. I was almost glad to find one such warning on a label not long ago: 'May cause soreness of gums'. For months my mouth had been full of the little ulcers that used to plague me as a child and now I knew why. There was nothing I could do about the ulcers except ignore them. Even as I write I have a mouthful of weeping ulcers.

They are a small price to pay for 'the new frontier of control' which I am striving for. The rips and tears in my gums, after fits in particular, become lined with ulcers. If these touch other parts of my mouth or if liquid runs over them, they become so sore that I want to cry.

Skin rashes are one misery reported by many people who take tegretol, but I suffer from them only intermittently. About once a month I find my neck red and itching. If I scratch it, I make it worse. If I can last a few days of the rash without reducing it to a raw mess, it goes away of its own accord. My body's anti-drug protests that take the form of rashes prefer my mouth as the scene for their exertions.

Weight gain is another unpleasant result of these drugs, caused by the slowing up of the metabolism, in time with the slowing up of the brain. I can't concentrate but I can expand. In fact, I have stayed pretty well the same in weight since becoming epileptic, though it is nice to have an excuse ready for my weaker patches.

On the whole, the side-effects I suffer as a result of tegretol are not worth much attention. The more I think about them, the more intrusive they become into my life, so it is best to pay them little heed. Exhaustion, aching, itching and soreness have quickly become as ordinary as breathing.

These side-effects, and those that inevitably result when the pills fail and I have seizures, are worse when I am about to have a period.

The only time I mentioned this fact to Professor C. he did not seem to think it was important. In my limited experience, doctors pay little attention to the relationship between hormonal and epileptic activity, and although I have a female doctor-friend who is always urging me to press for more help in this respect I have some sympathy with the standard medical indifference to the question.

In fact, as the subject is such a complicated and delicate one, I think I would rather settle for indifference than experiment. That applies to the drugs concerned as well as the condition they are supposed to ease. Occasionally my bottles of anti-convulsants have had warnings written on them about loss of sexual desire being one of the drug's main hazards. Fortunately, I have never found that the drug affects my sexual feelings. I confess, however, that I find it hard to read or think about such feelings analytically. It makes me laugh.

I dare say some epileptics find the earnest approach, with more analysis and discussion of their problems, more helpful. I can only speak for myself when I say that my best way of surviving the side-effects of drugs and after-effects of fits is to keep them as a minor issue. It is not always easy and I do not always manage it, but it is always worth a try.

CHAPTER EIGHT

Help from Home and Friends

There is nothing like looking after oneself. When I married Mark, over ten years ago, I acquired three teenaged step-children, one of whom now works in Africa, so we see little of him. The other two, a nurse and a neurologist, live within a couple of hours' drive and we see them quite often.

I have done well out of their useful qualifications, though it embarrasses me to admit it and it is never on purpose. To take an example at random, once when Catherine was staying at home, in her room next to ours, I flung myself out of bed during a fit. It was very early in the morning and I think Mark must have gone downstairs to get a coffee, so there was no-one there to keep me in bed when I started convulsing. No doubt I landed with quite a thump. It was enough to wake Catherine, who ran in and shoved a pillow under my head, saving me from doing anything too drastic.

When I woke up, or rather opened one eye, late that evening, everyone else was eating fish and chips. I had been planning to buy a piece of fish in the market and cook a good dinner for Catherine, who is a vegetarian. That plan had faded along with my consciousness. Peter was delighted. He much preferred fish and chips and came to offer me a congratulatory chip to go with my evening injection. I don't think anyone minded too much, though I will inflict my planned dinner on Catherine next time she comes, God willing.

Friday, the day I had that series of fits, is a bad day to have them. I like going into the market in town on Fridays and looking for fish or seafood for dinner, the remains of which I can make into a starter for Saturday's meal. If I miss out on a Friday, it means I have to stagger into town amid the weekend shopping throng or limit my efforts to whatever we have in the fridge. By the time Saturday is over and I have stopped feeling my way round like a relic, we have nothing left for Sunday except old vegetables, liquidised into soup. Mondays are gruesome by nature. At least on weekdays during term, Mark gets lunch in college and Peter gets lunch at school.

It is the details that hover and bother, stupid though that is. Whenever I regain consciousness after having a fit, the first thing I see has always been Mark sitting on the floor, trying to do some work that he has brought home. I am not going to pretend that this is always glamorous. The view of Mark from above usually consists of the bald patch on top of his head and the shaggy grey hair just below the patch, almost long enough to hide the dirty shirt collar I should have washed. Last time, the first thing I saw when I opened my eyes was some Xeroxed documents of twelfth-century canon law, reflected in Mark spectacles.

Even so, my first feeling was surprise and pleasure at being alive, then gratitude to God, Mark and any other nearby Bentleys for their part in that, then guilt at the nuisance I'd caused and worry at the things I'd failed to do: shopping, cooking, washing shirts for work and for football matches – that kind of thing. I'm much more likely to harbour some nagging memory of having to buy fish than to remember that I have to go down to London and interview someone. If I had been going to do a serious job, like an interview or an article in London, I know Mark or someone else at home can postpone or cancel it for me if need be. A small, domestic chore like buying fish, however, is up to me. If the burden of it is removed by buying fish and chips or Mark making his excellent omelettes, it weighs on my conscience.

The last time Mat, my neurologist step-son, was here during a long series of my fits, he insisted that I have the bedroom curtains drawn all day as well as all night. Why? Because the council had just finished putting an automatic pedestrian crossing outside the house and he was worried that its flashing lights might induce more fits in me while I was in a vulnerable phase.

Until then, I had not really taken in the fact that one epileptic attack increases the likelihood of another. The more fits you have, the more you are likely to have and the harder they are to treat. Armed with this cheerful knowledge, I had no defence against Mat's expertise and was happy to sleep all day rather than lie and regret the dark.

I think that this is the nearest I've let Mat get to exercising his professional prowess at home. I hope so. I can't remember another example, though I've no doubt Mark taps him for advice if he thinks it would help.

Peter is now ten years old and I'm not sure whether he has seen me in a fierce epileptic fit or not. He knows what they are, which I think is important if he is going to stay calm, as he is now, about them. He has seen me semi-conscious and out of control during attacks of hypoglycaemia, caused by my diabetes, but they must be less frightening because in the end they can be put right by giving me a piece of chocolate or a sugary drink.

That is easier said than done, especially for a child. The last time Peter saw me crash to the ground, I did a fair bit of thrashing around; all his efforts to give me a sweet drink ended in smashed mugs and puddles of orange squash. I slid down into unconsciousness and he could not wake me, so he rang Mark in college and was lucky enough to find him in his room. Mark came back, forced some sugar into me and within five minutes I was well enough to start cleaning up the mess.

Peter knows Mark's phone number in college, and it is pinned up by our telephone, along with the number of the college porters' lodge and the numbers of our local GP and the hospital. It all looks reassuringly simple on paper. How it might work out in the event of a fit, we don't know. An impersonal answering service would be discouraging and, no doubt, slow, leaving Peter alone with his convulsing mother. He is reasonably used to convulsions, in their weaker, hypoglycaemic form; my only fear is that, unable to distinguish between those and epileptic convulsions, he might try to put something sugary into my mouth. I could easily bite through his fingers.

Since I started writing this book, I have had some convulsions downstairs at home, in the kitchen, and not only did Peter work out that they were not sugar-induced, but he was proud of himself for doing so. They were a strange set of fits, one in a series that had started during the night and lasted into the early morning. Mark was outside for a moment and I was awake enough, despite all the sedatives he had given me, to come down and try to make myself a coffee.

Peter came into the kitchen and found me lying on the floor, my head leaking blood. I must have fallen and cut it on the corner of the sink when I went to fill the kettle. Peter may have been frightened, but he was matter-of-fact. He got out of my handbag my excellent new diabetic gadget for finger pricking and blood sugar testing. Finding that the sugar level was quite high, he realised I must have had an epileptic fit, not a hypoglycaemic one.

Having got that far, there was no further to go. I was unconscious and too heavy to move. He could not wake me up, but found Mark, who managed to shake me into a sort of half-awake state, alive enough to be driven down to the hospital and have the top of my head stitched together by a doctor in Casualty. Before we went, I made a misguided effort to comb my hair, breaking teeth out of the comb in the process. That hurt more than the cut itself, which was numb for several days.

I was interested to see how pleased Peter was at coping with an epileptic fit on his own, as far as was possible. Maybe next time he would even prefer to shove one of the rods of Valium into my bottom. It would be embarrassing, but it might make him feel more useful. Whether or not he could do that while I was having convulsions, rather than in the aftermath of convulsions, I don't know. He would probably be best in partnership with Mark, the first time at any rate.

Six of the nine instructions on my little plastic membership card for the British Epilepsy Association tell people what not to do if they witness a fit. The only positive instructions are those telling people to leave a clear space round a person convulsing, loosen the person's collar and put something soft under their head.

By the time onlookers have rummaged around in my handbag until they have found and read these instructions, it would probably be too late to help me anyway, by doing or not doing anything.

Only two of my friends have ever asked me what they should do if I have a fit. Most people are pleased to think that there is little that can be done; it is one of those times when helplessness is a relief.

My epilepsy may get harder, not easier, for Peter to cope with as he gets older and finds it more embarrassing. It remains to be seen whether he will be relieved or frustrated, or both, by his inability to do much about it. With luck, familiarity will lessen the embarrassment it is likely to cause him as he grows older.

The only time I have known him declare himself upset by my epilepsy was when I found by chance a piece of paper containing a list his class at school had been told to make of things that frightened them. I don't know why they had to make the list; it was part of an English prep, so it was more likely to have been for grammatical than emotional reasons. Peter's list contained all the usual things, like fierce dogs – citing in particular the bad-tempered Alsatian that used to live, viciously, next door, and the thought of being struck by lightning. The item I had not expected was the only one not described in detail; it just said: 'My mother's epilepsy and diabetes frightens me.'

Still, I am sure it would be more frightening to be shielded from it so that it became a source of frightened speculation in his mind, with no certain explanation or definition.

Peter lives a protected life, being in effect an only child in a stable setting. It could even be that learning to live with a rough problem like this will make him feel tougher.

The only other expression I have ever seen of Peter's fear of my epilepsy, apart from his mention of it in his 'fear list', was not when I was having fits but when a friend was trying to help me stop having them. Peter did not like it.

This friend is a Dominican friar called David, who likes to do things whole-heartedly. I can't remember exactly when it was – at least two years ago, at a time when I was having lots of fits. When I asked David if he could spare me a few minutes, he agreed unhesitatingly. I had never spoken to him on my own about anything religious, though I had often been to his talks, joined in his discussions, laughed at the jokes in his sermons, played cricket with him and had him to dinner.

It was different talking to him alone and I was surprised by some of the answers he gave to my questions. I told him I felt guilty about being such a burden on Mark. I had one or two recent, full-blooded examples on hand, to show him what I meant by being a burden, and was disconcerted when he made light of them.

'Oh, don't worry about that! It makes him feel useful.'

I was cross and gave a disappointed smile. It is the sort of problem, in my experience, that women understand much more easily than men. I was too tired to be cross when I got home later, told Mark what David had said and he agreed with it triumphantly.

'Quite right. Good for David. Maybe now you'll believe me when I tell you the same thing.'

Back at Blackfriars, when the issue of being a burden had been brushed aside, I got down to asking David for his advice. Did he think it would be good to pray to be healed or was it better to pray, as I did, along 'Thy will be done' lines?

David was slower answering that, but clear. He said that although he respected much about the totally trusting, never questioning, religious education I had been given at the convent where I went to school, he thought it tended to be too submissive. If it was in my nature to fight, the thing to do was fight. If I wanted to ask for healing, I should ask for it.

I didn't want to. I had never prayed to get better. Until I

developed epilepsy, it had never occurred to me that I should. I suppose I thought my diabetes must have been given to me for some reason, so the thing to ask for was help in getting something good out of it.

I think my epilepsy, too, must have been given me for some reason, but I find it harder to accept, I want to get better more than anything else on earth and I would be fooling myself to think I have got much good out of it. Even so, at least part of me would have been happier if David had left me with my submissive approach, which brings little risk of disappointment.

No such luck. David pointed out that silence can be cowardly. He is a Biblical scholar and I knew I would not get away without Biblical examples to back up what he said. He gave many Old Testament ones and chose the New Testament one about the Canaanite woman who came up to Jesus and begged Him to heal her daughter, who was possessed by a demon. 'But He did not answer her a word.' She kept on asking. The disciples begged Him to get rid of her 'for she never stops pleading with us.' So He told her to go; He was the saviour of Israelites, not Canaanites. She still pestered Him. He spelt out that He had no intention of helping her, saying that helping her would be like giving humans' bread to dogs. Nothing if not persistent, the woman pursued her point; surely dogs could eat the crumbs that fall off their master's table. Jesus gave up and did as she asked. He healed her daughter. (Matthew, xv, 21-28).

The woman in question had done nothing less than bully Jesus into giving her the answer she wanted. In case I produced counter-examples of more submissive prayers, David reminded me that this kind of direct prayer for one answer was not incompatible with 'Thy will be done' prayers. Before the crucifixion, in the Garden of Olives, Jesus prayed for what He wanted: 'Father, if it is possible, let this cup pass away from me.' Then He added a prayer of acceptance, come what may: 'Yet, let not My will but Thy will be done.' (Matthew, xxvi, 39)

I got the answer I had been hoping for, but it was also the one I had been afraid of getting: I should pray to get better. I still don't pray to God to cure me of diabetes, which has become a fact of everyday life, like going to the lavatory, not worth supernatural re-arrangement. I do pray nowadays, though, for my epilepsy to be cured, or at least made gentler. I only pray for that once in a while, without any real belief or hope that it will happen, just a shaft of slightly frantic hope hidden in an opaque cloud, more out of duty than conviction. Perhaps I only get that far partly because I know that containment, if not a cure can sometimes happen with medical help, not requiring miraculous help, so it does not seem so preposterous a request.

I have an atheist friend who reckons I am doing no more than insuring myself against all eventualities; whether I get better or not, I can claim that my prayers have been answered, in one way or another. I suppose he is right, but then that is in the nature of prayer; if there is a benevolent God, presumably it is the nature rather than the existence of the answer that is hard to understand, especially at the time.

David the Dominican decided it was time I had my cowardly commitment to the whole business galvanised by a visible, communal prayer for healing and strength. I gulped. However, he was thinking of what the Catholic Church used to call extreme unction and now calls the sacrament of the sick; I did not mind that. I was curious. I had always supposed extreme unction to be no more than a last-minute possibility, but I had read some recent articles about the changes it had undergone over the centuries before arriving at that status. It seems that in the early Christian Church the sacrament had been primarily one of healing and that is what David wanted it to be for me.

When I asked Mark about it, I thought he would be upset, but if he was, he did not show it. His first reaction to the idea was intellectual, as I had expected it to be. He agreed that the early sacrament had been as much one of healing as last blessing, so the proposal was true to history, which means a lot to Mark. Emotionally, I think he may have been helped by the support his first wife, who was a Protestant, had gained from a service of healing and blessing she had been given when she was dying of cancer. It had not saved her life, but she had often mentioned it as a source of strength in the cruel period of life left to her.

I was full of doubts about the sacrament I was to be given, but also full of interest and delighted when Mark said he would join in with it. Neither of us knew exactly what it would entail, but David told us to choose a gospel reading; it was not hard to choose the one about the healing of the epileptic boy. My friend Kate, who had come on my forgotten holiday to Greece with me, was staying with us at the time and did the reading.

We were in the sitting-room, by the fire. There were just four of us: myself, Mark, Kate and David, who arrived in his Dominican habit. His only hesitation before beginning was for a brief attempt to involve Peter, who did not want to be there. Peter knows David well, though not closely. This time he did not want to talk to him. He looked determinedly down at a comic. I showed more interest than he did when David showed us the pyx, the tiny container for the communion host, which I had encountered in catechism questions and answers about the sacraments when I was Peter's age.

Peter wanted nothing to do with the sacrament, so we left him downstairs with a packet of crisps, reading a book. He cheered up afterwards when David came to dinner.

I have one main memory of the sacrament: David stretching out his hands and putting them on my head, leaving them there for what felt like a long time but I think was only about half a minute, while he prayed quietly. So did I, for healing and for help. The only thing I could hear was the fire burning.

Hands-on-head must be a basic healing gesture and, with David's hands, it felt like an attacking one, too, trying to meet a challenge. I did not feel physically different or better afterwards, but I did feel blessed. Although I was not sur- prised, I was disappointed when I started having fits again soon afterwards. David looked sad when I told him about them.

I'm sure he is right that the sacrament should be a rare, not a regular event. All I can do now is back it up with prayers that it stays with me – preferably in the straightforward way which gives me the glorious weeks I have been enjoying more often recently, with nothing to do but live. Failing that, in the obscure way that makes it a painful victory to open my eyes and realise I am alive.

CHAPTER NINE

Help from Elsewhere

I thought my mother was joking when she rang up and told me that I was entitled to reduced train fares because of my epilepsy. When I laughed, she assured me it was true. She had turned on too early for a television programme and seen the last few minutes of an information bulletin for the disabled, who apparently count me as one of their number in matters of transport. With a 'disabled person's railcard' I could travel cheaply; or at any rate more cheaply than usual.

I did not believe I would qualify for such a card but went to the station, where they gave me a leaflet about it. The necessary qualifications made a daunting list: blind or deaf; reduced to driving an invalid's three-wheeled vehicle; at least 80% disabled due to war injuries. . . Only one disability was required, but many were mentioned and all were grievous. I hurried down to the end of the list, where I found I was eligible for a card if I had 'epilepsy with a continuing liability to seizures'. All I had to do was pay £12 and get a confirmatory letter from Professor C. to go with my application.

I suppose it is because epilepsy with seizures means I am not allowed to drive that public transport is made cheaper; it is the only form of transport I can use on my own. The laws on epilepsy and driving were eased in August 1994. A qualified driver who had to stop because of epilepsy can now return to driving when he or she has had one year without daytime seizures. The minimum period used to be two years. Both are in cloud cuckoo land for me.

I got my railcard and I use it a lot. No rail official has ever looked too surprised when not only I but also one accompanying passenger, both of us in good health, have travelled at reduced prices. I need an escort in case I have a fit. The only reason for regret is that the price of the card has risen while the discount has fallen; but it is still worthwhile.

Why stop at trains? I rang the County Council, who told me to go to my local Council office, armed with medical confirmation of my condition, if I wanted a concessionary bus pass. When they said the cost of a bus pass was only £5 and was soon to be reduced to £3.50 in special cases like mine, I knew something was due to go wrong.

I cycled across town to the nearest Council offices and queued for over twenty minutes before the lady behind the shatterproof glass screen told me my medical letter was no good because it was from the hospital consultant, not my family doctor. I told her it was the consultant who looked after my epilepsy.

'Yes, but not your health,' she replied.

'Well, it's my epilepsy that prevents me from driving, so shouldn't it be his letter I show you for a medically induced bus pass?'

'I wouldn't know about that. You'd better try Benefits.'

'Benefits' meant the Social Security office further down the road and I walked there apprehensively, stopping on the way to buy a delicious magazine because I knew that waiting there would be more like camping than queueing. It is an open-plan office with an atmosphere of failure, deepened by the clients clustering around nowhere in particular, looking as if they've failed even before they've begun. I was sure I should not be in Benefits for my bus-pass.

So was the lady behind the screen, who told me that Benefits was not for me and that Transport had moved temporarily to Housing, which was a long way further down the road.

'Housing?'

'Don't stare at me. It's not my idea. I've had people at me all day. Go to Housing and get at them.'

I went. I was just about at the point where it was worth

sticking it out, whatever the nuisance, to vindicate the effort I'd already put in. On the other hand, of course, I use the bike more often than I use the bus . . .

But by now I had reached Housing and they made short work of my query, directing me back to the offices where I had started. There a different lady behind a different screen not only accepted Professor C.'s letter but said they must keep it to copy on to their computer file, so they could refer to it each year and be nice and fast producing a pass, which only cost £3.50. I cycled home, pass in pocket, impatient to use it.

All I needed on the traffic front now was something for the car. But even I blushed a bit at the thought of asking for a disabled car-parking sticker (sounds daft, like the 'disabled toilet' across the road), having received my other disabled cards on the basis of not being able to drive. Still, I own our car and the fact that I can only go in it with a driver made it easy for me to get an orange badge, in case I need an unscheduled stop.

We hardly ever use the card. The only time our use of it has ever provoked doubt was when Mark, not I, started limping in order to look disabled. We had arrived late at Chelmsford cricket ground, where I was due to do a midday interview with Graham Gooch, then Captain of England, for my newspaper. It was midday before we arrived at the ground, unable to find a parking space. After exhaustive searching, we gave up and went for one of the empty spaces in the 'disabled' section of the multi-storey car park next to the ground.

The space was on the ground floor, so I took the stuff I needed to do the interview and ran off, flashing my press-card at the man on the gate and charging up the stairs separating me from Gooch. Mark was embarrassed at displaying the disabled card while I zoomed off, so he started limping, to the amazement of the car-park attendant, who did not believe either of us was disabled. A fast moving passenger – surely not; a suddenly crippled driver – certainly not.

I have stopped short of displaying one of my disabled cards on the bike, to help gate-crash an entry into the exclusively pedestrian central area of town. I might be able to justify my vehicular intrusion by arguing that as I am disabled I cannot walk. But on a bike such an argument would be tempting providence.

Riding bikes in busy areas is one of the many activities discouraged for epileptics whose attacks can happen without warning. It is easy to see why, but as my attacks start with a nocturnal introduction, I am never bike-borne when I have fits. I find diabetes, with its day-and-night potential for causing trouble, much more risky than epilepsy.

Motorcycle-riding, flying aircraft, testing military aircraft, travelling in light aircraft, hang-gliding, parachuting, mountaineering, diving, vehicle-racing and horse-racing are activities which even the insurance company used by the British Epilepsy Association, providing special support for epileptics, excludes from its personal accident policies. For obvious reasons.

Some less dramatic sports are dangerous for less obvious reasons. 'Never fish alone,' warns the BEA leaflet, *Epilepsy, Sport and Leisure*, though solitude is part of the appeal of fishing. An epileptic must fish in a life-jacket, with a companion who knows what to do if he has a seizure. I doubt if many epileptics follow that advice, or the equally depressing admonition not to go for long walks alone.

Life insurance for epileptics is at least as complicated a matter as accident insurance, the close connection between the two being more than usually full of possible hazards when a person has epilepsy. Less than a century ago, on October 5th 1904, the great neurologist Sir William Gowers exhilarated the Life Assurance Medical Officers' Association with a paper called *Insanity and Epilepsy in Relation to Life Assurance*. Using a huge haul of insurance statistics gathered by the Scottish Widows Fund over a period of twenty years, he found that epilepsy was 'a rare cause for insurance claims', but he still concluded his speech with the question: 'Is an epileptic insurable?' and the hard answer: 'Possibly, if extra is charged.'

The reason for this answer was that insurers then found

epilepsy seldom a direct but more often an indirect cause of death, which is the ultimate expense for insurers. Drowning and falling were the two causes of death that Gowers cited as the most common, along with one which I have never come across anywhere else but which makes obvious sense: turning over in bed and suffocating with the face in the pillow. This is an epileptic version of 'cot-death', particularly dangerous for people sleeping alone, with no-one to pull them free to breathe.

Today many post-mortems performed on epileptics who have died in their sleep still produce this 'cot-death' verdict, but in the last few years people have questioned and criticised the verdict as a 'cover-up'. Dr Stephen Brown of the David Lewis Centre, which assesses and cares for chronic epileptics, is one of the few doctors unhappy with the 'cot-death' interpretation; he is trying to find out what it is that causes the sudden death of some epileptics.

'There's not a shred of evidence that anyone has suffocated on a pillow,' he said, keen to point out that as many as 1,500 people a year in Britain die of Sudep (Sudden Unexpected Death in Epilepsy). Possible causes of death are hard to pin down, particularly when one is working with a tiny research budget – only about £360,000 government money a year – and little sophisticated equipment to examine brain and heart activity in epileptics.

However, Dr Brown is about to publish a paper which he thinks will show some evidence that victims of Sudep have abnormal brain and heart waves at the time of their death. He is uncertain what results his work will generate.

Doctors are reluctant to admit how many epileptics, most of them men under forty years of age, die suddenly during fits. Few doctors can explain these deaths or suggest ways of preventing them. Neither local epileptic groups nor ill-equipped hospitals like to give sudden epileptic deaths much publicity; an accidental, unavoidable cause of death, such as suffocation, is the least troublesome verdict to give after such deaths.

It was relatives of Sudep victims who set up a support group, Epilepsy Bereaved, in 1991 to discuss their losses and see how best to press for more research into the subject. This last is a hard task. Great hopes are being pinned by the National Society for Epilepsy on the eventual progress that may be made by the world's first magnetic resonance imaging (MRI) unit, paid for by a charitable appeal and set up at the NSE's headquarters in Chalfont St Giles, Buckinghamshire.

The NSE fights brave campaigns in the sorry field of epileptic care, to help epileptics find better information, advice or treatment. As the leading epileptic medical organisation in the country, it provides treatment itself. Its new MRI unit is an ultra-sensitive brain scanner, which has a massive electromagnet capable of stimulating the brain to give radio signals of its activity, even if the signal is no more than one millimetre big.

Researchers like Dr Brown and Professor Simon Shorvon, medical director of the NSE, hope that the minute detail it gives of a brain's structure and activity may help to explain the processes of epileptic activity and fatalities. But it will be a long time before that is likely to be within easy range of doctors interested in research into subjects as unpopular as sudden death in epilepsy.

Drowning in the bath is a household disaster easily caused by epilepsy. Like suffocating, it cannot be singled out for public prevention, only private education to increase awareness of the dangers. I remember a middle-aged nurse at the hospital clinic giving me knowing looks and tips not to lock the door when I had a bath.

'One good shudder and that's that. Choked and drowned at one go and you'd know nothing about it.'

I suppose she's right. I never lock the bathroom door anyway, so, short of giving up baths altogether, there is not much else I can do. Out of interest, I rang four life insurance companies and asked about the possibility of getting a policy with them, in view of the fact that I have epilepsy. All four said they would need more medical information before giving me an answer. That was fair. Two companies rang back as they had promised, after collecting some more details and asking higher members of staff for their opinions. Both paid more attention to my diabetes than my epilepsy, which also seemed fair.

The company which asked the most questions about what the lady called 'this sensitive subject' thought that life insurance might be possible, 'but it would mean quite heavy loading', just as Gowers had concluded a century ago. We did not get as far as picking out areas which would be thought to entail special risk and thus invite especially high 'loading', but water and air are areas of work where epileptics often have trouble getting jobs.

I'm probably letting down my epileptic brethren by saying so, but I have a lot of sympathy with the employers. Even if the epilepsy is well controlled and the person only has infrequent attacks which amount to no more than brief 'absences', epilepsy makes possible death-traps of jobs like sailing and working at sea, or those which require constant balance, like using high scaffolding, or jobs where a momentary loss of concentration could be fatal, like fire fighting. The worst thing is that the death-trap can catch other people besides the one with epilepsy.

That must also be true of work requiring minutely accurate skills; surgery comes straight to mind as a risky prospect when performed by an epileptic; but then so might sitting by a fire. How does one know where to draw the line between caution and neurosis? If an epileptic has his first seizure in years when crossing a road, thereby causing a car crash and killing someone, surely that does not mean he should have stayed at home and never gone out. Everything in life has its hazards; only the most obvious epileptic risks deserve to be singled out for avoidance.

I supported the *Civil Rights (Disabled Persons) Bill*, 'talked out' by the government in March 1994, because it opposed discrimination against disabled people, including epileptics, if the discrimination were purely because of their disability.

If their disability stopped them doing a job, living in a flat, fulfilling a contract, whatever was required – fair enough; someone else should get preference. In all other cases, the promoters of the Bill hoped, disability would be ranked alongside sex and skin colour as insufficient grounds for automatic discrimination.

With the failure of that Bill, parliamentary efforts to help epileptics have had to make do with pressing for better hospital services, including more specialised epilepsy clinics rather than general neurology clinics where epilepsy is one of many interests. John Battle, MP for Leeds West, is a vigorous champion of that cause. Doubtless his championship is spurred on by the fact that Leeds is home not only to his constituency but also to the British Epilepsy Association, a fearless body.

The BEA does not waste time trying to develop a glamorous image. Its quarterly magazine sports the uncompromising title *Epilepsy Today*, which does not make it casual reading for passers-by or those who feel like a change from *Vogue*. When I got diabetes, I was given a copy of the British Diabetic Association's magazine, originally called *The Diabetic Journal*, then after the war changed to a milder tone and a new title, *Balance*. This was thought to suggest interest in the management of carbohydrate levels in the blood and also in the management of diabetic public relations.

Epilepsy Today has no such modifications. Its name has a ghastly splendour which makes me laugh whenever I pick the magazine up, which is not often. I find it full of 'pinball' offerings from epileptics all over the world describing the mistreatment their condition has brought them. There are details of countless conferences, drugs, medical and media items, social and fund-raising events concerned with epilepsy. It would be a relief to find someone now and then who appeared less devoted to the task of looking normal, though I understand the cause.

A recent issue of *Epilepsy Today* deplored the fact that in a twelve-month 'media monitoring exercise', organised by the BEA to see how often ordinary newspapers and magazines mentioned epilepsy, 'around 35% of the clippings did, however, label people with epilepsy as epileptic or epileptics.' Sounds reasonable to me, but apparently it threatens those people's normality. The BEA regards the terms as 'unhelpful, and often misleading'.

I know what they mean about the drawbacks of labelling people, but my normality smothers me if I pursue it too consciously or too long and I would rather read about some of the BEA's other offerings.

At the heart of them is information. The BEA writes, prints and distributes a prodigious number of leaflets each year, aiming to fulfil the 'right to information' which it includes in its *Charter for People with Epilepsy*, a manifesto of epileptic rights. When I was told I had epilepsy, I was not given any information about the condition, except for Professor C.'s unprogrammed talk on the day of my diagnosis, an oasis of explanation in all my ignorant misery. I would like to say that the few granules of fact I have extracted from the hospital since then have removed my misery, but they have not; they have filled it out.

The diabetic clinic is wallpapered with teaching about diabetes and all that goes with it. There is a chiropodist, a dietician and a nursing sister, each in her own office, overflowing with advice. By comparison, the epilepsy clinic is bare. It is hard to discuss anything about either diabetes or epilepsy with a hospital doctor because it is clear they have not got the time. The difference is that facts about diabetes look accessible, indeed almost inescapable, to those attending the clinic, whereas facts about epilepsy have the air of privileged information. Hence the crusading attitude of the BEA.

Though I am happiest with the minimum of information, I would rather understand, in principle if not in detail, what is happening to me, so I can ask questions when it goes wrong. Information on the scale provided by the BEA for those who want it is admirable, but it is often too much for me. Its 'literature list' boasts among many possible purchases a marvellously sleazy-sounding item, the 'adult's information package'. This contains a video called *Not as Frightening as it Sounds* and 'a new leaflet about managing your epilepsy, including a weekly seizure diary'.

Heady stuff.

The great range of available information is entwined with moral support, both assets indispensable to the public as well as the epileptic if the condition is to grow out of its image as an evil too frightening to treat. Information lines at the BEA give pre-recorded telephone answers to the most common questions asked about epilepsy, including ones about employment, children and driving. More frantic questions can be answered 'live' on their Freephone helpline.

In the interests of this chapter, I made myself go to a meeting of the BEA's local group, held in a Quaker meeting-hall not far from where we live. This excellent place hires itself out to a wide variety of societies, on days when it is not being used by the Quakers. That weekend the ground floor was the scene for the Young Astronomers' Monthly Meeting, to which I have taken Peter on many a Saturday morning. Upstairs there was the BEA monthly meeting, signposted by a blackboard bleakly chalked EPILEPSY.

An arrow pointed upwards, so up I went, full of dread. I was agreeably surprised by the many piles of BEA pamphlets on display, for me to choose not to read. A smart, friendly lady who was drinking coffee and browsing through the pamphlets, said she would have liked to know more about her epilepsy but was told nothing about it or about the drugs she was given to combat it. Now she looked at pamphlets every so often, when she felt up to it. Casting a baleful eye on the *Epilepsy and Alcohol* offering, she said she thought we would do better without it. I agreed. We both knew, through bitter experience, that wine neutralises our anti-convulsants, but also that one small drink of some other sort, as long as it is not wine, usually does no harm.

'No-one's going to take away my gin and tonic,' said the lady, turning that little pile of pamphlets upside-down.

She was only too pleased to hear that a small quantity of

alcohol, with its relaxing properties, can be reckoned to be positively anti-convulsant. It is larger quantities that can have a dangerous effect, hours later, lowering the blood sugar and so raising the likelihood of fits. I don't know why wine is the villain of the piece, but everyone there agreed that it is. I find that even one glass is sometimes one glass too many.

The friendly lady advised me with a smile, 'Stick to gin, dear.'

I didn't oppress her with all the diabetic complications I have to take into account if I am offered a drink. Any such talk could quickly have turned into a contest about the number of difficult conditions in each of our lives. I thought we were feeling quite sorry enough for ourselves already, without showing off any more of our reasons.

Being a small group, six of us, with intermittent visits from the mildly epileptic daughter of the lady in charge, it was easy to swop details of our epilepsies. I had been sure this would be ghastly, with competitive lashings of misery, but in fact it was not so much miserable as pathetic, most of the time. Everyone said they would have liked to know more about their epilepsy and how best to live with it. Everyone felt a burden on the people they lived with or went out with. The only question was whether to try to turn that feeling into a fight for improvement or a serene acceptance.

The couple running the group – Mr and Mrs G. – were of the fighting school. When Mr G. was told by his local hospital that there was nothing left to lighten the heavy burden of his fits, except resignation, he walked out and presented himself at Queen Square in London. There, he said, they have treated him much better and his epilepsy has got much better. The point to which he and his wife attached most importance was the willingness of Queen Square to prescribe new drugs. There are several new anti-convulsants reputed to be far more effective than the old ones, but they are so expensive that they are usually only prescribed in special cases in special hospitals, hardly ever in the neurology clinics of general hospitals.

Recitals of drugs' achievements ensued. I listened

unhappily. I am probably predisposed to doubt such druggish glories, having aggravated my diabetes and brought on my epilepsy by falling for the reported triumphs of human insulin. I should have stayed on my animal insulin, as my consultant advised. I was glad to get back to it after a hectic spell of the new human glory, so these new anti-convulsant promises struck a warning note. Just as well when I have to deal with a hospital dismissed by Mrs G. as 'short on money and drugs, so all you get is what they've got'.

I was less sure in my anger than Mrs G., who described with appetite how her husband was wired up to a machine for five days, to test the electrical over-activity of his brain. This had only happened when he had moved on to 'higher' hospitals. When these tests failed to show clear answers, he was given one of the new anti-convulsants anyway. Needless to say, it had transformed his life. An excess of caution and a lack of funds were decried as obvious faults of the local hospital system, particularly where drugs were concerned, though Mrs G. did acknowledge that one set of new drugs prescribed for her husband 'sent him bonkers, so he came off that lot double quick'.

What did she mean by bonkers?

'Oh, you know, made him bad-tempered; one day he picked me up and tried to chuck me under a bus.'

Yet even the dangers of being made bonkers on that scale could not compare with the advantages of the new drug on which Mr G. now lived and thrived. Evidently he had failed in his chucking. Mrs G. is strong and would be a serious proposition for getting under a bus, even with the help of extra epileptic aggression. Mr and Mrs G. had no doubt that when it came to drugs it was better to try a change if need be, rather than refrain from having a go.

With my hard-won attitude of doubt towards having a medical go, I kept quiet, wondering whether any of this could be helping the rest of the group. It was unsettling, which I suppose might prompt people in search of help to ask their doctors more questions, but which can also be frightening.

The mood of the meeting was vigorous. Though drug-changing looked like something of a one-family issue, the desire for more knowledge was unanimous. I even found myself agreeing to pay part of the cost of an information video about epilepsy, for the next meeting. I had not intended to go to the next meeting, but it would have been mean to refuse.

I was told to look out for a pamphlet about 'mobility grants', to which it was thought I might be entitled. If it is not safe for me to be left on my own for more than two weeks, I may be able to claim the cost of hiring a night-time guardian, if I do have to be left that long. The money does not have to be spent on that but, as Mrs G. put it crisply, 'If the loot is sitting there, you might as well use it.'

Even so, I hope I never have to be a fortnight without Mark and I know two meetings of this group will do. I was glad to leave. I am not a natural disciple of public meetings, even meetings of alliance or common interest. I have no doubt that I would wilt if I went to many conferences and meetings about epilepsy. I lack the public commitment displayed by Mr and Mrs G.

There is an impressive number of voluntary local groups like this one all over Britain, each with its own special angle on the merciless sentence to which epilepsy sentences its recruits. Some help people deal with epilepsy as a rare, distressing syndrome afflicting children. At the more unusual end of the range is a new group called 'Support Dogs', set up to get epilepsy recognised as one of the disabilities for which guide dogs are trained and supplied. Nothing is beyond consideration.

It made me nervous and it was humbling, attending a meeting run with diligence on the scale shown by the Gs. It sounded as if most of their excursions so far have been restricted to this country, but there is no reason they should stay like that. Epileptic Internet is now a fact of life. Personal international discussion of epilepsy exists. Doctors, medical and pharmaceutical experts attend international meetings and

I dare say representatives of epileptic street-life can get themselves included if they want.

One of the most recent international conferences on epilepsy took as its topic 'epilepsy and society', reflecting the growth of official and popular interest in this aspect of the condition. It was held in autumn 1994 in Veldhoven, just outside Eindhoven in Holland, with the help of the International Bureau for Epilepsy, a 1960s off-shoot of the BEA. The IBE shares with its parent body the same determination to teach all sorts of people about epilepsy, so that those who suffer from it can more easily flourish as human beings.

CHAPTER TEN

St Piers Hospital School

It must be the helmets. I've always hated the protective helmets that chronic epileptics need to wear. A few are made of
padded metal, with wires across the face, not unlike the helmets worn by batsmen facing dangerous bowling. Most are
made of hard rubber, with a strong band of it, at least an
inch thick, encircling the head, just above the eyes. From there
the fearful possibilities are many: ear-pads; straps and pads
under the chin; further buckled-on bands; black, brown or
bright coloured rubber all over the top of the head.

I am a coward about helmets. I understand how they help
to protect someone who is having violent seizures – but I am
appalled by them. When I went recently to look round the
old 'colony' for epileptics, now St Piers Hospital School, in
the village where I grew up, I was impressed by it and by
what I saw there, but I was appalled by the helmets. I associate them with the epileptic children's blubbering and the sad
stares that used to frighten me as a child. I have grown up a bit
about those, but I will need a lot more practice and self-control
before I can claim to have grown up about helmets.

I think familiarity is probably the key to the process. After
spending a day at the hospital school I felt better than I had
done when I started. I began my tour by going to one of the
classrooms for children aged only five or six, in the 'very
low ability' category. There were four children, none of them
capable of any sort of speech, all releasing drones and whoops
every so often from their helmeted heads.

In some funny way, I did not mind the classroom of 'minimum ability' pupils as much. The two girls there, who were

several years older than those in the first classroom, were strapped into wheelchairs; their helmets were huge and reinforced with metal; their teachers seemed to be communicating with them only by kindly touching and stroking. Perhaps the fact that these girls looked so severely handicapped physically as well as mentally resigned me to their need for helmets. Here headgear was only one among many horrors. With the less severely handicapped children, the helmets were cruel scars on young, handsome appearances that engendered false hopes.

Half an hour after arriving at St Piers Hospital School, my feelings about it were as painful as I remembered them being in my childhood, but they were closer range, with new poignancy. Before, I had only been at St Piers as a domestic help or cleaner, to earn money. Now I was there for more personal reasons, meeting staff and pupils, talking to them, eating with them, liking them, feeling for them.

The staff asked me to call the place St Piers, which has always been its name but one that has only recently come into widespread use. They regard it as a gentler name than the one it used to be known by: The Colony, or the name that took over from that: The Hospital School. The name St Piers does not spell out with such brutal clarity exactly what the place is. No-one knows who St Piers was, in life or in legend, or why The Hospital School was named after him, but the name is presumed to be an English version of the French name St Pierre.

Over the centuries, many saints have been prayed to on behalf of epileptics, but their number has never, as far as I know, included St Peter. St Piers therefore remains an ideal mystery name, where nothing can be proved or disproved. Not just Lingfield's Hospital School but also the lane leading to it are called after him. When I first lived in Lingfield, about forty years ago, the lane was almost always called Colony Lane, occasionally St Piers Lane if one was talking formally or to outsiders.

Dr Besag, today's medical director of St Piers, looks like

the brilliant psychiatrist that he is, charming and distant. He was not very interested in the question of names and pointed out to me crisply that St Piers was not a new name he was trying to impose upon the place, but an old name he was trying to give back to it. So he was a reformer and a traditionalist at the same time.

The prime expert at combining these two positions is the lady who welcomed me with a coffee before I started my tour of St Piers. Mrs Luksepp has been working there for almost forty years. Her life-long knowledge of the place is an asset in itself. As part of her amiable personality it suggests a valuable stability, untroubled by change.

'The biggest change I have seen here is not one specific thing, like a building or a person, but the overall atmosphere. The whole set-up used to be more cut off from the outside world.'

Back in the 1960s, when the pupils were first allowed to swop their thick, dark grey uniform shirts for colourful Marks and Spencer's T-shirts, the more cheerful impression this made was largely wasted on the public because the public hardly ever saw the pupils.

St Piers has only one chapel. There is a Christian chaplain, a jolly looking lady who hurried past us as we talked. She has the advantage of having been a nurse at Great Ormond Street Hospital.

St Piers was founded in 1896 by the Christian Union for Social Service. The Union, unusually for the time, was made up of clergy of all Christian denominations. There was always a strong Christian motive behind The Colony, which had the original purpose of training both farm labourers and epileptics, then in 1912 was dedicated solely to the care of epileptics.

There are still many Christian pupils there, among staff and children, but since 1963 The Hospital School, given that name instead of The Colony in 1957, has been an independent voluntary school with no official Christian allegiance.

Back in the 1960s, when the Roman Catholic pupils used to come into the village for mass on Sundays, they were kept in a group together, apart from the rest of us. I think it was thought fairer to all alike – public, pupils and nervous nurses – to keep everyone in the areas they were used to, where they would not feel so awkward if things went wrong. For the pupils this meant the back rows of the church, out of sight.

Dr Besag echoed Mrs Luksepp's delight at the fuller integration of St Piers life and village life nowadays.

'The village is used to these children and kind to them. If a mishap occurs, a child is often found having a cup of tea in a shop.'

This could have been no more than benevolent propaganda, but I had stayed the night before with my parents, who still live in Lingfield and have no reason to tell me anything but the truth about St Piers, and they had said the same as Dr Besag.

Getting used to the physical horrors of epilepsy seems to be helping villagers to cope with them. There is just about nothing that can or should be done if someone starts having a seizure, except perhaps loosening their collar so they don't choke, or putting a jacket under their head so they don't smash it to pieces. But staying calm enough to be kind, to find chairs to sit on and tea to drink afterwards, is a tremendous bonus. It may not make much difference medically, but it must help psychologically. The patient still feels like a monster, but only a second-class monster and the person who has survived the monster's worst offerings feels more confident. If there is a next time, neither of them will be so upset by it.

St Piers is what my parents call 'a fair walk' from the village. It is no more than a mile past Notre Dame School, where I spent many happy years of my life persecuting the nuns who used to – but no longer – teach there. But Notre Dame is about a mile past the village, so the 'fair walk' must be something in the region of two miles. A left turn off the small main road out of Lingfield boasts only Notre Dame, then a tiny sprinkling of uncertain buildings and then The Hospital School. St Piers Lane never had any intention of going anywhere except its Hospital School. Actually it can also be used as a back way through to Edenbridge, a small town with a factory estate, about eight miles away, so it is not a dead end.

But, as a Lingfield patriot nurse at St Piers asked me with a shrug and a chuckle, 'Who on earth wants to go the back way to Edenbridge?'

If Lingfield villagers want a pleasant walk, there is plenty of pretty country round about; they do not go down St Piers Lane. It is the St Piers pupils who have to do the 'fair walk' to the village, which is all the more of an achievement given that 'the average mental level of the pupils has dropped about 50% while the level of communication has risen about 50% since the time you lived here', in the words of one St Piers teacher. Many of the pupils are severely mentally and perhaps also physically handicapped, but they manage to get out and about more often, to work as well as play. A few of the older ones do part-time work in the banana-packing factory near Lingfield Station. My mother always says hello to one girl from St Piers who does short stints in the supermarket, stacking things on shelves.

I would like to think that the worsening in the level of mental ability is an indication of milder epileptics being more often and more easily looked after at home these days, with no more need to board them out. This would leave hospital schools free to concentrate on more serious cases. The staff were keen to lend me a video about the changes at St Piers since the time when I knew it. We have not got a video-player, but the tape delivered much of its message in the title written on the box holding it: *Stigma and After*. Would that this were the 'After' era. Stigma has had long enough.

I was struck by the fact that back home in Cambridge, several people in the local shops asked me about epilepsy, after seeing a recent television programme about it. Television exposure is a popular modern push towards public acceptance and accessibility in general, a distant aim but one worth fighting for. I got the definite impression at St Piers that pupils feel more readily accepted now than when I remember them as objects of fear and amazement.

The sadder interpretation of the low mental level of St Piers pupils is that there is nowhere else for children with such severe disabilities to be looked after. It is less common to hide them away at home and heart-breakingly difficult to find them help at a suitable school. Britain has three big epilepsy assessment centres, at York, Oxford and Chalfont St Peter in Buckinghamshire. It has only two residential homes for epileptics, one in London and one in Cheshire, and only three hospital schools like St Piers, for children too badly afflicted to be cared for at home.

The only one of these that I have seen is St Piers, which has 225 pupils, from as far away as Switzerland, Ireland and the Channel Islands. It is a non-maintained charity and sending a child there would be a heavy expense for a local education authority trying to cut its costs. The cost of places is bound to be high. At St Piers anything classed as a 'special project', beyond normal running requirements, has to be paid for by voluntary contributions. At present, St Piers has about three million pounds to raise, to pay for a 'special project' putting into practice what Dr Besag described as 'the new schemes of an adventurous architect'.

My parents and their friends are happy to go all the time to fêtes, fairs, sales and any events that raise money for St Piers, just as people have been happily giving money to it ever since it started. If the event is, as it were, a home fixture, it also gives an on-the-spot view of the work for which the money is needed.

I had fleeting glimpses of a big, new building under construction, but did not have time to get a good look at any of it, except the bare bones of its roof, silhouetted against the sky. The only building I saw at close quarters was one of the school houses, where I had lunch. It was nothing like my memories of St Piers school houses, more like a holiday chalet. Its over-riding advantage is that it has only six or seven pupils living there; I'm not sure exactly how many because they weren't all back from half-term when I was there, but it is a small number.

None of the houses has more than sixteen pupils living in it. Each has at least one domestic assistant and seven 'care' staff. Where the children need more intensive individual care, there are fewer children and more staff. Farmhouse, where I had lunch, has a live-in member of staff, whose room is in the same bright, light-wood, loud-duvet style as the individual rooms of the teenagers with whom she lives.

Like all the houses, Farmhouse has its own kitchen, where a couple of house members were cooking themselves snacks from the food they had just come back from buying in the village. Dean was tucking into a pizza which he had given a well-timed spell under the grill, until its cheese was at that perfect combination of the long and the gooey. He gave me some of the grapes he was going to have as a second course. The pupils told me they are only allowed to use the oven if a member of staff is in the house. I can see why. I have the same make of oven at home and the perils of its unreliable inner fittings are many, without the obvious added dangers if the person using it were suddenly to fall out of action or unconscious.

One Farmhouse girl, Claire, had been appointed by the school management as my guide for the morning and, after fetching lunch for both of us from the staff kitchens nearby, she showed me proudly round the house. I won't go on about it in detail. What matters is to give a sense of the independence reflected in all its most attractive points, from the kitchen available for everyone to use to the luxurious bathroom, its shelves lined with bottles of Body Shop lotions.

Farmhouse is a house for the oldest and most able pupils. Claire is in this 'maximum ability' group, a world away from the first groups I saw on my tour. Despite being paralysed all down her right side, which means she has a blind right eye, Claire is doing an Open University course in computer studies, backed up by the excellent I.T. teaching of the St Piers further education unit.

It was not always like that. Claire told me that when she first came to the Hospital School, it was much more of a hospital than a school for her because she had seizures constantly. As she showed me round the woodwork, metalwork, I.T., domestic science and craft and design departments of the further education unit, she was greeted everywhere as an old friend, known of old through many troubles.

The man teaching metalwork told me, above the shrill scream of saw-blades cutting tin, 'Different noises bring different students seizures. This sort of high-pitched sound can easily start seizures.'

Claire nodded. 'Used to do it with me.'

'Anything did it with you,' he said with a dry smile.

You couldn't have heard a reply even if Claire made one. I felt a bit nervous, but both the helmeted pupils who were using saw-blades looked all right. One was making a hanging basket for flowers, the other a weather vane. Another boy at a different table was slowly screwing together strips of metal and looked more tentative.

Claire told me she has not had a seizure for two and a half years. Dean and the two young men I met in Farmhouse had never had a seizure.

'Don't ask me what they're in here for,' snorted Claire. Though she was tired by the time we had finished our mammoth tour – which I suspect was one among several with which she had been burdened in recent weeks – she was in good spirits.

Claire is a show-case for St Piers' triple purpose, triply expensive to put into effect, but all the more satisfying the more it can achieve. It seeks to be a combination of hospital, school and care centre. I confess to an instinctive distrust of the term 'care', the same sort of distrust I have of the term 'counselling', because I am not sure what they mean. The terms are often used with a slightly aggressive air, to suggest forces at once relevant, public and undefined, disguised in jargon.

The principal care officer at St Piers, described by Dr Besag as 'a great character' and by my parents as 'a saint', won me on to the side of care within a minute of our meeting, with his dulcet greeting, 'Ah, yes, grand to see you. I last saw Ms McLean in a betting shop, about twenty-five years ago. Welcome back.'

How could I resist?

One of the care officers in his department told me about the vital part care had to play at St Piers. 'Social skills are at the heart of it.'

I recoiled inwardly in case these skills were left without further description, but he went on, crisp and clear.

'That means we help severely handicapped children to walk, talk, eat without help, perhaps in groups with friends, dress themselves, keep themselves clean and hygienic, respond when people talk to them.'

The list was long and the range was wide. We had just come from looking at the lowest ability class, which stinks because the pupils are incontinent and all the problems are horrifyingly obvious. At the other end of the range, where abilities are highest, problems are more subtly apparent and thus need sensitive help from care officers if they are to be solved.

Claire no longer finds it a daunting task to write a letter, operate a computer or fill in forms and job applications, thanks to the combined efforts of doctors who have eased her epilepsy, teachers who have got her up to a high enough academic level to pass useful public examinations, and care officers who have taught her to make the most of these gains. They have transformed her life. In future, when I feel catty on the subject of care, I'll think of what the care officers at St Piers have given their lives to doing for the pupils there and bite my lip. On purpose.

The ratio of staff to pupils is extremely high, often one to one, or even two staff to one pupil if need be. It was only to be expected, though it still came as a shock, that St Piers has at least 480 staff, sometimes with many more part-time staff as well, for its 225 pupils. In the same way as I seem to have spent the whole time since I got epilepsy meeting people who have family or friends with epilepsy, the one night I spent

with my parents in Lingfield seemed to be full of local people
who worked at St Piers. The woman next door, who chats to
my mother over the garden hedge, turns out to do part-time
work at St Piers. The whole neighbourhood abounds in
St Piers employees.

Not wanting to be a wet blanket, I thought I ought to ask
how often all this high level of help leads older pupils to jobs
and interesting occupations after school. Looking at everything the pupils were managing to do, I had visions of them
sitting at home when they had left St Piers, alone and frustrated, with no-one willing to give them a job and all the skills
they had acquired going to waste.

I asked Mr Brown, a senior teacher at St Piers, about this
and he sighed.

'I always felt this is an area where we should do more.
They normally leave at nineteen and a lot of pupils go back
to their home area. The principal child care officer did a
follow-up study of those who left in 1991. It was quite interesting and quite disheartening. After spending as much as fourteen years down here, they go out into the world and their
fate is left to careers officers and social workers in their home
area and it all depends on how much is going on in that
area.'

He shrugged. I shrugged in sympathy. I was glad when we
reached another of the teaching units, away from our silence
as we walked.

If life is going to be shit, you might as well get the best bit
of shit within your range. St Piers' policy is to encourage its
pupils to do as much as they possibly can, even if the work
technically counts as dangerous and may lead to no more
obvious advantage than the invaluable 'growth of self-esteem'
beloved of care spokesmen.

To name but a few activities on offer at St Piers, some
requiring courses outside the school: horse-riding, canoeing,
swimming, mountaineering, work in the large school farm and
gardens or, for the naturally hearty, on the 'confidence course'
set up there for them by the army, with opportunities to swing

from ropes between trees or pick a balanced way across a swinging bridge.

My parents thought they remembered one of the pupils at St Piers being killed a few years ago, while involved in an activity. But as my father remarked, 'You could be killed as you fell, anywhere, any time. It was ill fortune.'

Thank God, it has not weakened the St Piers philosophy that as long as pupils are closely and carefully supervised, they should do as much as they can.

The nearest I got to seeing medical troubles at St Piers was seeing a very few seizures here and there, which must surely rank not as troubles or risks but facts of life at a hospital school for those with severe epilepsy.

I was in the kitchen buying some chutney made by the pupils, picking one out of a neat row of jars on a shelf, each jar neatly topped with a chequered cloth. Four pupils were planning their recipes for the rest of term when one of them seemed to be pulled down off her chair, to press against the ground in a tight knot. Within a minute she had regained consciousness and was helped to sit up.

'All right then, Sheilah? That's not like you, is it, love? You haven't had one of those for ages.'

I smiled at her but I don't think she saw me.

The technical facilities in the kitchen, as everywhere in the school, are excellent. The supervisor showed me what she called a 'split-level cooker', useful for people who have difficulty in bending down or are frightened of cooking. When the oven door opens, it can become a high shelf for food taken out of the oven, before the food is put on the table. I was ashamed to find that by the time I left the domestic science department I had pretty well reached saturation point with split-level cookers and soft-touch tin-openers.

It was a saturation with admiration. Every teaching unit I had seen, from classroom to kitchen, had a small number of pupils and a large number of special extras, skilfully used by a large number of expert teachers, some of whom were also nurses.

One such experienced member of staff gave her nearest pupil a stroke on the head, while showing me her classroom, and said quietly, 'They're very demanding, you see.'

When the boy smiled up at her in a contorted way, as if he could not shape his mouth properly, I was touched with dislike for people being talked about in the third person, as if they are not there or cannot hear. I had heard almost nothing else at St Piers and I know it is fair, but I don't like it. Staff used to bring visitors round the classrooms when I was at school, sweeping in through the door and saying, 'Here they are writing a short story. We try to keep writing and reading closely associated, so both develop . . .'

Or some such twaddle. We were exhibits, for display, not contact, and I resented it. The recent radio programme for and about people with disabilities had a title pinpointing what I mean: 'Does He Take Sugar?' I know that most of the time I was visiting St Piers my discomfort was ill-placed, but I still felt it a little.

I doubt if the nursing sister who showed me round the hospital block after lunch would have had much time for such fussing. She is a small dynamo, neatly strapped in at the waist, too busy to waste time on anything that does not deserve time. The boy rolling and suddenly uttering swallowed shrieks on the sofa in the corridor was a useful example of the point she was making at the time about the need to sort out seizures with a physical base from seizures induced by boredom, rage, fright, shock or a mass of other mental triggers. The boy in front of us had been having absences all morning, she said, but would calm down by the evening when he got used to the idea of being back at school again. That meant they did not need to treat him heavily with drugs.

A nurse lifted him into a padded wheelchair, smiling kindly as she said, 'Come on, young chap. Let's get you somewhere better than this.'

The aim of the hospital is to get all its patients back into the general run of school life as soon as possible after seizures. If possible the staff try to pre-empt seizures with drugs or some kind of therapy. As long as the seizure has not broken a bone, torn a muscle too badly or led to too elaborate a use of tranquillisers, there is no reason a pupil should not get back into action as soon as possible afterwards. I doubt if lying in bed helps to fight post-fit depression at all; if anything, it makes it worse.

It looked to me as if they fight fits well at St Piers. I had seen that most strikingly in the person of Claire, free now of the fits that used to wreck her life. The hospital has its own EEG department, its own pharmacy and can treat all sorts of illnesses, though it does not have the resources to become a general hospital on a large scale and, if a case of general illness looks too serious to be cared for there, it is sent to a local hospital.

It was late February when I was there, too early in the year to see the 100 acres of lovely grounds at their most exuberant. The whole place gave a sense of weary triumph at sticking to the fight, however high the risks and overpowering the odds. A tiny, mis-shapen girl limped through the hospital door on the arm of a nurse, just as we were leaving.

'That's the stuff,' said her nurse and they both grinned.

I shook hands with the dynamo sister and left.

One of the staff kindly offered to run me to the station, so I could catch the next London train and get a good start on my journey back to Cambridge. I had a few spare minutes in the reception area of the administration block, where one of the decorations hanging on the wall is a hand-drawn plan of St Piers in 1931. Then, as now, it was a whole community in itself. Its farmlands, ponds, gardens, woods and paths were drawn in as much detail as its buildings. The unexpected item on the plan that caught my eye was a women's cricket pitch, not far from the men's cricket pitch, occupied by girls in the heat of battle, the one at the crease poised in a dead straight forward defensive.

Restrictions of time and weather had stopped me seeing as much as I would have liked of the modern sporting facilities at St Piers. Obviously sports there these days are adventurous.

The old plan of the grounds would seem to be evidence that in this aspect they follow a noble tradition. Maybe the women's cricket was a plan that never came into being, but at least someone wanted it. Even back in bitter days when pupils were kept in protected gangs out of the way, someone was willing to let both sexes risk a whack on the head with a ball, for the sake of a good game.

I left St Piers with mixed feelings. It is a marvellous place and I respect and admire it. The atmosphere is infinitely more cheerful than in the days when I used to trudge down St Piers Lane to do my little stints of drying-up in the school houses, praying that none of the pupils would start writhing at my feet. It does not feel like a colony any more. Its staff stay and work there for long periods of time, committed to it.

But, as I said, I am a coward. I dreamt for nights afterwards of being carried away in a van to a nice, friendly place which would bring out the best in me. A place where everyone smiled and I was given a high-speed wheelchair in which to zoom over to the raw materials department of the further education unit. There I could get my head measured up for a thick, bright covering of rubber, in any colour I liked, and one of the boys in the workshop would mould it into a trendy helmet for me, face-cage optional.

CHAPTER ELEVEN

The Future for Epilepsy

The future for epilepsy – it is hard to think of anything less attractive to discuss, except perhaps bowel disorders, worthy causes and politicians. I set off to discuss the future for epilepsy with a heavy heart. I find the past and present enough of a burden, without venturing into a third dimension that does not yet exist.

I wrote and asked for an interview with Dr John Duncan, head of the Epileptic Research Group at Queen Square National Neurological Centre. To my surprise, almost to my disappointment, he agreed to an interview which, unfortunately, turned out to be a fiasco. My diabetes, tired of playing second fiddle to my epilepsy, chose this as the perfect vengeful moment to let my brain run low in sugar.

It was a sunny day and I had my sandwich lunch in the Square's quiet gardens, which were full of student doctors and nurses having picnics, occasional patients walking or wheelchairing their way past. Falsely feeling fully sugared after a starchy lunch, I went in to see Dr Duncan, in a section of the hospital marked 'neurological research'.

For some reason I had expected Dr Duncan to have a beard, with a face framed by curly hair and obscured by immense knowledge. In fact he is an informal and accessible man, with a clean-shaven, positively shiny face. He looks no more than young middle-aged and when I saw him he was casually dressed, friendly, glad to share his immense knowledge with as many people as possible. He warned me that he had only half an hour to spare before going off to talk to someone from television about neurology.

'People don't know what to do about epilepsy; that's part of the trouble. We need to improve public education, public awareness. We try to do quite a lot about that, directly and indirectly. We use the media: TV, radio, books, articles. It's a drip-drip effect. If you hear it ten times, it sinks in.'

He lured me into visions of epilepsy in the future being as easily accepted as 'flu. I imagined women in shopping centres chatting:

'Gill had one of her sessions yesterday, so I had to leave her in the grocer's while I finished the shopping. She's better today though.'

'There's a lot of it about at the moment; fits and throats. It's the time of year, isn't it?'

Dr Duncan would probably find no reason to doubt or discourage such a scene. The stigma attached to epilepsy is meaningless to him. Though he listened to all my enquiries carefully and tried to answer them in terms I would understand, he was puzzled when I said I thought the name epilepsy was a problem in itself because of its frightening associations. He did not think it a question worth asking or answering.

At the time I was going 'hypo'; my brain was starved of the sugar it needs to work properly, so it went into decline. I could manage the basic tasks I needed to do, like sitting down and listening to some of Dr Duncan's simple statements, but anything demanding real intelligence was too much for my under-nourished brain to organise.

I looked at the sensible questions I had prepared, but I could not understand or ask them. Instead I asked a few incoherent questions, for which I had to write and apologise to Dr Duncan afterwards. Some were rude; some were pointless; all were inconsequential. Mercifully, Dr Duncan did not seem to mind and answered even the most offensive of these questions, albeit briefly. He is obviously an old hand at answering the uninformed queries of people from the media, so perhaps my efforts counted as no more than the usual small change.

He tried to overcome my silence, as I sat speechless, faced

by my own questions, by emphasising the important help that could be given to epileptics by writers like myself and people from the media. When that drew nothing but a weak smile from me, he moved the emphasis to the help he could give to epileptics.

'My work in epilepsy encompasses neurology, neurosurgery, zoology, brain imaging, psychology, psychiatry and some social work. We have an inter-disciplinary approach.'

It was only when I had got my blood sugar back to normal and felt well again, long after the interview, that it occurred to me to follow up Dr Duncan's mention of zoology. I wrote and asked him what part zoology played in his research and he wrote back, explaining that animals are used to test the effectiveness and the side-effects of anti-epileptic drugs before the drugs are used on humans.

I know there is opposition to the use of animals in this way. Only a certain number of the animals in this particular research are naturally epileptic; the others suffer from 'induced seizures'. I have never been against this sort of research, which aims to help the treatment of human illness. Making animals' life a misery in order to produce better soap, skin-cream and make-up is grotesque, but when it is in order to improve human health, it seems to me nasty but defensible.

Had I been functioning more normally when talking to Dr Duncan, I might have gone further with the subject of animals and epilepsy, in a more extraordinary direction that has been receiving some publicity lately. A few weeks ago I heard an epileptic woman on a radio programme describing an incident when her dog had started fussing around her and dragging her home, despite her efforts to stop him. As soon as she got home, she had an epileptic seizure. She said her dog was not just a pet but also an advance warning system for her epileptic seizures.

Somehow, the story sounded too cosy to be scientifically true. I was surprised to see that the respected Support Dogs charity, which trains dogs to help blind, deaf and physically disabled people, has been organising a small pilot study to investigate the feasibility of training dogs to detect oncoming epileptic seizures and warn the people about to have them. It remains to be seen what results this study, which will rely mainly on monitoring videotapes of owners and dogs, with veterinary advice, will produce.

I knew before I asked Dr Duncan, in my letter following our meeting, that he would not think much of the notion of seizure-sensitive dogs. He thought it 'a nice story – unlikely to be substantiated'.

I expect he is right, but I would not be surprised if more people started using dogs in this way. Pets are loved as much as drugs are hated and animal help, like plant help, can be thought of as a 'natural' reaction against the chemical nature of modern anti-epileptic medicine, heavily dependent on drugs bringing foul side-effects with them.

I have little faith or hope in 'alternative' approaches to medicine, but I have no trouble understanding them. I know there can be a close enough bond between a dog and its owner for the dog to sense something unusual in its owner's behaviour – not a chemical sensitivity, but an emotional one, outside the range of Dr Duncan's work.

Luckily, the advanced, scientific nature of his work did not make Dr Duncan hard to talk to. My increasing dimness as I became more and more 'hypo' was more of a problem. I asked him slow, vague questions.

'Is epilepsy a condition or an illness?'

'Well, it's whatever you call it really. You can call it a disorder, a disease, an illness, a condition; what have you.'

'It can change the way you think about it.'

'Maybe.' He shrugged. It was time I asked him about facts, not little threads of theory.

On the other side of Queen Square's quiet gardens is an outbuilding of this relatively small hospital, labelled 'Brain Imaging'. It houses a branch of neurology that has come a long way since the days when surgeons pressed bits of the brain to see how each bit reacted to pressure and, by doing that, endeavoured to discover what purpose each bit served.

By 'brain imaging' Dr Duncan said, he meant developing
detailed pictures of the brain, so the functions and chemical
influences of epilepsy on all parts of the brain could be examined and understood and, if necessary, operated on.

Present-day brain imaging is infinitely careful, controlled
and meticulous and all the technical processes involved in it
are developing fast.

Dr Duncan put this last point simply. 'This year's scanners
are better than last year's scanners.'

I reminded myself that this was the man who is always
keen on developing new methods of brain examination, the
man who has removed and deep frozen a defective bit of a
young woman's brain, curing her of her epilepsy in the process. He told me that they do one or two of these ultra-accurate
operations each week in Queen Square.

'Successfully?'

'Not bad. But not 100%. About 70% of those undergoing
the operations at Queen Square are cured of their epilepsy.'

If I had been in better condition, I would have asked him
on the spot what happened to the other 30%. When I asked
him in my letter afterwards he said that 15-20% of this minority group show 'a marked improvement in their seizures –
i.e. 90% or more reduction'. About one per cent may have
their seizures worsened and the rest experience no change.
Perhaps this is because they are dead, but as he did not say
so, I had better give him the benefit of the doubt.

Micro-surgery on the brain is one of the areas of epileptic
treatment that will grow as quickly as supplies of equipment
and doctors with specialised training allow it to grow. It is
true that, as Dr Duncan said, 'the stakes are high', but the
other way of looking at it is that the life at stake can be so
lacerated by epilepsy that it might be worth gambling that
life, whatever the odds, if a cure is possible.

With few facilities for specialised brain surgery available in
this country, and with few epileptics ranking in this desperate
category, most doctors still prefer to treat epilepsy with drugs.
Before I could give a patient's persecuted sigh on the subject

of drugs, Dr Duncan rapidly mentioned drugs as one of the areas of epileptic treatment that is being improved. It is about time.

The benefits of new preparations such as gabapentin (which produces virtually no side-effects) and lamotrigine (extremely effective at controlling a wide range of epilepsies, including convulsions) are much publicised in the press. But they are new and expensive drugs and the NHS is cautious and short of money. That situation may change. Even if it does, better drugs are not the universal answer to controlling epilepsy.

If there is a theme in what Dr Duncan told me and what I have heard other specialists in neurology say, it is that epilepsy is a personal condition and treatment must deal with each case individually if it is to succeed. In its conference this year, celebrating its forty-fifth birthday, the BEA is emphasising that a wider range of medical help would mean that help could be more personal and attentive to individual needs.

The BEA intends to encourage GPs to set up epileptic clinics, smaller and more frequent than hospital clinics, run by doctors who know their patients well. That will be quite a task, requiring extra tuition in epilepsy for willing doctors.

Apparently the new weapons for this will be Sapphire nurses. The 'Sapphire Squad' are specialists in epilepsy; as well as helping GPs, they will help to teach epileptics about their condition and help doctors in outpatient departments with the treatment of people who have had black-outs and may be epileptics. The BEA 'officially launched' these nurses on to their awesome labours in late June 1994.

I would welcome a more personal approach to my epilepsy, away from the all-engulfing anonymity of the hospital, but there are frightening tensions between local and hospital treatment. I could not go into these questions while I was talking to Dr Duncan, partly because I was too dopey to string any useful questions together and partly because it seemed a waste when he was a specialist in neurosurgery and brain imaging. I felt I should ask about those.

In the event I heard myself come out with an improbable question.

'Are you good at your job?'

He replied, 'I suppose you shouldn't ask me.'

I cackled with hungry laughter. 'Oh, you mean ask the corpses for their views.'

Though he did not know what was wrong with me, Dr Duncan could obviously see it was time to calm me down and he killed that line of enquiry with splendid confidence.

My neurologist step-son Mat, who worked for a time at Queen Square, told me afterwards that I had been talking to one of the most brilliant neurologists in the world who cannot often have been asked questions like those. Fortunately, he took a generous view of them.

'I guess if I thought I wasn't doing any good, I'd go and do something else.'

Talking about possibilities appealed to Dr Duncan and he rapidly steered the possibilities back to the world of epilepsy.

'There have been great advances in neurosurgery over the last two or three years, for example.'

This launched me into one of my periodic excursions into lucidity. 'So you are optimistic about the future of treating epilepsy?'

'Oh yes.'

I showed the doubt of those on the receiving end of medicine.

'Really? I said. 'To the extent that you mean you think it will be completely controlled or even. . .'

'Whether there will ever be a cure for a person with epilepsy is as difficult to say as whether there will be a cure for a person with cancer. Some forms of cancer are curable now that weren't curable five years ago. Other forms are incurable on present knowledge. Epilepsy isn't just one diagnosis. Some forms of epilepsy are as difficult to treat as some forms of cancer or forms of headache, if not adequately understood.

'But treatments could improve. There are constant advances in drugs and technology.

'This last is very important, as much for the correct diagnosis as the treatment.'

Diagnosis is a treacherous side of epilepsy, for doctors as well as patients. Epilepsy is notoriously difficult to identify correctly. How is an epileptic absence to be distinguished from a fainting fit, or an epileptic seizure from a hysterical seizure? Dr Pamela Crawford, consultant neurologist at the Bootham Park Hospital's Special Centre for Epilepsy in York, reckons that about a third of the patients brought before her there, diagnosed as having epilepsy, have nothing serious wrong with them. The mis-diagnosis is usually made because the patients are incontinent or hard to revive after a fainting fit.

The technical developments which Dr Duncan thinks will help doctors to avoid this sort of mis-diagnosis bring with them their own troubles because people demand more of doctors when they realise that more is possible. They become less tolerant of mistakes.

In one case I heard about recently, a young woman started having fits, was diagnosed as epileptic and put on anti-convulsants. The fits continued and every time she went to the neurology clinic, her dose was increased. It was only after eight years of futile drugs, continued convulsions and the birth of two brain-damaged children that genetic tests apparently showed that she had never been epileptic at all. No-one in this situation can be pronounced at fault until every single medical detail is known, and even then how can one judge when ignorance or fear become neglect?

Everyone is a loser in such a situation and I am afraid that there will be many more like it as we come to expect more of our doctors with all their refined equipment.

Minute refinements of neurosurgical technology seemed to cheer up Dr Duncan, who was on his home ground talking about them. I asked him if the importance of medical technology and the importance of absorbing it into the existing system means that one's chance of better treatment varies according to which part of the country one lives in.

He said, 'I think it's true; neurology services are patchy. In some areas neurology provision is very limited.'

Then he smiled, 'But it is greatly improving.' He added, with a regretful air, 'However, there is a resource problem.'

I blundered in relentlessly, 'It's expensive, isn't it?'

'Yes, but the equipment here is paid for by grants from bodies such as Charity Action Research or the Medical Research Council. There are legacies and so on; bits of government money. At least in somewhere like Queen Square we have a live chemical practice of research.'

Unlike me, Dr Duncan stops talking when he has nothing more to say.

There were silences.

I consoled myself later with the thought that he was used to patients with unreliable brains, but that was weak consolation. They are patients, not people from the media who are usually ready to soak up reverentially his every hint, sub-reference or morsel of mention. I played a more pointless game.

Eventually Dr Duncan looked at his watch and warned me that he had only five minutes left. I apologised for my undemanding questions which offered him no challenge.

He smiled. 'That's okay. I don't want to leave you with questions unanswered.'

As a finale, he gave me a grand chorus of advances exchanged at meetings of the International League Against Epilepsy (ILAE). 'If one is trying to look forward, one has to look around because in the future medicine can be more international. The ILAE is a professional organisation for doctors, not a voluntary one.'

At the ILAE's biennial meetings, Dr Duncan talks to his colleagues from Hamburg, Zurich, Ontario and other centres of epileptic research. Experts can exchange news of what they have discovered since their last meeting. Dr Duncan is looking forward to the next one in Sydney.

Queen Square struck me as a hospital still dedicated to the pursuit of ideas. It was founded as a research hospital and its doctors make enough progress to keep its research going.

Constant exchange of ideas and discussion of developments play an important part in stimulating the doctors' efforts.

I smiled to myself when I saw the Sydney International Conference advertised in *Epilepsy Today* with a picture of Sydney Opera House in the sunlight, romantic and spectacular. The advert recommended luxurious ways of travelling across the world to get there. It is a long way, in every sense, from Dr Duncan's den of scholarship in London, which does not spend much time on appearances.

The stairs leading to Dr Duncan's upstairs room, where he deals with the media, are steep and narrow, covered with lino stuck down by black tape. When I left, Dr Duncan went down before me, but I don't know whether this was because the stairs are always slippery or because I had shown myself so clearly to be a liability.

I pondered on what an extraordinary unit the brain is. I was encouraged in principle by the doctor's thoughts on progress in neurology but in practice I reflected sadly on his parting remark: 'There is never going to be a panacea for epilepsy, any more than there is for cancer. It's learning how to treat each individual person.'

I have never expected anything wonderfully cheerful for the future of epilepsy, my own or anyone else's. I expect to go on having bad times with my epilepsy, however much I manage to rescue it from diabetic provocation. Doubtless that attitude means I will have bad times but I don't think I am being completely defeatist: more like resigned.

However, resignation does not suit me. Writing this book has made me think about my epilepsy, as it were, full on, and I admit that I do need to put up some whole-hearted resistance against the foul thing. In my heart of hearts, I already knew that, but it is such a frightening fight, against such an overwhelming, shameful foe, that I feel drained of all spirit just at the thought of it.

Perhaps the starting point for strong resistance against epilepsy should be reminding myself that even if I fail to stop fits, at least I can make sure I do not give in to misery.

I need to admit how much I hate my epilepsy, and fight against it by refusing to let it dominate my life. It will continue to distort my life with fits, and God knows what other horrors but, faced with tough resistance, the distortions will not take my life over, merely re-shape it.

Select Bibliography

Most of the publications listed below are out of print; the publisher's name, therefore, has only been given where a book is currently available.

WORKS ON EPILEPSY

Andrée, John. Cases of the Epileptic. Hysteric Fits and St Vitus's Dance, 1753

Barker, Wayne. Brain Storms, A Study of Human Spontaneity. New York. 1968

Beddoes,Thomas. (1760–1808). Essay on the Nature and Prevention of Some of the Disorders. Commonly Called Nervous

Billings, J. S. The Surgical Treatment of Epilepsy. Cincinnati Lancet and Observer Vol. 4, 1861

Black, W. G. Folk Medicine. A Chapter in the History of Culture. Publications of the Folklore Society XII. 1883

Brain, Walter Russell. Contribution of Medicine to Our Idea of the Mind. 1952

——Disorders of the Nervous System. 1969

Bunker, Henry Alden. The Sacred Disease. 1928

Casaubon, Meric. A Treatise Concerning Enthusiasm, as It is an Effect of Nature: But is Mistaken by Many for Either Divine Inspiration, or Diabollical Possession. 1656

Celsus, Aulius Cornelius: De Medicina.

Clarke, Edwin. Doctrine of the Hollow Nerve in the 17th and 18th Centuries: in Medicine, Science and Culture, ed. Lloyd G. Stevenson and Robert P. Multhauf, Baltimore. 1968

Comrie, J. D. History of Scottish Medicine. 1932

Crawford, Raymond. The Blessing of Cramp-Rings. A Chapter in the History of the Treatment of Epilepsy. Studies in the History and Method of Science, ed. Charles Singer

Crawthorne, Terence. Jesus Christ and the Falling Sickness. Proceedings of the Royal Society of Medicine. 1958

Delasiauvre. Traite de L'Epilepsie. 1854

Esquirol. Des Maladies Mentales. Paris. 1838

Evans, Margiad: A Ray of Darkness. John Calder, 1952

Ferriss, Greg, S. Treatment of Epilepsy Today. New Jersey. 1978

French, J. D. and Darling, Louise: Surgical treatment of Epilepsy in 1861. Journal of the International College of Surgeons Vol. 34, 1960

Fulton, J. F. History of Focal Epilepsy. International Journal of Neurology. 1959

Garrison, F. H. Introduction to the History of Medicine. 1929

Gowers, William. The Borderlands of Epilepsy. 1907

——Epilepsy and Other Convulsive Diseases. 1901

——Insanity and Epilepsy in Relation to Life Assurance. 1904

——A Manual of Diseases of the Nervous System. 1970

Greenblatt, S. H. Major. Influences on the Early Life and Works of John Hughlings Jackson. Bulletin of Medical History Vol. 39, 1965

Hazeldine, Peter. Epilepsy. 1986

Heberden, William. Commentaries on the History and Cure of Disease. 1962

Henslow, G. Fourteenth Century Medical Works. 1899

Hippocrates. The Sacred Disease, trans. Jones, W. H. S. 1928

Hoch, Paul and Knight, Robert. History of Epilepsy. 1965

——History of Epileptic Treatment.

Holmes, Gordon. Evolution of Clinical Medicine, as Illustrated by the History of Epilepsy. British Medical Journal Vol. 2. 1946

Hopkins, Anthony. Epilepsy, The Facts. 1981

——The Facts About Epilepsy. 1984

Horsley, Victor. Brain Surgery. British Medical Journal Vol. 2. 1886

Howden, J. C. Religious Sentiment in Epileptics. Journal of Mental Science Vol. 18. 1873

Hunter. Neurological Biographies. 1958

Jackson, John Hughlings. A Study of Convulsions. 1870

Jackson, Richard. Epilepsy. 1992

Jeavons, P. M. Infantile Spasms. 1964

——Photosensitive Epilepsy. 1975

——Epileptic Reference Book. Harper & Row 1985

Jefferson, G. Selected Papers. 1960

Kanner, Leo. Folklore and Cultural History of Epilepsy. Medical
    Life Vol. 37. 1930
——Names of the Falling Sickness. Human Biology Vol. 2. 1930
King, Lester S. The Growth of Medical Thought. 1963
——The Medical World of the 18th Century. 1958

Laidlaw, John. Textbook of Epilepsy. 1980
Laidlaw, Mary and John. People with Epilepsy. 1984
Lechtenberg, Richard. Epilepsy, What is it, what causes it and
    advice on diagnosis and treatment. 1985
Lemnius, Levinus (1508–68). Ucculta Naturae Miracula
Lennox, W. G. Science and Seizures. 1941
——Epilepsy and Related Disorders. 1960
Livingstone, Samuel. Epileptic Management in Infancy, Childhood
    and Adolescence. 1972
Lombroso, Cesare (1836–1909). The Man of Genius
——L'Homme Criminel
——After Death, What?
Lucretius; De Rerum Natura. transd. Sir Robert Allen. 1925

MacEwen, William. An Address on Surgery of the Brain and Spinal
    Cord. British Medical Journal Vol. 2. 1888
Maudsley, Henry. Responsibility in Mental Disease. New York 1874
McGovern, Shelagh. The Epileptic Handbook. 1982
Mead, Richard. Medica Sacra
Mingazzini, G. Some Strange Cases of Epileptic Behaviour in Birds.
    Archives of Neurology and Psychiatry Vol. 9. 1923
Murphy, L. Saints of Epilepsy. Medical History Vol. 3. 1959

Nathan, P. The Nervous System. 1969

Pagel, Walter. Religious Motives in the Medical Biology of the 17th
    Century. Bulletin of the History of Medicine Vol. 3. 1935

Rolleston, J. D. The Folklore of Epilepsy. 1943
Rondeletius, Guilielmus. Methodus Curandorum Omnium Mor-
    borum Corporis Humani. Frankfurt 1592
Rose, Steven. The Conscious Brain. 1976

Sander Lev and Thompson Pam. Epilepsy. 1989
Scott, Donald. Understanding EEG. 1976
——About Epilepsy. 1984
Sieveking, Edward H. On Epilepsy and Epileptiform Seizures. 1858

Spratley, Violet A. and Stern E. S. Epilepsy and Its Treatment. 1904

Storch, T. C. Von. An Essay on the History of Epilepsy. 1930

Temkin, Owsei. The Falling Sickness. John Hopkins University Press 1971

Zilborg, Gregory. A History of Medical Psychology. New York 1941

BIOGRAPHIES AND BIOGRAPHICAL WRITING

BYRON
Thomas Moore ed., Letters and Journals of Byron. 1830
L. A. Marchand, Byron, A Portrait. 1970

BRIGGS, JOHNNY
Wisden 1900
By His Own Hand, David Frith. 1990

CAESAR, JULIUS
Caesar and the Falling Sickness, by Terence Cawthorne in Proceedings of the Royal Society of Medicine, Vol. 51. 1958
Caesar, by M. Grant
Caesar, by Major-Gen. J. F. C. Fuller

DOSTOEVSKY, FYODOR
Dostoevsky's Letters and Diaries
Dostoevsky – Biografiia, by Strakhov
Dostoevsky and the Healing Art, by James Rice

FLAUBERT, GUSTAVE
Gustave Flaubert in his Works and Correspondence, J. C. Tarver. 1895
Gustave Flaubert, H. Lottman. 1989
Flaubert's Youth, L. P. Shanks. 1927

GREIG, TONY
Tony Greig (with Alan Lee): My Story. 1980

JOHNSON, DR
Boswell's Life of Johnson

LEAR, EDWARD
Edward Lear, Peter Levi. 1995
——Mr Nonsense, Emery Kelen. 1973
——Edward Lear in South Italy, ed. P. Quennell. 1964

MOHAMMED
Mohammed, Michael Cork. 1983

Mohammed, Maxime Rodinson. 1991
Muhammad, ed. Keith Thomas
Mohammed, The Man and his Faith, Tor Andrae

MORRIS, WILLIAM
William, Morris, Letters to Family and Friends, ed. Philip Henderson, 1950
William Morris, Life, Work and Friends, Philip Henderson. 1967

PAGANINI
A Biography of Paganini, Alan Kendal. 1982

PETER THE GREAT
Peter the Great, Letters and Papers
Peter the Great, Constantin de Grunwald
Peter the Great, Steven Graham
Peter the Great, Ian Grey. 1960

POPE PIUS IX
Story of the Life of Pius IX, Alfred Owen Legge. 1875
Pius IX, Frank J. Cappa. 1979

PYTHAGORAS
Pythagoras, Peter Gorman
Pythagoras, Ward Rutherford

SWINBURNE, ALGERNON CHARLES
Swinburne, A Critical Biography, Jean Overton Fuller

VAN GOGH, VINCENT
The Man Who Loved The Sun, Jack Raymond Jones
Van Gogh, Sa Vie, Sa Maladie et Son Oeuvre, F. Minowska. 1963

ZOLA, EMILE
The Human Beast, ed. Dr Hericourt
Zola, Oeuvres Complètes, ed. H. Mitterand. 1890, transd. Alec Brown. 1958

Sources of Useful Information on Epilepsy

National Society for Epilepsy
Chalfont Centre for Epilepsy
Chalfont St Peter
Gerrards Cross
Bucks SL9 0RJ

British Epilepsy Association
40 Hanover Square
Leeds LS3 1BE

Index

Numbers in *italic* refer to illustrations